"Nadler is a talented writer and . . . an excellent journalist. . . . [There is] brilliant writing here on the aftermath of Serb atrocities and NATO bombings in Kosovo." —*National Post*

"The perfect modern parable of that tortured region's conflict, a real-life Romeo and Juliet story. . . . Quite a tale."
—*Toronto Star*

"As a good journalist, obviously well informed and surrounded by good local sources, Nadler creates an impressive mosaic of testimonies told by primary witnesses. Whether he is talking about the air-strikes drama through the eyes of the Serb, or about the Kosovo Albanians' long journey through the mountains, Nadler stands solidly with both feet on the ground. The picture of the Belgrade underground is powerful and authentic, as are the accounts of the executions of the citizens of Rezallë. . . . Nobody can be immune to the moving, somber picture of a period that left deep and visible scars on the face of the Balkans." —*The Globe and Mail*

"Nadler is a fluid and lucid writer. He adroitly places his search-for-a-lost-lover story against the background of the complex relationship between politics, ethnicity, and religion that inflamed—and still enflames—the Kosovo-Serbia-Albania axis."
—*Winnipeg Free Press*

"Spare and vivid . . . He has an eye for local detail."
—*The Gazette* (Montreal)

"Nadler wonderfully mixes the dense, complicated political history of the region with the personal stories of war and its aftermath. And though that history includes ethnic cleansing, paramilitary punks, corrupt leaders, and petty criminals and their victims, Nadler refrains from explicit condemnation. It is a remarkably brave and endearing approach."

—*Quill & Quire*

"Riveting. . . . As a commentary on the brutality of war, Nadler's first-hand account is valuable and moving. . . . His reporter's eye—and a memorable supporting cast of Balkan characters—give the book its best moments and its real strength."

—*Edmonton Journal*

"John Nadler's *Searching for Sofia* strikes the perfect balance between drama and contemporary history. This engaging and heartbreaking tale brings to life the human cost of corrupt politics and war, and stands as a testament to those who history, at its own peril, so quickly forgets."

—Olen Steinhauer, author of *The Bridge of Sighs*

"Nadler's book is a stroke of originality among the legion of journalists' memoirs of the Balkan wars. In terms of portraying the impact of ethnic division on individual human lives, there is little better to be read on any conflict, not only the former Yugoslavia."   —Neil Barnett, correspondent for *Jane's Defence Weekly*

JOHN NADLER

Searching for Sofia

a TALE of OBSESSION,

MURDER and WAR

ANCHOR CANADA

National Library of Canada Cataloguing in Publication

Nadler, John
   Searching for Sofia : a tale of obsession, murder and war / John Nadler.

ISBN 0-385-65823-0

1. Kosovo (Serbia)—Ethnic relations. 2. Kosovo (Serbia)—History—Civil
War, 1998–1999—Atrocities. 3. Interethnic dating—Serbia—Kosovo. I. Title.

DR2087.7.N33 2004   949.71   C2004-900637-1

As indicated in the Author's Note, names of the people who appear in this
book have been changed or otherwise obscured to protect their identities.

Cover image: Jerry Cooke/CORBIS/MAGMA
Text design: Carla Kean
Printed and bound in Canada

Published in Canada by
Anchor Canada, a division of
Random House of Canada Limited

Visit Random House of Canada Limited's website: www.randomhouse.ca

TRANS   10 9 8 7 6 5 4 3 2 1

For Norma

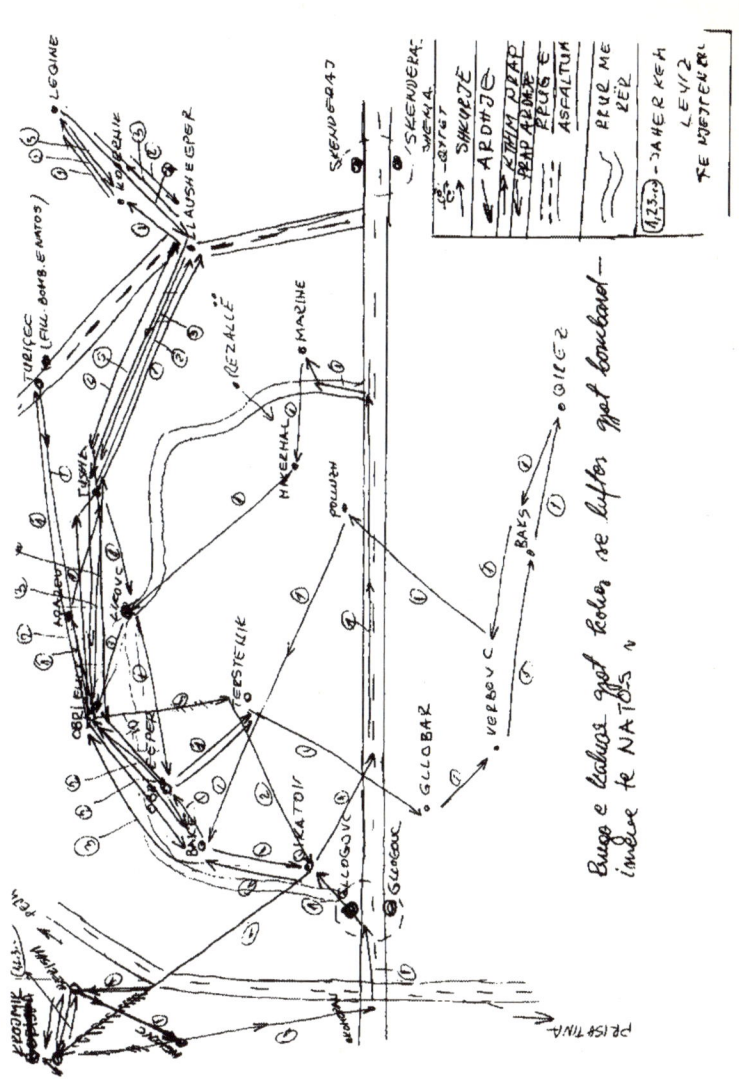

Hand-drawn map of Gjorg's wanderings.

Contents

Memory tells us not what we choose but what it pleases.
—*Montaigne*

Crossing the Ibar

I sat on the ground cross-legged in front of the Albanian boy Gjorg. A war had just ended; Gjorg's house lay in ruins off to the side. An onerous Balkan sun pressed down on us. But Gjorg had not sat me down on the cool grass of his farm in central Kosovo to escape the heat.

He wanted to tell me something, I was certain of it. I hadn't known Gjorg for long. But the fateful circumstances of our meeting had created an understanding and intimacy between us, and I knew when something was on his mind. Today Gjorg made no secret of it. He stared at his hands, plucked grass from the ground, and gazed out at the fields that stretched like a warped chessboard across the Drenica Valley before turning to me and declaring:

"I want to find Sofia."

I was astonished and speechless. Just the fact that Gjorg had uttered Sofia's name in my presence—easily, and without prompting—was startling. Yes, I had known about Sofia for as long as I knew Gjorg. Sofia was the first secret Gjorg had shared with me after we met in the refugee city behind rebel lines in August 1998. But that had been a year ago. An eternity had passed since then, and in that time I thought that Gjorg had given up on Sofia. In fact, he had told me she was dead to him. But now he was telling me he was changing his mind.

"I tried to find her before," Gjorg said. "Before, when you and I met. But it was hard."

I knew how hard it was for Gjorg, and that is what astonished me. He had been displaced for months before and during the war, that period known as the NATO air strikes against Yugoslavia, only to return home to a devastating revelation. A massacre had occurred in his village, and his fiancée Sofia—yes, gentle Sofia—was implicated as an accessory in the high crime of being her father's daughter.

"I believed I would never see Sofia again," Gjorg said, staring north as if fixing his gaze on the very horizon Sofia was lost in. "I tried to forget about her. But now everything has changed. I want her back . . ."

Before I could figure out exactly what had changed, Gjorg asked the question.

"Will you help me find her . . . Will you do this?"

*

Standing at the bridge over the Ibar River in the city of Kosovska Mitrovica, I went over this conversation again and again, replaying it in my mind like a video on an endless loop.

Will you help me find her? Will you do this?

Will I? . . . I didn't have an answer.

Standing near the bridge, I gazed through the razor wire of the French army checkpoint, and stared into the river's waters. The Ibar was a fitting metaphor for Sofia's disappearance. Down below, eddies grew, swirled, and disappeared like faces in a mob. The water passed like moments. Every ripple glimpsed was instantly gone—like Gjorg's innocence, like the dead in Gjorg's village, like Sofia.

Like me, these waters had travelled far to get here. The Ibar rose from mountains in eastern Kosovo, and snaked endless kilometres before passing under this bridge. My work as a journalist had brought me to Kosovo. But I had come to the Ibar for a different reason. My destination was the last place Gjorg had seen Sofia before she vanished, the ethnic-Serb enclave on the far bank.

I mounted the bridge, showed my credentials to the French peacekeepers, and seconds later set foot on the hot concrete of north Mitrovica. This was where Gjorg had met Sofia in 1994. It was the place where they had spent three passionate and perilous years together. This is where they feared Sofia's father and awaited the war.

Sofia had been here once, but I held no illusions that I would find her that day. I was certain she was long gone. Instead, I had come today to inspect the place where their relationship had begun, and to decide whether I would honour my new friend's request to find the missing girl.

North Mitrovica. If setting truly dictates character, the romance between Sofia and Gjorg was more complicated than I had imagined, because Mitrovica's complexities defied easy comprehension. The Dolce Vita off to my left was a case in point. The Dolce Vita was a café. And if you believed the rumours, it was really a hangout for war criminals, plain-clothes cops, and racist ruffians who fuelled bad ideas with caffeine and *rakija* plum brandy.

On this day the Dolce Vita was quiet. The only man in sight was a severe character with the heft of a TV wrestler who sat in a chair in the middle of a nearby square. I guessed this man belonged to the Bridge Guard, a cryptic corps of locals who stood vigil near Mitrovica's bridges and radioed for reinforcements (a mob) if any *persona non grata* (an Albanian) attempted to cross the bridge into their part of town.

Ironically, except for a few kids skipping rope and an arthritic dog that woofed at me from the shadows, there was no sign of a mob anywhere, which made north Mitrovica distinct from the southern half of the city. Stepping off the bus in south Mitrovica thirty minutes before and making my way on foot to the bridge, I had waded through a sea of people—women clad in head scarves, walking arm in arm with their daughters, men strolling and smoking, and sitting and smoking; and smells—boiling coffee, frying *qebaps*; and sounds—cries of sellers, prayers echoing from minarets.

South Mitrovica was indeed different from the north. It was Albanian, Muslim, and an echo of the long-dead Ottoman Empire. North Mitrovica, where I now stood, was Serbian, and the epoch it conjured up was the imposing concrete and paranoia of Communist-era Yugoslavia. Mitrovica was divided north from south. The river was the fault line, but the Ibar had not always been a Balkan Berlin Wall separating Albanians and Serbs. Before the NATO air war against Yugoslavia, Mitrovica had been a single metropolis. But when NATO arrived a year before and unleashed new Albanian violence, thousands of Serb civilians south of the river fled to the north, where a large Serbian community already lived, and dug in. Similarly, Albanians in the Serb-dominated north ran south. The ancient metropolis of Kosovska Mitrovica had become two cities separated by a muddy river and enough hate to fill an ocean.

Leaving the security of the Ibar, I sought out those few and precious landmarks of Sofia's life with Gjorg. My first stop was Mitrovica's hospital, located at the end of a tree-lined street in the hills above the city. The hospital was where Gjorg had met Sofia and her father six years before. Here Gjorg became fascinated with the daughter and fearful of the father. This was the place where it all began—their secret affair, a decade-long obsession, and all those lies. Dusk had arrived by the time I wandered onto the hospital grounds, but the buildings were still visible in the grey light. Some windows were broken, and most were dark. I searched for the window where Gjorg told me he had stood and waited for Sofia's visits. In the jungle of elms and tall grass between the buildings, I tried to imagine the spot where the two had crept off to be alone, and I was almost able to manufacture their silhouettes.

I left the hospital, descended the leafy hill into town, and tried to find the corner where the lover's café was supposed to have been. Sadly, the café was no longer there. But I did see a few young women on the street, and I found myself staring deeply into the face of every one.

I was looking for the *mark*—a thin scar above Sofia's left eye, the result of a childhood abrasion. I passed a young woman with brown eyes and fleshy cheeks, and immediately I stopped. Her thick hair shook as she emoted to a girlfriend. This girl was beautiful, and blithe, and above one eye I saw a sliver of a mark, and for a moment, a long moment, I thought I had found Sofia. Then, an instant later, I snapped out of my daydream and realized I had been projecting Sofia's characteristics onto someone else. This girl was too young to be Sofia, and the scar I imagined on her brow was actually a wrinkle that appeared when she laughed.

This was not the only familiar face I encountered that day. I saw something of Sofia in every young woman in Mitrovica, partly because the image I carried of Gjorg's fiancée was faceless. At least, it had been an hour ago. Before coming here, Sofia had existed in my mind's eye as a shadow, an eddy in the Ibar. Now Sofia had somehow taken on substance. I still couldn't make out the details, but since crossing the river and visiting her last known whereabouts and passing people on the street who might have known her, I had gained a sense of her.

As the sky darkened, I headed back to the river. But before mounting the bridge, I turned my back to the Ibar, gazed north, and considered what had to be done if I was to grant Gjorg's request and look for Sofia.

At that moment I faced Yugoslavia, Eastern Europe's last police state. It was a two-republic federation—the two being Serbia and Montenegro—governed by the moon-faced dictator Slobodan Milošević, who had led his country into four losing wars over the span of ten years. The last war, the Kosovo conflict, had been lost the previous June. But at that moment future conflicts simmered on the Kosovo border and in Belgrade as rumours of civil war intensified.

A decade of chaos and violence had left its scars on the country and its citizens. Yugoslavia had become a land of brutality and suffering and hope and courage and defiance and denial. A lot of denial. Very simply, Yugoslavia sat on the southern extremity of Europe like a walled fortress. I was standing on the moat—a frontier guarded by diseased hounds and fanatical sentries. And somewhere in this strange land there was a young woman. She was twenty-four years old, and she was hidden among 10.5 million Serbs and 680,000 Montenegrins and countless refugees within 102,136 square kilometres. There were as many doubts and obstacles on the road to finding her as kilometres. And there were many uncertainties.

But one thing was now clear to me. Before, Gjorg had asked me: Will you help me find her? I decided I would. I would try to find Sofia. I owed it to Gjorg, and Sofia, and all the other lives I had traversed and trampled in my work. I would not exit these two lives immediately after deadline. I would stick around and see this story to its conclusion. And the only conclusion was to find Sofia.

Clearly, locating her would be no easy feat. To find this girl I would have to travel into Yugoslavia as it edged towards upheaval. And in retrospect, I know that finding her necessitated seeking the help of murderers, and Mafiosi, and dear, extraordinary people—like Zoran the Fixer, Sasha, and Boris. I would ask for their trust and help, and lie to them.

All these people and events were in my future. It was impossible to conceive at that moment, but over the next year all of our lives would collide and come together for a brief period in an extraordinary project: the Search for Sofia Neznanović.

PART I

Glimpsing Her

CHAPTER I

Setting Out

September 2000

I awoke early, and stuffed notebooks and a change of clothes into a knapsack—enough supplies to last me for a weekend road trip. I made sure the security wallet buckled to my waist contained my passport, and enough Deutschmarks and dinars to finance the trip.

As I waited for my travel mates Sasha and Zoran to arrive, I wasn't hopeful that this trip would yield anything about Sofia or her father, Momo. I had already been in Belgrade for more than two weeks, and I had found nothing on the father and daughter I was seeking. Similarly, I had uncovered nothing on the crime—the mass murder that had occurred in Rezallë in central Kosovo in April 1999—to which both were linked.

Instead I had found a city that was skittish and tense during the day, and joyfully raucous at night. During daylight hours people went about their business. They went to work. They sat for hour after hour in cafés. Habits were unbroken, but the mood was far from normal. The strain was building. Something awful—a crackdown, a civil war, all triggered by an election only days away—was coming, and everyone seemed to know it. I sensed it every time I left the dark and airless apartment I rented, which I kept locked, sealed, and curtained due to my own paranoia that as a western journalist I was an unwanted alien surrounded by enemies, cops, and potential informers.

Sipping a coffee, I heard my mobile phone ring. It was Sasha. "We are gonna be little late," she said. "Zoran has just come for me, but the traffic is bad from Novi Beograd. I call you when we get to your place."

That was fine. I had time for another coffee, and a chance to plan. I was desperate, but going to Kraljevo was not a shot in the dark. After weeks combing Belgrade for clues on the whereabouts of Sofia Neznanović and her father, I had finally been informed that there was every reason to believe I could pick up their trail in southern Serbia. Boris, my third travelling companion, was from Kraljevo. He had knowledge of the local scene, and a lifetime of contacts there.

After my second coffee, the phone rang again. It was Zoran. "We are on the street outside," he said. Within a minute I was sitting in the back seat of Zoran's 1987 BMW as he wove through Belgrade traffic. "Sorry for being late, but the traffic, it was bad," he said, confirming Sasha's initial report. Zoran drove like he moved and talked—with supreme confidence and a devilishly bad attitude. By trade, Zoran was a translator and journalist's assistant, an occupation known as a "fixer." Zoran looked like a gangster. He had the leather jacket and Italian shoes and smattering of gold jewellery. But he was a unique animal. He was Zoran. He had self-assuredness, but he also had wet eyes that looked almost sensitive, and a voice that flirted, seduced, and boasted but never seemed to shout.

As we drove, Sasha sat sideways in the front passenger seat so she could speak to both of us. But she didn't say a thing. Judging by the pillow imprint in her closely cropped black hair, I guessed she was too tired to talk. Instead, she held a smoking cigarette between two fingers as delicate as surgical scissors, stared at me through swollen eyes, and smiled. That said it all. Sasha wore no lipstick or rouge, but not because there hadn't been time this morning. Sasha never wore makeup; at least, she hadn't during the last two weeks. Far from diminishing her femininity, however, the minimalist style she struck seemed to unfurl her natural elegance and grace. Like the perfect woman, Sasha was rife with mystery. Since coming to Belgrade, I had run the gamut with her—from distrust and fear to unconditional confidence and admiration. The latter two emotions were what I felt for her at that moment.

"I called Boris," Sasha finally said, with a slight hoarseness in her voice. "He waits for us."

Sure enough, a few minutes later Zoran pulled over, the door opposite me flew open, and in climbed big Boris. "Hey, guy," Boris said to me in a voice that sounded like the low F blast from a tenor sax. And then he went about stowing his bag and getting comfortable, and in the ensuing commotion you might have thought a grizzly had been let loose in the car. His enthusiasm was visible in his every gesture. It echoed in his voice. He was the type of guy who might suddenly break into song. When he was joyfully wired—like now—words escaped him like wind from an accordion, and it was easy to think Boris was singing when he was simply speaking or laughing. "Ah, I am happy," Boris said, slapping the fabric of the car seat. "Tonight I will be at my home. I did not tell my parents I am coming. I want it to be surprise."

We made one last stop before leaving Belgrade and getting underway. Zoran drove to his parents' place, where his brother lived, and exchanged his BMW for a 1979 model Volvo, a gold-coloured tank of a car. Zoran expected the worst in southern Serbia, and he didn't want to risk his precious

BMW. It wasn't just the dilapidated roads and car thieves that worried Zoran. He was also mindful of the unrest brewing as a result of the upcoming presidential and parliamentary elections, which were just over a week away, and the mounting tensions. That public opinion polls placed the underdog opposition in the lead in the last run-up to the election had ratcheted up pressure in Belgrade. But Kraljevo was both hard on the Kosovo border and home to an impassioned opposition movement. This placed it squarely on the fault line if unrest did indeed break out. For most Serbs, calamity—civil war or bloody government crackdown—seemed unavoidable.

The pessimists had good cause to fear election day. Earlier in the summer Yugoslavia's president, Slobodan Milošević, whose coterie exercised utter control over Serbia, had called elections, putting his job and those of the deputies in the federal parliament up for grabs. At the time, Milošević's position seemed unassailable. By mid-2000, Yugoslavia, made up of the republics of Serbia and tiny Montenegro, was at its weakest, and Milošević at his strongest. Though he ruled a four-party coalition, he compromised and manipulated political allies like mercurial Vojislav Šešelj of the Serbian Radical Party (SRS), who supported Milošević's Serbian Socialist Party in the republic's parliament. Nearly every opposition politician of any stature was either hopelessly flawed, chronically handicapped after years of slander from state TV, or deftly compromised by the leader himself.

But then something unexpected happened. Soon after the election call, Serbia's fragmented opposition united into an eighteen-party alliance, the Democratic Opposition of Serbia (DOS). They appointed a retiring law professor, Vojislav Koštunica, as their candidate for president, and launched a vigorous campaign. When I first arrived in Belgrade, I attended the convention officially kicking off the DOS campaign at Belgrade's palatial Sava Centre, and heard

Kostunica's maiden speech. Kostunica wasn't offering Yugoslavs the moon. His ten-point platform, a Contract with Serbia, delivered in a speech as wooden as a rostrum, promised "honest" government, economic development, anti-crime measures, a peaceful resolution to the crisis in Montenegro, and "fair wages for honest work." Back home, the Contract would have been your garden-variety list of political promises. In Serbia it was the first bit of sober common sense uttered by a politician in a generation, and voters were paying attention. Kostunica's popularity grew, primarily by word of mouth. By the morning of our departure, Kostunica and his DOS movement were favoured to win the election. Not that anyone believed Milošević would accept defeat. Which is why Zoran was leaving his BMW at home.

So we transferred our bags into the Volvo and climbed aboard. Minutes later we were underway. Eventually we broke through the barrier of grey tenements on the outskirts of Belgrade, and bushy hills took shape in the car windows. Leaving the city behind, I also cleared my mind of politics, and focused on the purpose of our trip: to find something that might lead us to Sofia, or her father. At one point I almost had to laugh. This project seemed so . . . *preposterous.* I looked around the car as Sasha and Zoran chatted in Serbian and Boris stared out the window, watching the countryside rush past.

We four were on a trip to find a girl whom none of us had met. None of us even knew for certain whether Sofia really existed. This situation would have been strange under normal circumstances. But Yugoslavia was a police state careening towards civil war. This search posed risks, particularly for my three new friends. Why were they doing it?

CHAPTER 2

Sasha

I wasn't sure of my own motives, but I guessed that each of us had a unique reason for being part of this quest. The real enigma, the person I understood the least, was Sasha. For the past two weeks she had been my main confidante in this project. When I stepped off the train at the Belgrade station in the middle of the night on August 30, greeted by taxi drivers calling for fares and shoeless tramps asleep on the platform, I hadn't yet identified a local collaborator for this project. Every friend, fixer, or translator I knew in Belgrade was gone or unavailable.

I was alone, and I was stumped. But like so many times before in the Sofia story, I didn't find the answer; the answer found me. The next morning I went for a walk. I headed up the hill from where I was staying, past the great decaying Hotel Moskva, past Republika Square, and onto the Knez Mihailova pedestrian street. The day was clear and sunny, and there were folks on the street—teenagers, young couples, children, and oldsters. They went about their business, but I sensed the strain. I spent the day taking in the city, trying to gauge its mood. In the evening I returned to the Astoria hotel, fell asleep, and was awoken by a call from the front desk. "A young woman phoned for you," the voice at reception said. "She left a number. Her name is Sasha."

I had hoped to hear from Sasha, but hadn't really expected to. I had emailed her, along with a couple of other Serbian acquaintances, telling her I was arriving and suggesting that we meet for coffee. But I hadn't heard from Sasha in months, and had no idea if she was still in the country. We had met on a previous visit at a film festival of all things, spoke at length between screenings, and exchanged addresses before I left the country. I had been intrigued that young Serbs like Sasha had enough hope left in them to concern themselves with luxuries like movies, and Sasha, who hadn't travelled from her isolated stigmatized nation in years, seemed delighted to chat with a foreigner.

After getting her message at the hotel, I called Sasha back, and suggested that we have a chat over a drink. Sasha agreed, and told me to meet her "at the horse." The horse was the equestrian statue of Prince Milos Obrenović at Republika Square, and it was one of Belgrade's more popular *rendezvous* spots. The next evening I arrived early, and stood off to the side so that I would see Sasha before she saw me. Since we barely knew each other, I wondered if she had changed. Would I even recognize her?

When she stepped onto the square, I saw that she had changed. She was slimmer. She had sheared her thick black mane and wore stovepipe jeans and owl-eye glasses. This twenty-five-year-old woman now had the appearance of a teenage schoolboy.

"Because of the heat," she said to me after I had asked about her hair. "Come on, I know a place where we can go."

My plan was to get a sense of the mood of Belgrade, and perhaps see if Sasha could recommend a translator—someone reliable whom she could vouch for. I didn't know much about Sasha. I would later learn she had a flawless Serbian pedigree. Her great-great grandfather had been a Serb Orthodox priest who was beheaded by the Turks. Her grandfather had died in prison, jailed for shooting a bear and a rare bird on royal territory. Two of her uncles were Serbian Orthodox priests. I would later learn she had studied literature, and had bravely saved her brothers during the Bosnian and Croatian civil wars. But that evening she was a friendly face in a strange city, and that was enough.

Sasha led me to an outdoor café—somewhere near the circular plaza everyone called Slavija. Facing me across a tall round table, Sasha told me she was glad to hear from me. I got the distinct feeling she was bored.

"So what are you doing here?" she asked.

"Covering the elections," I said. "I'll be around for the next three weeks. I was sure you weren't around. I thought you were getting a job in western Europe?"

If there had been a job opportunity, it hadn't worked out. "I'm still here," she said, and shrugged.

Being *here*—in Serbia—made Sasha a minority of sorts. Serb history speaks of several migrations. There was the Velika Seoba, or Great Migration, of 1690, when thousands of Serbs fled Kosovo after an Austrian-inspired revolt was put down by their Turkish occupiers. But arguably a greater exodus began in the early 1990s, when nationalist hysteria and war seized Yugoslavia. Between 100,000 and 300,000 young Serbs left the country at that time. Many were young men escaping the draft. Others were evading the chaos, crime, and ensuing poverty.[1] The evacuees included many of the brightest and best of the young generation. Those who remained did so because they couldn't get out, or else they stayed to change things. Sasha was one of the latter. She had spent most of her young adult life in the trenches.

Talk of this election quickly spread to past votes. She told me that in 1992 she had worked to elect Milan Panic, the

Serb-American tycoon who ran against Milošević for the Serbian presidency. After Panic lost, Sasha supported the Zajedno opposition alliance in elections in late 1996. She took to the streets after the regime failed to recognize Zajedno victories in municipal elections, and was one of thousands who for months banged pots and pans, blew whistles, tossed eggs, and presented flowers to riot police. Protestors like Sasha eventually forced the regime to capitulate, only to be betrayed by leaders like Vuk Drašković, who compromised himself by accepting a lucrative job with the regime.

Milošević emerged from the protests stronger than ever. By the summer of 1997 he had moved into one of Tito's official residences. Sasha was unemployed and living with her mother.

Eventually the topic swung back to politics. "What do you think is going to happen?" I asked.

"War," she told me. "You can't start four wars in your neighbourhood without having one in your house. This is why I think we'll have a civil war here."

"A fifth war?" I said.

"Serbs are tough," she replied. "That's the way they are raised. They're a warrior people . . . Sometimes I tutor kids who are fifteen, sixteen, seventeen years old. They've never left the country. They've never been anywhere except Serbia and Montenegro. This is all they know—this situation. They know what they see on TV, and they know war. For them it's normal. It's life."

"There's no hope Slobo will lose without a war?"

"I hope," she said. "I hoped before. Hope is something that gets weaker every time you lose it."

I had come to ask Sasha to recommend an assistant. But when she told me she didn't have students at the moment or any work in particular it occurred to me I didn't need to. "I'm here for three weeks," I said. "I need a translator. Are you interested in a job?"

Sasha paused and gave me a startled look. She looked pleased that I asked, and seemed like she needed cash badly. "I want to do a story on refugees, Serbian refugees from Kosovo," I said, easing into the subject of my real purpose in Serbia. "Do you think you can find someone for me to talk to?"

Sasha said she thought she could help. "But just one thing I want to know," she said, after pausing and reflecting a moment. "Why do you want to hire me?"

I told her I thought she was talented and I wanted to work with someone young. I didn't tell her I was desperate for help, and that so far she was my only friend in Yugoslavia.

My plan in the beginning was to elicit Sasha's help without revealing Sofia, Momo, or the search. I was painfully aware that I could hide my agenda from Sasha only by lying. This I did not want to do, but Gjorg's fears and Sofia's fragile anonymity made me ultra-sensitive about security, and about protecting Sofia's identity and past. The truth is: there were too many things I didn't know. Because I didn't know where Sofia was I didn't know whether she could be hurt if even a single person in her current life knew about Gjorg. I didn't know how much I could trust Sasha to be discreet. So I decided to give information to her on a need-to-know basis. But almost immediately after we started I realized that it would be impossible to conduct a proper investigation if I were keeping the essential truth from her. So I confided in Sasha about Sofia, but I did so at precisely the moment I began to fear my trust was misplaced.

We started work two days later. Sasha said her uncles the priests would be able to help. The Serbian Church was providing relief for thousands of displaced Serbs from Kosovo, and through her family Sasha identified the priest who led the church's effort to care for Kosovo's Serbian diaspora. She contacted him. And he refused to speak to her beyond the offer of some friendly advice: *Little girl, be careful what you are getting yourself into.* She contacted a friend from Kosovska Mitrovica,[2] a Kosovar Serb attending university in Belgrade. He refused to speak to a foreign journalist. It had been little over a year since the NATO bombings of Yugoslavia, and it was evident the level of anger and suspicion towards westerners was great. Even those Serbs who didn't resent the western-inspired trade sanctions and bombings surely felt the impact of a generation of propaganda over the state-controlled media that labelled western countries, like the one I hailed from, the enemy. Clearly no Serb was going to talk to me. Sasha would have to make enquiries for me, which she couldn't do without knowing the full story.

So, on our second frustrating day trying to locate Serbs from Kosovo, we retreated to a student café called the Plato, nestled along a square beside the downtown campus of Belgrade University. This had been the congregating spot for the whistle-blowing students who agitated against Milošević in 1996 and 1997, and it had since been boarded off by the police to prevent a repeat performance.

Despite the drizzle of late summer rain, we sat at an outdoor table and huddled under the sun umbrella. The story I had told Sasha was that I wanted to find refugees from Kosovo, particularly from Mitrovica or villages to the north. I had lied, telling her I had met Serbs from this area during the war and wanted to locate them to do a "Where Are They Now?" story. Now she asked me their names. I told her I didn't really know them. I was lying clumsily, and she sensed something was wrong. I realized it would be impossible to work with her without telling her more.

"Can I trust you with something?" I asked. "It's something very important."

*

The story I told Sasha began fifteen months before—on June 14, 1999. Sometime in late morning I was in a car with three other journalists lumbering along a dirt road in central Kosovo. NATO troops and armour had begun pouring across the border two days before, and with them came reporters like ourselves. The day was fiercely hot. As I stared at the farm fields that stretched on both sides of the road, I remember thinking it was difficult to imagine a terrible war had taken place here. But terrible it had been. We had left the capital, Priština, forty-five minutes before, and the entire way we passed debris. Torched ruins that had once been homes. Houses reduced to chimneys, standing like sad totems over piles of rubble. Villagers—sad, skeletal folks—plodding along the roadside, returning to homes they hadn't seen for months.

And the fighting was still going on. A ceasefire had been sealed between NATO and Yugoslavia, but the hills of the Drenica Valley were rife with guerrillas of the Kosovo Liberation Army, known by their Albanian initials UÇK (pronounced *Oo-chee-KAH*). Like most things in the Balkans, the UÇK was indefinable. How you viewed them depended on where you stood. To Serbian cops and soldiers, they were an ubiquitous and vicious enemy. To Serbian civilians, they were not only terrorists, but mystical bogeymen—killer Albanians with guns, and as such the embodiment of every Kosovo Serb's nightmare. To Albanian villagers, they were heroes. And to the rest of us in the world they were as flawed and contradictory. A convincing money trail seemed to link the UÇK to Albanian organized crime and narcotic smuggling rings operating across Europe. Did this make the guerrillas a front for Balkan-based organized crime? Or did this mafia link make the UÇK highly pragmatic—willing to put dirty money to good use? I myself had been associated with the Kosovo story long enough to know that all these assertions were both wrong and right. The reality seemed to be there was no single definition of the UÇK for the simple reason there was no single UÇK. Since the force's appearance sixteen months before, many groups rose from Kosovo's hard soil wearing the UÇK insignia. Some were killers and smugglers. Others were local village men with the best intentions banded together in home-defence militias. Still others were the closest thing Kosovo had to a disciplined professional army.

Whatever UÇK was holed up in the hills of the Drenica Valley, rumours flew like bullets that they were still battling retreating Serbian forces. We wanted to find a guerrilla camp and learn what was happening. And we wanted to know what had happened over the past eighty days.

This was the assignment that had brought us to this quiet bend in Drenica, and as peaceful as the road looked, we knew that terrors resided just beneath the surface.

We had been warned that the roads were mined. We had turned off the tarmac and ventured onto this country road only because we had spotted a tractor ahead of us. Gambling that the locals knew which roads were safe and which were not, we pursued the tractor, and caught up with the rickety machine just as we rounded a bend on the outskirts of Rezallë. We stopped. The tractor stopped. And three Kosovar men riding in the wagon leapt to the ground and sauntered up to our car. From the back, where I sat, I saw their soiled, bony faces peering in the front passenger window.

The car's driver, a Hungarian photographer, asked if any of them spoke English. One boy said yes. "Is there mines on the road?" the driver asked. The English-speaking boy clenched his face in concentration. But instead of answering, he shifted his gaze from the driver to me. Giving me a once-over, he smiled with his eyes and asked: "Are you John Nadler?"

I was stunned. The seventy-eight-day bombardment of Yugoslavia had just ended. The NATO invasion and the Yugoslav withdrawal were underway. I was a foreign reporter, in Kosovo for barely forty-eight hours, and suddenly I'm recognized and asked this implausible question.

"Yes," I said. *But how in the world do you know this?*

Then the boy uttered the sound, "Cheerez." He stretched the skin of that face into a wide smile and said it again. *Cheerez.*

The sound was familiar, but I couldn't place it. And then a wind blew in my memory, shutters opened, and figures took shape—crooked mahogany-faced men in white skullcaps, aid workers in cargo pants. *Qirez*, I realized. He was talking about a village less than ten kilometres away. I had been there almost a year ago—before the air campaign and everything else. Between Qirez and this bend I had travelled a lot of miles and met a lot of people—refugees, victims, cops, guerrillas. I had encountered them in homes, at funerals, in tents and camps, in flight, and in despair. How many faces had I seen covering this story—dozens, hundreds, thousands? I couldn't begin to count. I was lost among those faces. And now this thin and dirty boy had identified me. But how could he know me?

Ten months earlier we had rolled into the village of Qirez in the rear of an aid convoy. I had come to Kosovo a week before to cover the recent outbreak of fighting between ethnic-Albanian guerrillas and Yugoslav security forces, and I journeyed to Qirez to chronicle the suffering the war had created.

Fighting had displaced several hundred thousand Kosovar Albanian villagers, and thousands of homeless had found safe haven in Qirez, one of the few villages in the Drenica Valley untouched by the violence. The UN had organized the convoy to bring food to the homeless, and had allowed hacks like me to tag along behind the flour trucks. We had parked our car on the outskirts of a compound, which consisted of two long buildings that served as a food warehouse and an administrative centre, a mosque on one end, a school at the other, and a bazaar in the centre that sold everything a refugee might need—bottle stoves, plastic tarps, and carton after carton of Marlboro, Lucky Strike, and HB cigarettes. There was even a barbershop. Dozens of people, mainly men, milled about—smoking, chatting, or standing silently by. The homeless in Qirez vastly outnumbered the local population. The displaced stayed in the school, crowded into the mosque, were billeted in homes, or found shelter under makeshift tents.

Getting out of the car, I blinked away the dust and resolved to find a refugee to speak to. After wandering through the crowd for twenty minutes or so, I heard a voice behind me ask, "Do you need help?"

I turned and found myself staring into the soiled face of a Kosovar man. The face was stern but honest, and appeared young. (At that moment I pegged the boy for seventeen; he would later tell me he was twenty-three.)

"I need help," I said.

He asked if I was a journalist and I said I was. "I have a story for you," he said. And then he told me that I was now speaking to a dead man, *a ghost.*

I later remembered this boy as "the ghost" because he wouldn't tell me his name, only the bizarre thing that had happened to him. The story began when Yugoslav security forces attacked the boy's village two weeks before. By that time most of the boy's neighbours had read the stars, antici-pated an invasion, and left. But the boy had stayed, gambling that the Yugoslav army and police might never invade.

But invade they did. "The Serbs came very fast," the boy told me. He had fled the village, joined up with a group of neighbours—and then he got to the point of his story. "I was in a field," he said. "The police did see me. They shot at me, and I fell down and pretended I was dead. My neighbours did hear the shooting, and they thought I am dead.

"They left and they did tell everyone they saw that I had been killed by Serb police. Somebody who heard this did tell my mother and family in Bajicë. Everybody did think I was dead. But I wasn't. I lay down very still for many hours, and then, when I was sure the police was not looking, I jumped up and run away." He told me he went to the village of Bajicë, where his family was staying. The first person he met was his sister-in-law. "She say to me, 'How can this be? The Serbs did kill you.' My mother and brothers did say this too. They all looked like they did see a ghost."

The boy paused, slipping into the word *ghost* like an exotic robe, and I scribbled the entire account down. It was a good yarn—the first cogent account I had heard of the cleansing of a village—and I wanted to include it in my article.

"How do I spell your name?" I asked.

"No," he said, "I do not want to give my name. What if the police read your report? Then they will come for me again." Of course I didn't think this a plausible fear, but I had nothing to fear and he had everything to lose. So I deferred to him, and asked if I could use his words without his name. He agreed. "I did tell you all this because it is important for people in your country to know what is happening here," he said. "The gun is no solution for nothing. My solution is peace. Peace for all." He hung this statement out like a child's poster written in crayon.

"I always did want peace between Serbs and Albanians," he continued. "My girlfriend and I did try to make peace between Serbs and Albanians." He stopped talking and I stopped writing.

"Your girlfriend and you tried what?" I asked.

"Yes," he said. "She and me did try. But it was so hard." Then he paused. "Look, if you want to know about the refugee people here in Qirez, I bring you to them."

The boy headed off in the direction of the school, at the far end of the compound. As he fought his way through the

27

crowd of unwashed exiles that swelled by the minute as news of the food convoy spread, he continued talking.

"This is not a way to live," he said, as I took notes. "War is not a way for people. The Albanian and the Serb do not have to fight. My girlfriend and me, we did try to show the Serb and Albanian can live in peace."

"Your girlfriend?" I said, remembering the earlier reference. "Tell me about your girlfriend." I then asked if she was in Qirez, and whether I could meet her.

The boy frowned and said no. His girlfriend wasn't with him, he told me. And then after a pause, he began another riff on peace. "I want that the world know what is happening in this war. I want that—"

"When was the last time you saw your girlfriend?" I asked. References to his girlfriend had caught my interest. I envisioned a human interest story: *Albanian couple who fought for peace now separated by war.*

He stopped and tensed his face. "I did not speak with her since before the war," he said, and I assumed he meant since the outbreak of hostilities that year.

"Why?" I asked.

"It was too dangerous," he said, pronouncing the word *dangers.*

By this time we had rounded the corner and stepped into the school building. We walked down a hall decorated by cracks and water stains. After wandering from room to room, where we saw a few white-capped old men reclining and smoking, the boy suggested we visit the mosque at the other end of the compound. As we left the school and re-entered the mob, I steered the boy back to his girlfriend.

"You say you haven't seen your girlfriend since before the war. Where is she now?"

He told me he girlfriend lived in a village in northern Kosovo. "Maybe she is there," he said. Because they studied together in Mitrovica, he said it was possible she had returned there to wait out the war.

"Or maybe in Belgrade," he said. "She told me once she would go to Belgrade."

Belgrade, I thought. *That's odd.* The war had created such bad blood between Serbs and Albanians that it was hard to understand how a Kosovar could consider Belgrade sanctuary. The boy must have sensed my confusion.

"My girlfriend is Serbian girl," he explained.

The mosque sat on a hill, and to get there we trudged up a track that ran alongside a graveyard of tilting headstones. I itched to ask more about this Serbian girlfriend. The revelation that this Albanian kid had a Serb lover was extraordinary. One of the first things that had startled me about Kosovo was the chasm between the communities. There was no single Kosovo; there was a Serbian one and an Albanian one, and almost no exchange between the two, except with mortar and shells. No Albanian I had met had a close Serb friend or lover he or she wanted to admit to, and vice versa. Before the civil wars of the 1990s, mixed marriages—Serb-Bosnian, Serb-Croat, and Bosnian-Croat—were common in Yugoslavia. But Serbs and Albanians were a different matter, which made this boy's love life so remarkable.

He and I wandered the mosque. I collected quotes and sad stories, and fifteen minutes later we headed back down the hill. "I will leave this place," the boy said. "I will go to the north. It will be dangers. But I must to go."

"To find your girlfriend?"

"Yes," he said.

"How are you going to get there?" I remembered the innumerable checkpoints and cops the convoy had passed to get here.

"By the fields," he said. "The police will not find me."

"When you last spoke to your girlfriend, what did she say?" I asked.

He looked away. "She tell to me we cannot meet. She say it is too dangers."

"Too dangerous for her?"

"She say it is dangers for me. She say she will not be the one to kill me. This was when the troubles did start. Everyone did know war is coming."

Before I could ask more, a colleague I had driven in with—a photographer named Andy—appeared from the mob. "The convoy's leaving, mate," he said, a camera slung over his shoulder like a rifle.

I nodded, and turned to the boy to tell him goodbye.

"Look," said the boy, "I cannot tell you my name now. But someday I can. Give to me your name and address, and after the war I will write you a letter."

I tore a page from my notebook, wrote down the information, and presented it to the boy.

"When this war is over," he said, "I will write to say to you that I am alive. Maybe we can be pen friends."

Minutes later I left the Refugee City not realizing I would revisit Qirez in my memory again and again.

*

I spoke for perhaps thirty minutes. I didn't tell Sasha everything, but I confided more to her than I would ever tell anyone else about my unorthodox mission. I told her about the girl Sofia, and that I was trying to locate her for the sake of a friend in Kosovo. "This is what I'm doing here," I said in conclusion.

Sasha listened quietly throughout, revealing no surprise at the things I told her. She did flash one expression—of disappointment in me for lying, for not telling her this from the beginning.

She rolled her eyes. "This will be very dangerous," she said. "I remember Bosnia. I heard many cases when girls were killed by their *fathers* . . ."

I told her about Sofia's father, Momo. "And there's a problem that may make it more dangerous. The boy thinks Momo was a cop—and not a normal cop, but UDB."

"DB?" Sasha said. "That's no problem. I know some DB guys. I'll talk to them. Maybe they can help."

DB were the Serbian initials for the state security service, Serbia's chief intelligence agency, the local version of the KGB or CIA. Given that Yugoslavia was a police state, the moment I had begun this endeavour I had been wary of Momo and his state security connection and the intolerable contingencies this connection posed. What if Momo, as a member of state security, had the ability to know when someone was looking for him and his daughter?

This paranoia had started to haunt me the moment I crossed the border into Yugoslavia, which is why I secretly panicked when Sasha so nonchalantly told me about her "DB guys."

"Jesus Christ," I thought. "Who have I just shared Sofia with?"

*

I didn't tell Sasha I was terrified by our last conversation, by her revelation she had "DB friends," associates within Serbian state security. I feared I had exposed Gjorg, Sofia, and myself to the Serbian police during my first hours in Belgrade.

But I didn't have an easy solution, so I did nothing. At my next meeting with Sasha, at the Plato a day later, I tried to ignore the topic. We were seated inside. It was late morning and there were a few students about. We spoke about several matters including our plan to use the Orthodox Church and aid agencies to assist us in locating the people we were after. We had all but decided to visit the Belgrade offices of the Red Cross and UNHCR when Sasha casually mentioned that she had asked her friends about Momo, the father with alleged state-security connections.

I felt ill. I hadn't wanted Sasha to ask them about our business, but I had been so allergic to the topic the other day that I hadn't told her not to.

"They said they would look," Sasha said. "But they did say the name Momo is familiar. It's unusual name, you know. They think they heard about him."

I looked into Sasha's long, almost Asian eyes and decided there was no way I could trust her—or anyone in Serbia. I would take the first train out, and pray I hadn't done anyone any lasting harm. But before going, I decided I had to know what was going on. I asked Sasha about her friends. She told me two stories about crime, the police, and punishment in Serbia that she said would make it all clear.

"About six months ago, I was at home and the bell rings," Sasha said. "I answered, and it was the police. They were looking for my brothers." Sasha had two older brothers, and the police visit brought Sasha back to the time when both lived like fugitives, hunted by the cops and the army.

Sasha explained that in 1991, when Yugoslavia started to come apart and war broke out in Croatia, police began coming to her family home. On every occasion the cops were looking to deliver draft notices to her brothers. But their intention wasn't just to deliver papers; they had come to take possession of the boys.

"That's how they always did it," Sasha said. "And how they still do it. When a boy is drafted into the army, they come to your flat or house to get you. And if they find a boy at home, they take away and he wouldn't come back until after he did his army duty. Sometimes the boy never came back at all."

Right from the beginning Sasha knew what the uniformed men were after. So no matter where her brothers were, she always said the same thing when the draft officials came to call. *No, they are not here,* she would say. *And I don't know where they are.*

"Usually, this was enough for the cops," Sasha said. "But once they said, 'Can we come in?' And I said, 'No, because he is not here and I don't know where he is.' But the cop really wanted to come in, so I stood in the door and said, 'You can't.' My dad, he is a lawyer, and he told me they cannot come in without a paper, a warrant.

"During Bosnia, the war there, they really pushed. I remember once, some VJ[3] guys, I think they were military police, came to my door and asked over and over, 'Where is your brother?' 'I don't know,' I said. 'Will you come with us to the station and sign a statement saying you don't know where he is?' 'Look, I'm a woman. I'm not going to war, and I don't want to go anywhere with you.' 'Will you sign a statement saying you don't know where he is?' 'I won't sign anything,' I said. Finally, I told them, 'I'm going to close this door. You can go to war if you want to. I'm going inside.'

"After a while I learned how to act with them. You had to be a little rude, and very strong. Once, these cops came to the door—it was during Bosnia too—they were pushing for me to tell them where one of my brothers lived. That's how it worked. Boys would hide from the army. They didn't want to go to war, so they lived in secret in other flats, with uncles or grandparents or girlfriends, so the police couldn't find them. These cops kept asking, 'Where is your brother?'

"Finally, I looked at one of these guys in the face, and I realized how young he was. I mean, he was the same age as my brother. I asked him, 'Do you know what you are doing? Do you really know?'

"He didn't say anything. He left right away. I wonder if he

did understand what he was doing, that he was sending Serb boys, just like him, to die?"

When Sasha had concluded, she stared at me sharply. Sasha read you like an obituary. I realized this because she suddenly told me I had nothing to worry about. I had said nothing, but she knew what I was afraid of.

"I know these guys for years," she said of her DB friends. "They're good guys. One lives in my building. The other guy lives in Novi Beograd. They watch out for me. DB friends will always do that . . . if you help them."

I seized on the words "help them," and asked her how.

"These guys are really smart, really educated," she said. "I give them books and CDs. They really appreciate it. They'll do anything for me if I'm in trouble."

Trouble?

"If I get a traffic ticket, if I go through a red light, I just give the ticket to them and they take care of it. When my father got his car stolen, the police never did nothing. So he went to them and they got it back."

Sasha told me she got to know her state security protectors through an old man she had met at a party years before. "He had white hair and was dressed elegantly, like a real gentleman, and he had this beautiful wife who was so much younger than he was. I never forget when we met, he took my hand and said: 'You are very beautiful.' And just then, when he said it, I saw that he was blind. He knew what I was thinking, because then he said, 'I can feel your beauty.'"

Somehow Sasha and the old man became friends. "He loved to talk about his life. He was special. He spoke languages, and he had travelled around the world."

And he had a secret. Sasha learned he had been recruited into state security in his late twenties. This was how he made money, and learned languages, and transformed himself into the man—the gentleman intelligence officer—who could charm her so completely. Only later did he explain his blindness.

"It's funny thing," Sasha said. "He told me what happened with his young wife standing right there. He told me this wife was not his first wife. He was married before. He came home unexpectedly and found her with his best friend. He shot and killed them both. And then he tried to kill himself. But he blinded himself instead."

That was that—how Sasha acquired her DB friends. "I'm not the only one," she said. "I think everyone has a DB guy. These days in Serbia you need them. To survive."

Suddenly I was no longer suspicious of Sasha, a young woman who had repeatedly defied the police, the army, and the regime to protect her brothers. I understood that in a society where authority is crumbling, you seek justice through friends in high places because there is no law, only influence. This influence transcended mundane matters like traffic fines. Sasha's "DB guys" provided a modicum of protection in a society that offered it no other way.

So I decided I didn't have to abandon Sasha, Serbia, or Gjorg's search. I said not a word about what I was thinking, but Sasha understood.

"Don't worry," she said. "I would never tell them about you. They hate all journalists."

CHAPTER 3

Zoran

As we sped south on Highway 23 towards Kragujevac, I glanced around the car. Of my three Serbian friends, I figured I understood Zoran's motives the most. Why was Zoran here? Because I was paying him.

That is why I needed Zoran—to fill in the gaps in a story I had learned in tantalizing pieces and whispers over the past year from a frightened Albanian boy.

I heard of Zoran long before I met him. A colleague had regaled me with stories of working with a translator who had amazing state-security contacts. When I had arrived in Belgrade two weeks before, this fixer was on my mind. I feared I would need the help of someone like Zoran, but for the sake of confidentiality I didn't want to involve more people in the search than necessary. So, after hooking up with Sasha, I called Zoran but told him nothing. Zoran and I worked on a few news stories—several concerning the upcoming presidential elections, and one about the abduction of Milošević's former friend and rival Ivan Stambolić.

During my first ten days in Belgrade, I had fallen into a pattern: I used Zoran for journalism and Sasha for the search. In the beginning I thought this system might work. Sasha had contacts in the relief arm of the Orthodox Church. She knew a young Kosovo Serb who was attending university in Belgrade. She came up with fine ideas like using the Red Cross (ICRC) and the UN's refugee agency (UNHCR) to find the people we were looking for.

But Sasha and I soon hit a wall. None of our leads yielded results, and faced with the prospect of failure, I had to consider conscripting Zoran. First, however, I needed to be sure. So one night I suggested that Zoran and I go out for a late dinner. We met outside the McDonald's on Terazija avenue and went straight to his car. Zoran led the way, limping. "I killed my knee a month ago." I braced myself for another story of blood and violence, but Zoran said he had pulled a muscle at the gym.

Zoran took me to a restaurant called the Frans, which he said was a popular Mafia hangout. Not long after we were seated at a table underneath a glass canopy, Zoran nudged me and pointed to a giant of a man sitting nearby. In front of the giant was a plate bearing a Neanderthal-sized serving of grilled meat. Beside the giant and his meat sat a fleshy-cheeked woman with blond hair of a hue not found in nature and a bottomless chasm of cleavage.

"That guy over there, I know him. He is with the Rakovcki gang," Zoran said, referring to a suburb of Belgrade. "He is into many things. I think he makes his money from stealing the cars."

This sighting led to other stories. After we finished our drinks, Zoran and I piled into his car and headed back across town. We passed a coffee shop, and Zoran told me how the proprietor was swindled out of 2 million Deutschmarks by Serbian state security in an oil-smuggling scam. Eventually we arrived at the Sava River and climbed aboard a near-empty barge restaurant.

We sat at a table on deck, and Zoran continued. "The guy who owns this place has another place too. This guy, he was a cop. Then he was state security, and his career went up and up and up. Anyway, this guy, his name is Goran.

"He was involved in a shooting two years ago. He's on this other ship club on the Sava where they always play national [Serbian] music." These two other guys come into the club. One guy was named Bojan and the other guy was Mija. They go up to Goran and they say something very ugly to him. And then they go away. Goran follows them outside and taps one of the guys on the shoulder, and as he turns, Goran shoots him in the face, and then he shoots the other guy in the face."

I was impressed by Zoran's stories and his seeming intimacy with the killers he spoke about. He had access to a brutal world where I might find Momo. Finally, I asked Zoran about the rumour he had once worked on an investigation of a Kosovar war criminal. Zoran told me the story was true. He had been on an assignment with a journalist, and found a Kosovo Serb cop who had been implicated in the killing of civilians in a city in southern Kosovo.

"On that operation it took me three days to find this guy," Zoran said. "You give me three days, I can find anyone in Serbia." Then, flashing a smile that seemed to curl at the ends like a handlebar moustache, Zoran said, "Hey, I'm the best."

I gave Zoran another once-over and decided he looked like no fixer I had ever met.

"I'm working on a project," I told him. "It's an investigation into some fighting that happened in a village in Kosovo during the war. We need to find VJ or police who were there. Do you think you can find somebody?" I would eventually tell Zoran about Sofia, but would give fewer details to him than I had to Sasha.

Zoran said he knew someone who had been Ministry of Interior (MUP) special forces and fought in Kosovo. In the meantime I asked him to accompany Boris, Sasha, and me to Kraljevo. In the hope that Zoran would be able to help us find someone who could shed light on the massacre. In fact, he would help us more than I ever imagined.

*

Gjorg had just returned to his village to begin his life anew. What he found was death. No sooner did he identify me on the road than he offered me a glimpse of war's horror.

"There is a massive grave near here," he said. "The Serbs did kill people here, and there are bodies. I can take you."

This was one of the things we had come to Drenica to see—the aftermath of the war. So we packed Gjorg into the front seat of the car. Under his directions we drove to a cemetery on the far side of town. A rebel stood in the grave-yard and stared into a void in the earth. We entered via a gate, and found two large mounds and the open pit the UÇK guerrilla was obsessing over. There was a corpse in the pit, but we knew this before looking; we could smell the rot yards away.

The corpse's appearance was as bad as the reek suggested. It was unrecognizable as human. The figure was bloated, putrid death stuffed inside blue jeans and a winter parka. Gjorg said more bodies lay beneath the nearby mounds.[1] I joined the guerrilla, took a spot on the edge of the pit, stared into that fetid hole, covered my mouth with my shirt sleeve, and felt not very much. The entire scene was so surreally obscene I had no scale within me to register it. I was able to respond to simple suffering, grief, and even death. But it was impossible to fathom this—rotting flesh, exposed for weeks, clothes the only remaining sign of humanity, exuding the worst odour I had ever inhaled. The stench said it all. It attacked your nose and eyes like gas, and seemed to hang on and follow you like a depression.

Gjorg chatted with a couple of locals and returned with

the news that there was another open grave in the neighbouring village. We climbed into the car, sped back to the main road, and turned right on another unmarked dirt track. Minutes later we stopped the car near a mound at yet another bend. Beneath the mound was a deep ditch, and inside it two bodies lay face down. Again there was the putrid sweet smell of decomposition. Like the unfortunate we had just seen, these two had been dead a long time, a month or more. Once again I had to exercise great imagination to picture them as living people. Only the trousers and sports clothes and coloured athletic shoes suggested humanity.

For reasons I have forgotten, there were flowers, only slightly withering, in the back seat of the car. Someone took a rose and placed it near the ditch. We lingered a moment longer, and then moved on.

The last stop was a nearby homestead—the location of the burial site Gjorg had heard rumours about. The farm consisted of a house, a leaning shed, and fruit trees. The focal point of the yard was a single-storey dwelling. Slavic graffiti painted on its walls was the only immediate evidence that Serb police had commandeered this farmhouse as a base. But there were other, more horrifying clues, shown to us by Habib, the elder of two brothers who owned the farm before the war. As soon as we got out of our vehicle, Habib led us to a charred strip of earth filled with soot and shards of red tile. Before the war, the shed stored grain, he said. But during the war, police had used it as a crematorium. Among the tiles, ashes, and embers, Habib had found the remains of neighbours. He fetched a white plastic fertilizer bag and opened it. The bag was filled with jewellery and shards of bones that were eerily recognizable as human. There was a finger; a large plate-like portion of a skull; the shattered piece of what might have been a shin bone; a few teeth; a wristwatch with a metal bracelet; and pieces of clothing.

One of Habib's cousins then wandered into the yard. We shook hands, but sadly, I do not remember the texture of his grip. Moments later this would be important. The man's name was Meha. He was about forty years old and stereotypically mustachioed, and he arrived with a story about these bones.

"When the Serbs came to this area in April, the men ran away and lived in the hills," Meha said. "I left my family behind because I believed the police would kill the men but they would spare the women and children. I hid in the forest, but I worried about my family. In the day I saw smoke coming from my village and others.

"I met others in the hills who were hiding from the Serbs. I asked everyone I met what was happening down there, and if they knew about my wife and children. No one knew, but one man told me a terrible thing. He said the police were killing our people and burning their bodies in the farm of Habib and his brother. Every day, I saw the smoke of the fire burning in this farm, and I worried about my family."

According to Meha, the sight of the pyre's smoke drove him mad. He came down from the hills and crept into the farmyard after the police had gone to sleep. Kneeling beside the hearth, he thrust his hands deep into the warm ashes and felt several fine, thin, smooth shards of . . . something. He pulled them from the ashes and probed them with his fingers.

"When I held these bones in my hand," Meha said, "I knew I was caressing my children."

But, happily, he was wrong. Meha's story ended well. His family had fled their home shortly after Meha had taken to the hills. His wife and kids survived the war. The bones Meha embraced that night might have been someone else's children.[2]

After Meha finished his tale, my colleagues signalled they wanted to get going. For the first time since our first meeting, I focused my attention back on Gjorg. I couldn't help but think that fate had caused our paths to cross, and I wanted to say and learn many things. I offered Gjorg a ride back to his home village, but he declined. His sister lived nearby. He wanted to visit and find out who had returned. So Gjorg and I walked away from the group to exchange a few words in private.

"Did you ever find your girlfriend, the Serb girl?" I asked.

"No," he said. "I did not find."

Someone from the group called out for me to hurry.

"Look," he said. "I want to tell you this story, about her."

I told Gjorg I wanted to hear it. He told me he lived near the bend of the road where we had stopped the tractor. I said goodbye. But before heading back to the car, I asked one last question.

"Your girlfriend . . . what was—is—her name?"

"Sofia," he said, after hesitating a moment. "Sofia Neznanović . . . Come back, John, and I will tell you."

I packed myself in the back seat of the car, and as we bounced out of this sad, morbid place, I looked back and caught a glimpse of Gjorg—as thin as shade—walking in long strides up a path.

It took me ten days, but I did go back to talk to Gjorg. I was curious about Sofia and wanted to hear "this story" he had to tell. I also felt a responsibility to continue our relationship. Chance had reunited Gjorg and me, and I believed it would be almost irreverent not to keep in touch with the young man.

But I was just too busy chronicling the daily convulsions that seized and altered Kosovo. After meeting Gjorg, I watched as Kosovo's Roma population fled the territory in panic, and *en masse*. They disappeared so suddenly, and their homes—in the city of Kosovska Mitrovica, at least—were torched so quickly after their departure, that it was as if Kosovo's Roma had been snatched up in a Biblical rapture. After meeting Gjorg, I watched Serb police, soldiers, and civilians stream out of the province in endless convoys as Kosovo re-invented itself as an Albanian-only state. It was a sad and ironic ending to the drama I had been witnessing since 1998. NATO had gone to war with Yugoslavia to prevent a human rights catastrophe. But as soon as the bombings began Kosovo saw hundreds of thousands of Albanians uprooted and driven from their homes. Now that NATO was entrenched on Kosovo soil, a reverse cleansing of the province's Serbs and Roma was going on. The scene was mad, and maddening.

I encountered a ragtag police *milicija* convoy that had stopped for rest and water on the outskirts of Štimlje. UÇK snipers had attacked the convoy on the road from Suva Reka, and the cops were jumpy and angry and didn't notice they had parked outside the gates of an insane asylum. Four patients, eccentric-looking and bedraggled, stood at the fence, and I can still remember the cheer they gave as the cops emerged from their cars and buses. "Serb-ij-a! Serb-ij-a! Serb-ij-a!" The mentally ill were not afraid to show their support for Kosovo's constabulary. Minutes later a tall cop with a walrus moustache gave me his general appraisal of the situation. "Fucking things, fucking things," he said. I could not have put it better.

I wasn't sure why so many Serbs were fleeing. Many had been threatened. But there were not enough Albanians back to chase away the thousands of Serbs that seemed to be streaming out of Kosovo by the day. I understood the exodus better the afternoon a Hungarian photographer and I visited a village in northern Kosovo. The Serbian villagers had just cleared out, fires were underway in most of their empty homes, and local Kosovars were carting away everything that wasn't burning. One young Kosovar wore a skin-diving mask on his forehead. He rooted through a heap of trinkets and assorted belongings dragged from a burning home. The letters 'UÇK' had been written in large orange letters on the walls.

Throughout this time I thought of Gjorg daily. Unable to schedule a day (or even a morning) to visit him, I eventually devised a plan that would give me a professional reason to pay him a visit. I made a pitch to my editor on a story about Gjorg's travails and his search for his Serb fiancée Sofia. My editor was enthusiastic. "It's a Balkan Romeo and Juliet," he told me. So, the morning after receiving the commission, I hired a car and driver, and rumbled into Gjorg's village with my photographer friend Andy, who would take photos for the article.

Andy and I found Gjorg in a tent on his family's farm, having received directions to the Isufi homestead by two kids cutting hay on the edge of town. As soon as we set foot on Gjorg's property, I realized this young man and his family still faced a world of hardship. The summer heat weighed down on us in waves, and the earth was so dry even the grass was dusty. Glancing around you could see Gjorg had little protection from either the sun or the dirt. Except for a dilapidated shed, the only structure left standing on the farm was a khaki-coloured army tent bearing the letters UNHCR. On the far left the Isufi family home lay in ruins. The Serb *milicija* had destroyed this house the previous summer, but the weeds growing among the heaps of bricks inside the foundation made this disaster look ancient.

We were greeted by a thin old woman with a lovely weathered face, and a lovelier smile that consisted of a single upper tooth. The woman spoke no English but seemed to understand our purpose, because she immediately called out, "Gjorg, Gjorg." Ten seconds later Gjorg emerged from the tent, grinning in surprise at the sight of us. This smile was the last of our visit.

During our entire stay Gjorg brooded. The euphoria of our reunion ten days before was gone. I wasn't sure why, except of course that life for him was far from easy. He currently shared his only shelter—this tent—with his mother (the woman who had greeted us) and aunt. He had four brothers who had yet to return, and one of his sister's sons was missing and feared dead. He had troubles that I could never have imagined when I was a twenty-four-year-old university student fretting about grades and beer money.

Despite his dark mood, Gjorg was a fine host. He introduced Andy and me to his elderly mother, to whom we presented a bag of groceries we had brought from Priština.

"Ah, why you bring this?" Gjorg said. "We do not need nothing."

Then his mother brewed tea over a tiny propane stove as Gjorg, Andy, and I sat on the grass and talked. We spoke about Gjorg's experiences during the war. "I did live in the mountains," he said. He had also spent a good deal of time fleeing from village to village in Drenica, staying out of the path of the police and army. He recited a long list of Kosovar place names that I neither understood nor retained.

"When did you get back to your village?" I asked, wondering how long Gjorg had been home.

"Then," he said. "Then when we did meet on the road."

If he was just arriving home when we met on the road, I asked him, how did he know about the dead body in the cemetery?

"Before, in Gllogovc[3] I did meet many people from my village and they did tell me about the massacre that did happen here."

Finally, I asked about Sofia. "While you were running . . . during the war . . . did you hear news of your friend?"

Gjorg glared. "You mean that person we did speak of before in Qirez?" he asked.

"Yes."

"No," he replied. "I do not speak of that now."

He jumped up and walked over to the women. Something was wrong, and I had no idea what. So when Gjorg returned

46

seconds later carrying two hourglass-shaped cups of tea, I asked him if we could speak in private. He led me to the far end of the garden, where a long field began that had in happier times yielded a crop of corn.

Gjorg did not wait for me to begin. "John, I do believe you and I are friends," he said.

"Sure," I said.

"That which we did speak of before, in Qirez," he said, "she must be a secret between I and you. You must tell no one about . . . her."

"OK," I said, blinking. "OK . . . But you said last time you had something to tell me about her."

"Look, this is what I did want to say to you," he said with finality. "You are the only person I tell about her. You must not tell nobody, and you must not ask about her."

As we travelled back to Priština, Andy asked, "What happened? Why didn't we do the story?"

I shrugged. I had no idea.

It would take me three weeks to learn that the answer involved the gruesome remains of murdered neighbours that had greeted Gjorg and me when we arrived at his village immediately after the war's end. Gjorg wanted Sofia to stay a secret because a bloody cord linked these remains with her.

CHAPTER 4

Boris

At 2:30 P.M. we arrived at the outskirts of Boris's hometown. As we passed a sign that bore the word *Kraljevo* and seven coats of arms—one for every Serbian monarch who had been crowned there—Boris declared: "Welcome to the City of Kings."

Boris shook with excitement. "Oh, I love always to come back here," he said. "I live in Belgrade, and maybe someday I go to Slovenia, the country of my father. But Kraljevo will always be my home."

Boris was not wrong when he described his birthplace as kingly. Known as Karanovac during the Ottoman times, the city was given its kingly name by Aleksandar Obrenović, Serbia's first monarch of the post-Turkish era, and a succession of kings was crowned there. In 1951, Communist leader Aleksandar Ranković, founder of the Yugoslav state security apparatus, renamed the city Rankovicevo in honour of himself. But it eventually reverted to Kraljevo, and kingly it has remained. During the Milošević era, Kraljevo's Serbian royalist tendencies made it a hotbed of the opposition, that is to say, the anti-Milošević movement. In elections in 1996, Kraljevo voted in a roster of anti-regime candidates to city hall. As payback, the regime harvested Kraljevo's manhood and used them as fodder in the 1999 war in Kosovo. As many as twenty thousand Kraljevo men were conscripted into the army, and Boris was one of them.

That was how chance had brought us together. During my first week in Belgrade, I had asked Sasha if she knew any veterans of the Kosovo war. "Why?" she asked. After giving Sasha the salient details of the attack on Rezallë, I told her I wanted to find Serbian VJ, *milicija,* or paramilitary who had been there on the day, who could give their side of the story. Short of a witness to the killings, I hoped to find someone who knew Momo, or at least knew of him. Momo, after all, was a state security cop. Like a bear protecting a cub, he could be dangerous if we encountered the father before the daughter. The question was: How dangerous? I had conscripted Zoran into the project to find this out, but I didn't think there would be any harm in putting Sasha to this task as well.

"I know a couple of guys who were there, in Kosovo," she said. "I will ask them." But any optimism I felt from that conversation dissolved a few days later when she reported that one friend had refused to meet. "He said he just doesn't want to speak about what happened. He said he just wants to forget."

I promptly forgot about the whole thing for close to a week. Then one morning, out of the blue, Sasha announced: "I found someone who was in Kosovo. He says he'll talk to us. He was VJ."

"Did he fight in the Drenica Valley?" I asked.

Sasha shrugged. "I think he was a lot of places," she said.

The next day we went to the café at the Dom omladine, and found the veteran waiting for us at an outdoor table. He was not alone. A couple of other acquaintances of Sasha were there too, smoking, talking, sipping coffee. I barely noticed the veteran in the company. Later I described him in my notebook: "Oval-faced, a prominent nose. His fleshy cheeks and girth gives him appeal."

I barely remember our introduction, just Sasha's voice saying: "This is Boris Postovnik."

Boris was reserved. I remember he said no more than "Hello" and then retreated back into his chair, watching and listening.

While Boris said nothing, I bided my time chatting with his friends. There were two of them, early twenties, dressed in black, and ragged like students in eastern Europe a decade before. One guy told me that he was involved in publicity for the DOS campaign.

I asked him, "What's going on? Everyone talks about Kostunica, but you never see him, except in posters. Why are there no rallies or marches, like Vuk Drašković used to have, to get the message out?"

Sure, Drašković in his day in the 1990s had been fighting a losing battle. He had taken on Milošević in an electoral system that the strongman controlled so completely it could only be called democratic under the most narrow of definitions. But still, the DOS publicist argued, Drašković's grandstanding had failed to inspire the people. It was different now.

"People notice that Kostunica does not do this," he said. "There are no ads on TV, no big posters. They say they like this better. Our whole advertising strategy is mouth-to-mouth. People are telling people." I had been only half-listening to most of this conversation, but at this point I blinked myself awake. For weeks I had considered this election a cynical show that looked exciting during the race, but which would be subverted by the regime at the finish line. But the DOS publicist was one of the first to hint (to me anyway) that Serbs themselves might not be willing to let this happen. I was trying to decide whether he was right when he and his friend stood up, said their goodbyes, and left Boris, Sasha, and me at the table.

Boris leaned back in his chair and continued to say nothing.

Looking back, I realize he was inspecting, judging, and coming to a decision—about me. Throughout the political chit-chat with his friends, I had been sizing Boris up as well. Boris was as big as a bear. He had heft and girth, but he was not threatening. He had the build of a sensualist, a man who loved to eat and drink. But his silence made it impossible to read much more. He may have arrived at some judgment based on the things I had said to his friends, but the fact that he had remained meant he hadn't made up his mind.

We huddled around the circular table outside the Dom. We ordered more coffee and mineral water. I started over. I introduced myself again, and stated my purpose. I told him I had been in Kosovo before and after what Serbs call "NATO aggression." I was investigating certain aspects of the war. I had heard the Albanian side of the story; I wanted to hear the Serbian side. I wanted the story directly from a veteran, some-one who was there. Boris's face eased a bit.

"You were in Kosovo?" I said.

"Yes," he replied. "I went to Kosovo shortly after the air strikes began, and left with the entire army in June. I was in a medical unit."

"Did you ever serve in Drenica?" I asked, with Momo in mind.

"No," he said. "I was in Klina and Orahovac."

I was disappointed.

Then silent Boris started to talk. In fluent English and a booming tenor voice, Boris vented anger, although he did it gently, without ranting or raving. Anger that war had come and that the Western world (NATO) was bombing his family and friends—his country, Yugoslavia.

Boris was a medical student. He had several years of study left to go. He would talk to me, he said. There were things he wanted to say. But he would relate his personal history only. The NATO alliance—which included my country—was still an enemy of Yugoslavia. He would not relate any military information. He would not name units or describe weaponry or provide numbers of troops. He would simply tell what had happened to him.

Boris had not been in Drenica. And he had been a medical officer. This was not the type of person I felt would be useful. I was looking for an active fighter, an ethnic cleanser. Someone who had been involved in the clearing of villages. I was both disappointed and relieved that Boris was essentially normal and humane. As much as I wanted to converse with a killer and find out the truth about Rezallë I dreaded the thought of meeting such a person. Simply being in their presence would be to enter an eerie and warped place where I hoped I wouldn't feel right. And I always wondered: if you visit such a place and fraternize with murderers (and perhaps somehow grow to like them), how much of yourself do you leave there, or how much of them do you take back with you?

No Boris wasn't the man I was looking for, but I decided to hear him out anyway. I was there, sitting in front of him, and really had no other choice but listen.

"I was very afraid," Boris began. Then he flew into his story. I never had to ask him a question. He vented. He raced. It was like he was whispering an aria. He would barrel forward and recount events, dates, feelings, fears, and doubts. He would pause every now and then to consider something. Often he paused because he was astounded by what he himself had just said. I quickly got the feeling that in telling me about Kosovo, Boris was remembering it for the first time since these things had happened to him.

He remembered the Albanians he considered enemies. "I was afraid about the UÇK, the terrorists," he said. "I don't have another name for them. People were passing on the road and they would attack them. They even attack their own." He remembered the Albanians he considered innocents. "When I went there, I was ashamed. Many [Albanian] people were afraid of me," he said. Afraid simply because he was a Serb in uniform. "I didn't know how to tell them I wouldn't hurt them." He remembered the carnage—a NATO attack on a VJ unit in early April, forty wounded, four or five dead. "One man was incinerated in a tank. A second man lost a leg."

Boris grew sombre and thoughtful remembering what he considered the worst moment of the war—a NATO attack that had annihilated a refugee column. He talked for five hours. Although he had not been in Drenica and had never witnessed the cleansing of a village, I found his tale fascinating. There was no doubt he was speaking honestly. Very quickly I found myself liking and admiring Boris, and I realized how fortunate I was to have met him. He had given me a glimpse of the Serbian side of the Kosovo war. He was humane and—by virtue of his decision to speak to us—brave. He had gone through a war and kept his sanity.

Boris gradually became part of our team. After a full afternoon of emoting and testifying, Boris decided that Sasha and I should be his guests for a meal. He had lightened up considerably over the course of the afternoon, shedding the Kevlar-like reserve that he wore in the beginning for protection, and revealing his true self—booming, laughing, boisterous Boris.

In the cab on the way to his home, Boris told us how the American TV series *M*A*S*H* had been aired in Yugoslavia, and he laughed and laughed recalling how members of his unit had been cast in these famous roles—the orderly they had called Klinger, the sex-starved gynecologist they called Hawkeye, and the unit's only female nurse who served as their Hot Lips. Boris was still laughing as he climbed out of the cab in front of the university residence where he lived.

Boris lived in a double room on the third floor. As soon as Sasha and I set foot in it, I marvelled at how much it looked like a college room back home, or anywhere in the Western world for that matter. Sketches and movie posters adorned the walls. The furniture consisted of two beds and two desks. Boris shared the room with a tough-looking guy with a shaved head, who was on his way out with a friend when we arrived. These two supplemented their meagre student income by gambling. They had discovered a way to beat slot machines, but their system only worked on machines with fruit dials. A new casino had opened up just outside the city, and they were on their way to check it out. If the machines' metres clocked fruit, they planned to come back with cash.

Sasha and I sat down on a sofa that folded out into a bed, and Boris went to forage for food. Before leaving, he invited some friends to join us. A sweet and fragile thing named Suzanna arrived, gave me a once-over, and cornered me with a question. "If Milošević wins the election, will NATO bomb our country again?" she asked. "I don't think I will survive if anyone bombs us again," she said.

Boris returned, and within minutes the coffee table in front of us displayed a fine makeshift feast. There were scrambled eggs, and *kajmak* cream, and fresh white bread. "This is your home," Boris said, motioning to the table. "Everything that you want, just take it. Don't even ask. Take, take. It's for you."

As we ate, Boris started talking about his home city, Kraljevo. *Kralj* means "king" in Serbia, and *Kraljevo* is the "City of Kings," he said. He talked about how pleasant his hometown used to be when he was young, and how unpleasant it had become. He said the place was lousy with Kosovar Serbs who had streamed across the border after the war.

"Do you know what it means, 'No place for my dog to piss'?" he asked. "That is Kraljevo now. We have so many from Kosovo, our dogs have no place to piss."

Boris explained that most Serbs who fled Kosovo did not flee far. They stayed as close as they could to the Kosovar border by finding refuge in southern cities like Kraljevo, Niš, and Kruševac. I would later learn from the UNHCR that there were 102,427 registered Kosovo Serb refugees in Kraljevo alone.

"They even moved Kosovska Mitrovica police department to Kraljevo," Boris said. "Now we have their Kosovo cops."

If I had been daydreaming, I was suddenly alert now. "What do you mean?" I said.

"When NATO came, all the police must leave Kosovo," Boris said. "These police offices are now in Serbia—Niš, Čačak, I don't know where. And the Kosovska Mitrovica police are in Kraljevo."

At that moment I realized it might be worthwhile to make enquiries in Kraljevo. Through Gjorg I had some reason to believe that Momo Neznanović was a cop—or somehow affiliated with the state security (SDB) apparatus of the Ministry of Interior—in the general area of Kosovska Mitrovica. He may have lived and worked in a town other than Mitrovica, but if he was a cop they would certainly know him in Kosovska Mitrovica.

With ten days to go before the vote, we left for Boris's City of Kings.

*

Three weeks passed before I found an explanation for Gjorg's refusal to speak of Sofia. I should have guessed. It was as obvious as the stench of decomposition that polluted the air the first time I visited Gjorg's village. But the devil is in the details. And the details behind Gjorg's change of heart were more personal and horrific than I could ever imagine.

The details came to light the next time I went to check on Gjorg. I rose early, purchased a few groceries, took a taxi to the outskirts of Rezallë, and stumbled into the Isufi yard after climbing the steep lane that led to the homestead. It was mid-July 1999. Gjorg, his mom, and his aunt were still living in a tent. But as I looked around, it was clear the family was making progress. Gjorg had erected a second tent, found a wood stove for cooking, and planted some vegetables.

But the greatest improvement was in Gjorg himself. He seemed relaxed, and happy to see me. As soon as I appeared, Gjorg ran up, grabbed my hand, and leaned to my cheek, giving me the traditional Albanian embrace between men.

"You come back," he said. "I am glad. I did think you go to Canada."

I apologized for not returning sooner.

"No, no, it is OK," he said, and began to show me around. He led me to the tomatoes and green peppers he had planted, but admitted he did not think the plants would prosper. "There is no enough water," he said.

Gjorg then led me back to the tents, sat me on the grass, and disappeared under a flap. He reappeared with a box of orange drink and a small yellow envelope. He poured me a glass of juice and handed me the envelope with my name and home address typed on the front. "I did think you go home, so I write to you this letter." I glanced at the envelope and stuffed it unopened into the knapsack I carried with me. "I am sorry I did not want to speak with you the last time."

"That's OK," I said.

"I am happy you come here," he said. "I write to you this letter because I did want to tell to you something."

"All right."

By this time Gjorg and I were sitting cross-legged on the

grass. His mother and aunt were nowhere in sight. We were completely alone.

"It is about that person we did speak of before," he said. "I want to find her. I want to find Sofia."

To my amazement Gjorg had changed his mind about Sofia.

"I did try to find her before," he explained. "Before, when you and I did meet. But it was so hard."

He confessed to me that he had run the gamut of emotions over Sofia. "I know I did tell you before we would not speak of her. I did say to you to keep her a secret, and not to tell no one. But I did have a reason for this. I was angry, I was. . . ." He paused and clenched his face into a fist. "Look, it was very bad for us, I and my family, in the war. I did want to hate her. But now, everything did change. The war is finish. And maybe it is possible for us to be together. Before, no. But maybe now it can be."

Clearly, Gjorg's perception of his possibilities was different from mine. When I looked around his farmyard and at his life, I saw squalor. His home lay in ruins, and he had no money and no job, and little prospect of getting one soon. But Gjorg saw things differently. Although he was poor and living in a tent, postwar Kosovo offered a host of new possibilities. For Gjorg, one such possibility was Sofia.

I asked him where he thought she might be. He repeated what he had told me in Qirez almost a year ago. He said she could be in her village, which was outside Mitrovica, or in Mitrovica itself, where she had worked and gone to school.

"Or maybe Belgrade," he said.

I was beginning to understand. Whether Sofia was in Mitrovica or Serbia proper, it didn't matter. All these places were north of the Ibar River, and the Ibar had become an unofficial but impenetrable barrier dividing Albanians and Serbs. If Sofia lived somewhere north of the river, Gjorg stood a better chance of getting into North Korea than of reaching her.

Then Gjorg repeated a question he had voiced earlier in the conversation, a request I had not answered because I was reeling from his sudden change of attitude. "Will you help me?" he asked. "Do you do this? Maybe you can write a report about us—she and I."

He was asking me to find Sofia, and to write about it. The first request was a tall order, but the second seemed strange, particularly in light of Gjorg's past sensitivity about his history with a Serbian woman. Gjorg must have read the perplexity in my face, because he answered the question without prompting.

"I think that people must know about it," he said, with so little hesitation it was obvious he had thought this answer through long before. "And . . . if I do not find her, Sofia, then maybe someday she could read this newspaper report and she will know that I looked for her and that I am alive."

"This is why you want to find her, to make sure she is alive?" I asked.

"Yes, I want to know what is with her," he said. "That she is OK. But . . . this is a new Kosovo, and maybe it will be different between Serbs and Albanians. Maybe now it is possible for us—she and I—to be together. Maybe now we can be married."

And then I asked Gjorg why he had changed his mind. Why had he reacted so coldly to the mere mention of Sofia when I had visited before? And that is when Gjorg confided a secret that he said he had told no one else.

*

The secret had to do with the dead who awaited us when we arrived in Rezallë two days after the end of the war. These grisly remains did not begin to reflect the magnitude of killing that had gone on. "There was a massacre here," Gjorg said. "So many from my village did die." This turned out to be a gross understatement. I had already learned that as many as eighty[1] of Gjorg's neighbours had been murdered in a frighteningly brief orgy of gunfire that took place in the first weeks of the air war, just down the road from where we sat.

"The people who the Serbs did kill were my family, my neighbours," he said. "When I hear what did happen here, I did hate all Serbs. I did try to hate Sofia."

But Gjorg, as he had just explained, experienced a change of heart. He decided he wanted Sofia back despite the ethnicity of the men believed to have committed this grave crime against his community. This magnanimity—a reflection of the depth of his attraction to Sofia—became all the more remarkable when Gjorg finally confessed to me the terrible secret he had been keeping about the massacre.

The invasion of Rezallë in April 1999 had been undertaken by a large contingent made up of at least three branches of the Yugoslav security forces. Gjorg had learned that among the men there had been a commander. He was not tall but was powerfully built. He wore a great beard and a haphazard uniform, and he glared at the doomed inhabitants of this village with fierce green eyes.

"Sofia's father was that man," Gjorg whispered. "Sofia's father did come here, and kill."

Gjorg told me that the shock of learning this had initially turned him against Sofia. Now he decided he wanted her back anyway, no matter the crimes of her father. But I also sensed he wanted to know for sure—was the father of his fiancée complicit in the murder of over eighty of his neighbours?

It would take months to finalize the project. We met the following spring, and again in June 2000. I took a pilgrimage to the Serbian enclave of north Mitrovica, the last place Gjorg had seen Sofia, and searched for her in the face of every young woman I encountered.

Two months later, after an intolerable period of waiting, I received a visa for Yugoslavia, and began searching for Sofia and Momo.

*

As we eased into the city centre of Kraljevo, uncharacteristically orderly for a southern Serbian city that traces its roots back to Turkish rule, Boris's excitement grew.

"I love the streets of this city," he said. "A teacher once told me that all of Kraljevo's streets are on right angles. It's the most well-planned city in the world."

Boris was not wrong. Large swaths of Kraljevo, including its former urban sprawl, had been levelled during the Second World War, and reconstructed according to the best-intentioned communist plan. And you could see that Tito and his followers had had a hand in Kraljevo's renewal. A wide pedestrian avenue dominated the centre of town, and flowed into Trg Srpskih Ratnika ("The Square of Serbian Warriors"), a circular space dominated by a colossal statue commemorating the Partisan fighters who defeated the Nazis, brought the Communists to power, and helped make Yugoslavia a model of inter-ethnic harmony.

We parked on the street, and left Boris to run home and see his family. Sasha, Zoran, and I started to work. Despite our lack of success with refugee agencies, I sent Zoran and Sasha to the local Red Cross office—just in case. I waited at an outdoor café near the square and watched kids motor around the stone *Partizan* in tiny electric cars, which you could rent on the spot. Twenty minutes later, Zoran and Sasha returned. They were back so quickly it was as if they had walked around the block and come back.

Zoran sighed. "They said they close at three," he said. "There was nobody there." He told me afterwards that he and Sasha had also tried the local UNHCR office at City Hall. It was also closed.

The next order of business was the real reason we had come to Kraljevo—to look for Momo among Mitrovica's exiled police force. Gjorg had told me Sofia came from a village north of Kosovska Mitrovica, but I figured he had to have worked with the Mitrovica headquarters in some capacity. We parked across the street from the police building. The building looked appropriately officious and bunker-like. Sasha and Zoran went in alone, and I waited in the car. Once inside, Sasha left Zoran at the door and wandered up to a desk.

"I'm looking for a girlfriend from Kosovo," she said to a cop. "Her father's a police officer in Mitrovica. Or around Mitrovica. His name is Neznanović?"

The cop thought for a moment and said he didn't know of any Neznanović. Then another cop walked up. He was obviously a commander. According to Sasha, he had the bulk of a wrestler but was dressed like a civilian, in blue jeans. "What's going on?" he asked. Sasha repeated her story.

"If anyone knows," he said, "it's the secretary who works in wages and accounts." The commander led her to a room on the second floor where a woman in her late thirties worked.

Sasha repeated the story. "I don't know if he's still a policeman," she said. "He was one six years ago, when I knew my friend."

The lady rifled through her files, and Sasha took notes. Minutes later, back at the car, Sasha read from her notebook and told me what happened.

She told me about the cop at the desk who didn't know any Neznanović. He could be lying, I thought. Then she described going upstairs and talking to the accounts secretary.

"She said, 'I don't know this name.'" Maybe he's not a cop now, but he was a cop in 1994, I thought.

Sasha said that she asked the secretary this same question. "She said to me, 'Look, I've worked here for the last fifteen years. There is no way I would not know his name if he worked here.'"

Now I didn't know what to think. Was the secretary lying? Perhaps Momo wasn't a cop. Perhaps he indeed belonged to a branch of state security, but one that did not fall under the jurisdiction—and records—of the local police department, even though the police and state security both operated under the umbrella of the interior ministry.

Zoran told me he chatted with another cop while Sasha inquired at the desk. "I ask him if it is possible the cop we are looking for is still in Kosovska Mitrovica," Zoran said. The inference: could Momo be working there undercover? "'No, he wouldn't be there,' the cop had said. 'All the Albanians know who we are. They'd kill us.'"

After the police station Sasha and Zoran went off to find a friend of Zoran's who offered to set him up with some Kosovo refugees, and I went to meet Boris. He had invited me to join him for a visit to his older sister, and on the way he chuckled about his visit with his parents. "I talked to them about election, and they say still they are voting for Milošević," Boris explained. "I can't believe. I say, 'Are you crazy? You must vote for DOS. That's our only future.' But my father say, 'Milošević is my president. I will vote for my president.' They're old people. They don't understand. They think if Kostunica wins, the next day there will be American soldiers on the street of Kraljevo."

From a distance Boris pointed out his sister, Snežana, at the kiosk café where she worked, sitting in a chair and chatting with a patron. Boris crept up behind her, pounced, and smothered her in a bear hug. There were cries of greeting, and laughter, and then Boris called me over. Snežana looked at me through oval eyeglasses, and greeted me in fine English, and immediately reminisced about Boris as a boy. "He was a disaster in a little package," she said. I could imagine it.

Boris told Snežana I was a journalist and that he had been telling me about the war. Snežana nodded and told me her story. She had been in Kraljevo during the air strikes and defended her country in her own way—by using her ham radio to relay information on the daily attacks to the nation's civil defence network. "I protected my children with my work," she said. "There was nothing else I could do. I couldn't hide my children.

"I was angry. The people in the West does not understand. We didn't have Albanians in Kosovo until the Turks came. In 1389 they started to come. They came from Albania and they settled and they had privileges under the Turks. But we were there before them.

"It's interesting, I don't hate anyone," she said, and I assumed she was referring to Westerners like myself. "I'm just sorry because no one understands what's happening here." How much did I have yet to understand?

Around this time Sasha called. They had met with Zoran's contact and had accomplished all they were going to accomplish today. "Where are you?" Sasha asked. I put Boris on the phone and he directed them to the kiosk. Within fifteen minutes they were sitting at the table.

Snežana went back to work, and Boris went off to visit the widow of a friend he had served with in Kosovo, a man named Srečko. Zoran, Sasha, and I could speak in private. "What happened?" I said. "Did you get anything?"

"Maybe," Sasha said. Zoran's local contact had found a woman who worked as a civilian administrator at the local VJ military base. She was from Mitrovica.

I sat up in my chair. This is very good, I thought. This woman was not only a Kosovo contact, she had access to VJ records. What if Momo wasn't a cop? What if Gjorg had got it slightly wrong, and Momo was with the Yugoslav army as a soldier, military policeman, or intelligence officer?

"Did you talk to her?" I asked.

"No," Zoran said. "But my friend, he only have her number at home. When I phone, there was no answer, so I think she was at work."

No problem, I thought. We would simply keep trying.

"Did you hear about Kostunica?" Sasha said.

"Is he here?" I said. "What about him?"

"They attacked him," she replied. Sasha explained how she had heard that Kostunica and his campaign had been in Kosovska Mitrovica that morning, and there had been trouble. As a community on the front lines, Mitrovica was radical, angry, and pro-regime. Despite the presence of NATO troops, Sasha heard there had been an altercation when Kostunica spoke at a rally. She didn't have many details. There were stories that a mob had turned on him and had attacked his motorcade with stones. If accurate, this was the first hint of violence against the opposition. I was shocked but not surprised. With Milošević trailing so far in the polls, there was conjecture—usually whispered—that Kostunica would never live to see election day.

I remember asking Zoran: if Milošević kills Kostunica or if Milošević steals the election and everyone knows it, will people go to the streets to take their votes back?

"No," Zoran said sadly. "Not after all the wars, not after the last ten years. He's destroyed out souls." As it would turn out, he was only half right.

That evening the three of us planned to go to the opposition rally in downtown Kraljevo. On our way, we stopped in at

Boris's Kraljevo home to meet his parents. I appreciated the invitation. Boris's father, Ivan, was a man I desperately wanted to meet. Boris had told me much about his dad.

As we entered Boris's mother appeared from an adjoining room and greeted us with a smile and lovely girlish giggle that belied her appearance—a stout body, and long grey hair that she wrapped like a turban on top of her head. She embraced Boris, greeted us one by one, and was giggling over something Boris had said when the father shuffled into the entranceway from the living room. I had feared Boris's father was a zealot, but what does a zealot look like? He was trim, with a healthy country-fed complexion and great dignity. You could see it in his conscientiously knotted necktie and the carefully pre-served knitted vest, which was as fastidiously clean and pressed as the man wearing it. Like almost every Serb I'd ever known, Boris's father evinced unqualified hospitality.

Boris introduced me to him, and when his father shook my hand, he looked me in the eye and gave away nothing but delight. He seemed unconcerned that not long ago I had been the enemy. Boris's father ushered us into the living room with a smile and expansive gestures. After we sat down and started talking, he hinted that his son's departure to war—and what-ever role he played in it—haunted him still. The conversation quickly got around to the air strikes.

"Old men should go to war," he told me, with the help of Boris, "not the young guys." He described how he had written a personal letter to nationalist icon Vojislav Šešelj of the Serbian Radical Party. Šešelj's movement had a paramilitary army, and Boris's father pleaded in his letter to be allowed to fight with them in Kosovo. "I was ready to die ten times over for Kosovo," he said. "And there were 500,000 Serbs ready to go to Kosovo to fight and die."

Then Boris's father described how he and his wife coped with the air strikes, and fear and shame filled the room like an icy draft. I felt it was time to say something. "Airplanes from my country attacked your country," I said. I told them I was sorry for this, and that I was happy they were safe.

Boris translated, and the old man nodded. "I can forgive this," he said. "I can never forget this."

Then we were treated to a fine meal of bread, creamy *kajmak,* peppers, sausage, and potatoes. Ivan poured me shots of homemade *rakija.* Between sips I noticed a portrait of Marshal Tito on the wall.

There were other images of Tito in the house. One was embroidered on cloth, handmade—I assumed—by Boris's mother. They made no secret of the fact they admired Tito then and supported Milošević now. Ivan tried to set us straight before we left to join the Kostunica rally. "We're older," he said. "We know about the world. And our president is right!" At first I thought he was talking about Tito, dead since 1980. It took me time to realize he was actually talking about Milošević, who had in a strange way become the current incarnation of Tito. It seemed strange to me that the president who had led Yugoslavia through successive decades of ethnic harmony, economic rejuvenation and diplomatic cosmopolitanism would be identified with the man who had presided over several years of bloody strife, fiscal ruin, and international isolation.

We had hurried through dinner and left Boris's parents soon after in order to get to the rally in time for Kostunica's arrival. When we walked into the central square, Kostunica was indeed already there. He stood on a podium only a short distance away, addressing a supportive but subdued crowd. As I strained to hear him speak, an American reporter from Belgrade came up to me.

"Kostunica's pissed," he said. And I could hear the anger in Kostunica's voice. The rumours, it appeared, were true.

Kostunica's convoy had been attacked. No one seemed to be hurt. But the tension was rising. Everyone wondered where this outbreak of violence would lead. Would Kostunica be murdered, arrested, or elected in ten days?

I dwelled on these questions that night and the next day. But within forty-eight hours something would happen that would make me forget utterly about the fate of Kostunica and Serbia, and that something was our first tantalizing brush with Sofia Neznanović. Ironically, we glimpsed the girl on the one day I wasn't looking for her.

We had arrived in Kraljevo on a Thursday. The next day we kicked around the city, chasing war veterans and Kosovo cops, but came up with nothing. Sasha tried again to call the VJ secretary, the Mitrovica woman who we hoped might confirm or deny Momo's status in the military in Kosovo, but again we weren't getting through. Unable to do more, on Friday night I decided on impulse to do something I had wanted to do for over a year, ever since Kosovo's occupation in June 1999. So the next morning, September 16, I announced to Zoran and Sasha that we were taking a day trip east—well actually south, but the journey felt as if it should be east—to the city of Novi Pazar.

Sasha offered me a puzzled stare. *Why Novi Pazar?* I had several reasons. The least important was personal interest. Outside of Kosovo, Novi Pazar, which means "New Market" in Serbo-Croatian, was in September 2000, the last bastion of Muslim Serbia. The Ottoman Turks had established Novi Pazar as a commercial centre along the route linking the trading metropolis of Ragusa (now the Croatian port of Dubrovnik) with Istanbul. Novi Pazar had sat in the centre of a Ottoman military district or *sancak,* which had remained in Ottoman hands until 1912, when the Serbs finally wrested it away and incorporated it—along with

Kosovo—within their fledgling kingdom. But the Serbs still called the area the *Sandžak* and eighty-eight years after its conquest the majority of the folks living there remained Muslim Slavs, with a healthy population of Albanians and Roma tossed into the mix.

Like some quarters of Kosovo, Novi Pazar had a Muslim character that gave it a "Turkey in Europe" appeal that should have made it an exotic and valued corner of the republic. Instead it was the odds-on favourite for the next civil war, which is why I told Zoran and Sasha we needed to go. Novi Pazar was being touted as a ethnic powder keg that—according to one doomsday scenario—Milošević would deliberately ignite in order to foment sufficient mayhem to scuttle the elections. It was the same bloody scenario being imagined for Montenegro and the Preševo Valley. But Novi Pazar seemed a more logical flashpoint because it was so vulnerable. The Presevo Valley was home to a new Albanian rebel force. Montenegro boasted a U.S.-equipped paramilitary constabulary that was rumoured to be aching for a fight. Novi Pazar had no army, and little practise in the art of war-making. But with Milošević running out of minorities to demonize, more than one Serb had told me in recent weeks they considered it inevitable Novi Pazar would be the next front. "I fought in Croatia and Bosnia," one army veteran told me in a café in Novi Beograd. "Before the end of the year I'll be fighting in the Sandžak." I had taken these premonitions seriously, seriously enough to take a look for myself.

On our drive south I sat in the back seat and thought in silence as Sasha and Zoran gossiped in the front seat. I was curious to experience Novi Pazar, and I wanted to file a story on this anachronism. But I hadn't yet told Sasha and Zoran that these were not the real reasons I wanted to visit. In Novi Pazar I hoped to find another, unrelated innocent who had gone missing during the war.

Much of our trip had been through rocky outcrops, covered by bush and pine trees as thorny as the region's history. But as we neared Novi Pazar itself, history quickly caught up with us and the scenery took on a decidedly oriental flavour. We sped by women in head scarves and men carrying peppers to market by bicycle and car. There was an entrepreneurial passion in the air that was clearly eastern, and Zoran noticed it too.

"Welcome to Turkey," he said as houses began to clutter the roadside and we approached the city limits. "These people are different. They're good at business because they have close family relationships and they help each other. Serbs are different. My uncles and cousins don't help me. They have their own problems. I'm just a burden for them. If I go to them they say, Zoran, fuck off. But these people here have close family and they help each other really."

Zoran was right. As we cruised into the city we immediately felt the mercantile buzz. Everything seemed to be for sale. And the prospect of civil war in Novi Pazar appeared far less realistic when we got out of the car and strolled around the city centre. Just like everyone else in Yugoslavia, Novi Pazar's citizens—Muslim, Albanian, and Serb alike—were edgy. But everyone seemed far too concerned with making money to bother with war or elections.

We strolled among the open kiosks of the market. I inspected the wares, Zoran gawked at the shapely olive-skinned local girls, and eventually we found ourselves at a café, where I confessed what I really wanted to do in Novi Pazar. "I'm looking for somebody," I said, "and it has nothing to do with Sofia and Momo." Nothing much fazed Zoran. He shrugged, and turned his attention to a hennaed redhead at a neighbouring table. Sasha stared at me with an expression that gave me the distinct impression she was beginning to doubt my mental stability.

"It's not about Sofia?" she said.

"No. It's about a gypsy kid I knew from Priština," I said. And then I told them the story. I explained that I wanted to find an old friend, a Roma boy whom I last saw around June 14, 1999, in Kosovo. When I first arrived in Priština in August 1998, this kid shined shoes and panhandled in front of the city's Grand Hotel, the main hostel for visiting reporters, relief workers, and diplomats.

I had befriended the kid that summer in 1998 when Kosovo—everywhere but in the capital—was embroiled in a Yugoslav Army military offensive aimed at eradicating the UÇK. The kid was of an indeterminate age. He was short as a stump and dirty as an oily rag. He looked about ten years old, but he conducted himself like a grown man. I got in the habit of passing the kid a ten-dinar note every morning as I entered the hotel on my way to the press centre. Every ten-dinar note elicited the same response: "Thanks, you my friend." Then he'd nod at me, as if to say, *Don't worry about a thing.* In the beginning the kiddie shtick charmed me. Later when his begging became relentless, I slipped him cash just to shut him up and keep him off my back. Eventually I saw the payments as protection. Most of the time the kid was in character, giving me the Artful-Dodger-in-the-Balkans routine. I got my first sensation I was actually being conned by a forty-year-old dwarf the morning he braced me for cash, and I found myself with no small notes in my wallet. "Not today," I said. "I've only got a hundred-dinar bill, and I'm not giving you a hundred dinars."

"No problem, no problem," he said. Then he pulled a thick wad of dinars from his pocket. With grubby, stubby fingers he deftly counted bills from the folded wad and gave me change. Then he nodded again, as if to say, *Come back again.*

This confidence impressed me, as did the crude knife hidden under his pant leg, which he probably revealed to me to make sure the dinars kept on coming. I had no doubt this kid would one day be running Priština, but in fact I grew fond of the kid because I recognized in him a good heart and a wily talent at self-preservation that one couldn't help but like. I worried about him during the air strikes. When I arrived to Priština on June 12, 1999, immediately after the war and slightly ahead of the NATO armour, I found the kid exactly where I had left him, at his post at the doors of the Grand Hotel. But he wasn't the same boy. He was frighteningly thin. His head had been shaved, for reasons of hygiene I suppose. But the biggest change was his demeanour. There were no more beggar-boy theatrics. He edged up to me without a word, and hugged my leg. "Are you OK?" I asked. He nodded. Then he looked at me with eyes that were painfully wise for his years, eyes that had witnessed things no child should ever see. If the kid had ever enjoyed any childish innocence it had been eradicated during the seventy-eight-day air war over Kosovo, and the mass deportations, looting, and torching that raged on the ground.

Then the kid was gone, along with almost every other Roma in Kosovo. They fled after Albanians began meting out retribution for alleged gypsy collaboration in the Serbian ethnic-cleansing campaign of Kosovo, a campaign that uprooted nearly every Kosovar in the province, and drove hundreds of thousands across the border. Some of the Roma barricaded themselves in a school in Kosovo Polje. Some moved north of the Ibar, settling in and around Mitrovica. Others fled to Serbia. I had no idea where this kid was. I visited the Kosovo Polje school, but had no luck finding him there. The only other clue I had to his whereabouts was a passing comment that he and his clan commuted on the weekends to Novi Pazar. For this reason I believed I could always find him there.

Once we were in Kraljevo, it was just too tempting to continue on to Novi Pazar and ask around. For some reason I expected it would be easy to find him. I figured he'd be standing under the awning of the local version of the Grand Hotel. I assumed he'd be widely known. He was now twelve years old—he'd own the town.

I didn't know the kid's name, nor did I have a photo. I did have a description, and again I thought this would be enough. How many three-foot beggars were there in Novi Pazar who had once ruled the front door of the Grand Hotel in Priština?

That afternoon we ventured into the hills overlooking the city, and negotiated a maze of narrow oriental streets in a desperate attempt to find Stari Ciganski Grad—Old Gypsy Town—where I thought the kid might live. There we made contact with a local named Zaim. We found Zaim in a café that was actually a single plastic table surrounded by men with long faces who were wearing Nike knock-offs and drinking bottles of beer. Zaim had the body of a wood stove. His great belly strained the buttons of his dirty shirt. We told Zaim about the Roma kid. He didn't know him, but he offered to accompany us to a nearby Roma neighbourhood where the kid might be.

He climbed in the front passenger seat of Zoran's car and pointed us in the right direction. I liked Zaim because he had no teeth, and when he smiled he had the gummy grin of a baby. And Zaim smiled a lot. He confessed he was a happy man. "I love all women," he said. "No matter if they are beautiful or if they are drunk from *rakija*."

"If I drank as much *rakija* as you did today," Zoran said, "they'd all look beautiful."

Zaim flashed another baby smile, and stayed on the topic of women. "I am a Muslim. I'm with this poor Serb girl. Ah, she's beautiful. I love her. But this is the thing: I want to marry her. But I was too poor even for her. So I borrowed three thousand Deutschmarks. I guaranteed the money with my life. I used it to buy food, you know."

Zoran pumped the steering wheel as if Novi Pazar were a video game, around potholes and corners and people, fast and then slow, barely avoiding collisions. Finally, Zaim told us we were there, and Zoran stopped the car in front of a few men loitering in a driveway. Zaim rolled down the window. The locals bent down and heard Zaim out. They had the swarthy complexion of Roma, and a perplexed look. It was the open-mouthed gape you might get when you wander into a neighbourhood that hasn't seen a stranger for years. And we *were* strange—a Volvo with Belgrade plates containing a gangster (Zoran), a pretty Serb girl (Sasha), and an alien (me). On top of it all there was Zaim, asking about some kid from Priština. The locals must have thought it preposterous, so they directed Zaim to somewhere else. Off we went.

"Wait, wait," he said. "Do you have something to drink?" Sasha passed him a bottle. "Water!" He looked like he was going to spit. "Don't you have beer? Hey, there's a store. Stop and I'll buy us a beer."

We didn't stop, and Zaim continued on about his love life. "Anyway, I use this money—this three thousand marks I guarantee my life for—to buy food, what I need to set myself up with this Serb girl. But I don't have a job, and that's the problem. I spend the money. I can't pay it back. Now my family has money, but they won't help me because I'm with a Serb girl. So I have to go to jail for a year."

We were all happy that Zaim didn't have to give his life in return for reneging on the three thousand marks. No one was more pleased than Zaim even though he would be going to prison instead. "It's not so bad," he said. "She'll wait for me."

We visited several spots around Novi Pazar—three shanties, and a tent city at the local dump. We did not find the beggar boy from Priština or anyone who would admit to knowing him. So we left Zaim on the side of the road. He was destined for a year in jail for the high crime of loving a Serb, but as we drove off he smiled like a newborn baby, probably because of the thirty Deutschmarks I had given him for his time.

Late that evening we had retreated to a restaurant in the Old City. The restaurant, wood-panelled and Turkish in style, was a traditional Serbian grill—Sasha's favourite cuisine. We sat at a table as solid as an Ottoman battlement while a waiter with a heavy moustache took our orders with just the right air of aloofness. I was disappointed by our failure to find the gypsy kid. Staring into a half-empty bottle of fleshy Montenegrin *Vranac* wine, I wondered if I would ever see him again to pay the dinars that had accrued since our last meeting. My hollow feeling might have been transference for the frustration I was feeling over Gjorg's search because an instant later something happened that caused me to forget about the poor Roma kid whom we had spent the day looking for.

Midway through her dinner of grilled chicken Sasha dropped her utensils, fished her notebook from her bag, and turned to me. She had remembered something. You could see the bulb flash above her head. She borrowed my mobile, dialled a number from her notebook, waited, and then started talking in a loud telephone voice. I had no idea whom she was calling, and I didn't pay much attention until Sasha put the phone down, and said: "I think we found her."

I couldn't quite believe what she was saying. But Sasha explained. She had called the home of the VJ secretary, the one whose number she had obtained from Zoran's contact. "I'm a journalist from Belgrade," Sasha told the secretary. "I'm looking for a friend from Kosovo. She's from a village in northern Kosovo, and I think she went to school in Kosovska Mitrovica for a couple of years."

"I'm from Kosovska Mitrovica," the secretary said.

Sasha said she decided to take a shot. "My friend's name is Sofia Neznanović," she said. "Have you heard of her? I'd really like to find her."

"Yes, I remember her," the secretary said. "She's the cousin of my best girlfriend. She lives in Belgrade now. She's an art student."

Sasha explained that she was in Novi Pazar on assignment and would be returning to Kraljevo in the morning. "Can we meet?" Sasha asked.

"Why not?" the secretary said. "I'll try to find out Sofia's phone number in Belgrade." Sasha agreed to call her on Sunday.

After recapping the conversation, Sasha added one last piece of information. "Oh yes," Sasha said. "She thinks Sofia's getting married."

The next morning we raced back through the lush hills of southwestern Serbia, and rolled into Kraljevo at about mid-day. Boris was long gone. He had taken a bus back to Belgrade the day before. Zoran parked downtown, and we took another table at one of the cafés near the Square of Warriors. The afternoon was bright and warm, and people were everywhere, strolling aimlessly, on their way to the family luncheons that were a Sunday institution across Serbia.

Once seated, Sasha called the VJ secretary from my mobile phone to arrange a meeting. Watching from across a soiled table cloth, I knew Sasha had made contact. She immediately started speaking Serbian rapid-fire, and loudly. But then she grew silent and listened. Opening a notebook with her free hand, she scribbled down a phone number.

Seconds after the call had ended, Sasha gave me news both good and bad. "The VJ secretary won't meet us any-more," she said.

"Why?" I asked. Sasha shrugged.

The secretary hadn't given a reason. But she had given Sasha something: the phone number of a relative of Sofia who was at that moment in Kosovo.

"She gave me the number of her friend, Sofia's cousin," Sasha said. Without a word Sasha picked up my phone, hammered the buttons with an index finger as narrow as a pencil, waited for contact, and launched right back into it. She talked, then looked away, listened, and talked some more. Finally, she said, "*Dobra, dobra.*" She picked up a pen and wrote down more information in Cyrillic. She ended the conversation with "*Puno vam hvala.*"

After a moment of rest or reflection, Sasha looked up at Zoran and me, and filled us in on what had just happened. She had just been speaking with Sofia's cousin. According to Sasha, the cousin was a Kosovo Serb now working for an NGO in Priština, but had grown up in Mitrovica. "Yes, I am in touch with Sofia Neznanović," she said. "She is in Belgrade." Sasha asked about Sofia's age, and home. The cousin said she was twenty-three years old. Sofia came from a village in northern Kosovo, she said. But she had gone to school in Mitrovica.

"Great," Sasha had said at this point of the conversation. "I'm an old friend of Sofia's from Belgrade. Can you give me a phone number and address where I can find her?"

"I can give you a phone number," she said. The cousin then explained there was a problem. Sofia has just moved into another apartment. The cousin hadn't spoken with her since the move, and did not know her new coordinates.

"What's this?" I said, pointing at a number she had written in her book.

"It's her old number," Sasha said.

"She said she thinks that Sofia will call her soon to give her new number. She said to call back in a week or so."

I leaned back computing, blinking, and struggling to

catch up with the changing events. From one moment to the next, the setting for this project had changed, as if someone had advanced a slide, and the projection on the wall behind us had just put us down in a new location. Until a moment ago Sofia Neznanović had lived exclusively in the sparse, stony, and dimly lit terrain of Gjorg's memory. Now she was a young woman with a talkative cousin who lived in Belgrade. If the VJ secretary was right, and I hoped she wasn't, she was even contemplating marriage. She had become both more tangible and closer. We almost had her, I thought. The next step was to go back to Belgrade, find her old address, and locate her new one. Propelled by this news, I stood up, and shepherded Sasha and Zoran back to the car. On the way, Sasha added one more fact.

"The cousin said Sofia's mother still lives in Kosovo," Sasha said. "She didn't have the number with her. She said I should phone her later for it."

Sofia's parents. After three weeks of searching, we not only had the daughter, we had the father.

PART II

Chasing Her

CHAPTER 5

Beginnings

The project to find Sofia didn't really begin on the cool grass of Gjorg's farm in July 1999. I was pulled into the search gradually. The process started about a month later, mid-August 1999, the moment I left Kosovo. I was boarding a plane in Thessaloniki after spending most of the year away from home when my mobile phone rang. It was Gjorg.

"I am at the bridge in Mitrovica," he said. "Please call me back." Gjorg was about to cross the Ibar into Serb-controlled north Mitrovica, and begin his own perilous search for Sofia in the villages of northern Kosovo. Obviously, he had phoned because he already considered me a confederate in the search, and he was calling to shore up his own courage as he embarked on a dangerous journey. I felt a twinge of panic in my stomach, the feeling you get watching a car careening out of control on a patch of ice, not knowing whether the car will regain a grip, or crash. There was a loneliness in his faraway voice. Perhaps it was nothing more than a quirk of the phone line itself, but it would haunt me for weeks. Gjorg stayed on the line long enough to recite his number.

But I was never able to get him. I tried repeatedly to call the number he had given me. I called from my mobile and a pay phone. I had a friend in Budapest call from her landline. But there was no getting through. All I could do was board my plane, and wonder. Did he make it into northern Kosovo? Did he find Sofia? Did Momo find him instead?

I had planned to return to Kosovo to ask him. But the real life I had been neglecting for the past six months overwhelmed me. Before I knew it, summer had ended, autumn had become winter, and the year was over. I had thought of Gjorg and his project, but with every passing month I became more reluctant to take it up. Looking back I'm not sure why I felt so ambivalent about Gjorg's hunt for his lost fiancée, but when I returned to Kosovo early in 2000, I stayed away from Gjorg and Rezallë like a minefield.

But by early spring curiosity had won the day, and during a routine assignment to Kosovo I took a taxi to Rezallë, and found Gjorg at home. Sitting on the porch of the partially constructed house he and his brothers had built the previous fall, Gjorg admitted that nothing had come of his Mitrovica foray. NATO peacekeepers had mercifully refused to let Gjorg cross the bridge for the infinitely sensible reason that it was too dangerous.

"Have you heard anything of Sofia since?" I asked.

Gjorg shook his head, and looked away. He clenched his face in that way he often did when speaking of Sofia. It was clear to me he still wanted her back. With the chill of winter still in the air, I told Gjorg I'd see what I could do. But something troubled me about the story. I just didn't understand it. I didn't understand the fear and paranoia. I needed advice. So I went to Priština and paid a to visit my old friend Shaban.

Shaban was a Kosovar Albanian. By trade he was an actor, and he looked the part. He had sharp features and olive-coloured skin, and a curly head of hair that would have made him perfect for roles as the youthful Mafioso or the Cuban trumpeter in Hollywood. I had become friends with Shaban after he invited me to a party at his home to research a retrospective I was writing on the war. The party was a reunion of friends and family who had evaded deportation, hiding together in Priština during the war. His had been an Albanian Anne Frank story—as many as six people crowded into a flat in the Sunny Hill district of Priština, waiting for the police to barge through the door.

That evening Shaban confided the worst of it. He had worried that his wife's milk would stop flowing from the terror of it all and his newborn daughter would starve. He eyed the refrigerator daily, knowing that if the child did die, the freezer would be her tomb until the war ended and they could leave the flat safely to bury her.

That evening had sealed a friendship between us. I trusted Shaban completely, and I knew that if anyone could help me to understand this situation, it was he. So I gave him a general outline of the story and asked him what he thought. Shaban barely hesitated before launching into a story. This topic—love, sex, and war between Albanians and Serbs—was dear to his heart.

"Right," Shaban said. "To understand all of this you have to understand what it was like before between Serbs and Albanians. It was a strange relationship, and it's hard to understand if you didn't live here at the time."

He leaned back in his chair. "The troubles started in 1989, right? Before '89 Kosovo was basically autonomous. It wasn't a republic, but it was like one. We Albanians had our own leaders, our own parliament. Everything was cool for us. But Kosovo was still Yugoslavia, and to really make it, an Albanian had to marry a Serb.

"You can investigate this yourself. But just about every big political leader from those days was married to a Serb. Or a Bosnian, or a Croat."

"A Slav," I said.

"Yes, a Slav," he said. "That's how they thought. To make a career in Yugoslavia you had to be like a Serb, and the best way for an Albanian to become a Serb was to marry one. This was the politicians and the leaders—the big guys. But in the nineties everyone started to feel that way. Before '89 we Albanians ran Kosovo. When I think back on it, it was like heaven, man. After '89, when Milošević came to power and changed things, Albanians were like second-class citizens. If a Serb and an Albanian applied for a job, the Serb always got it. We had no jobs, no money. The regime was keeping us down, and it affected us, it affected our confidence.

"We really felt inferior, and in a way this made the Serbs, especially Serb girls for us men, more attractive. Albanian girls are beautiful, but for us they were normal. We could have one whenever we wanted. But we couldn't have a Serb. They were almost impossible. They were . . . forbidden fruit, and so they were the ones we wanted most."

Shaban leaned forward and raised both hands in the air to make his point. "I mean, you could get hotter for a Serb girl than any Albanian. First of all, there was sex. Albanian girls tend to be conservative. And there was a time, man, when the Serb girls were totally up for it. Sometime in the eighties there was this trend with Serb girls to have Albanian lovers. Albanian boys were forbidden fruit, just like Serb girls to us. It wasn't such a big problem in the seventies or eighties. Technically, a Serb and Albanian could be together, and nothing really bad would happen. But in the nineties it was dangerous. Things got so bad between us Albanians and Serbs, if a Serb girl was with an Albanian and somebody found out, say her father, or a brother heard a rumour about it, or a Serb friend saw the girl with an Albanian, the girl would fall into heavy shit. To get herself out of trouble, she could say the Albanian boy raped her. Even if he didn't." Shaban's voice turned gravely serious. "If this happened, there was no hope, man. The Albanian boy would go to prison, just like that. For a fuckin' long time. And these things happened. It almost happened to me.

"I'll tell you a story," he said, leaning towards me. "When I was in school, back when Serbs and Albanians went to school together, I was chosen to go to a poetry-reading festival for all of Yugoslavia. I decided to read an Albanian poem for the competition. Everybody said to me, 'Why are you reading in Albanian instead of Serb-Croat?' and I said, 'Because the poem is an Albanian poem. That's the poem, and that's my language. That's how I read it.' The judges and the audience loved it. I was given second place.

"Anyway, I came back to school a hero. There was this Serb girl. She was the prettiest in our school. I mean, she was beautiful. She was hot for me. I was a star because of the contest. And I was a volcano for her. I mean, I really really wanted this girl. I wanted her so bad. And I could tell she wanted me. We both knew we had to be careful. We got together once, and . . . we kissed and . . . nothing happened.

"Even though I wanted her so fuckin' bad, even though it was so cool to have a beautiful Serb girl interested in me, an Albanian—I couldn't do it. I thought I could, but in the end I decided, no. Because I knew, if it went too far, if we made love, it could mean my life. Just like that, I could go to jail for fifteen years.

"So. I can understand this kid. He's from Drenica. It's poor. It's like the poorest part of Kovoso. And it's been oppressed more than any other part of Kosovo. This is what the kid has been living with. And there is this Serb girl showing interest in him, and it must have been something, something else for him. It must have lifted him right up high, because through this girl's eyes, suddenly, for the first time in his life . . . he's as good as a Serb."

I knew a little bit about the climate of tension in Kosovo. I knew that from the Albanian point of view troubles began in 1989, when Milošević forced a constitutional amendment through the Serbian national assembly stripping Kosovo of autonomy, a right it had enjoyed since 1974. Albanians in the province took to the streets. Belgrade imposed "emergency measures," tantamount to martial law, and Kosovars fought back passively with a campaign of civil disobedience that evolved into an armed insurgency by 1998. I also knew that from the Serb point of view tensions with the Albanian majority predated 1989, and at times took on a weird sexual manifestation.

In 1985 a Kosovar Serb farmer named Đorđe Martinović was admitted to a Priština hospital with a broken bottle in his anus. Authorities ruled it a creative attempt at masturbation that had gone painfully wrong. Martinović charged he had been attacked and impaled by Albanians, and suddenly a private act of self-abuse became a national act of flagellation. The incident was debated in the Yugoslav federal assembly. In 1986 a Belgrade journalist published a thick book called *The Martinović Case*.

Martinović did not happen in a vacuum. Rape hysteria was already gripping Kosovo and Yugoslavia. As early as 1984 an Orthodox clergyman raged against the rape of girls, elderly women, and nuns in Kosovo. Other commentators piped in. The media fuelled the flames, and overnight an ethnicity was redefined. "In the mainstream Serbian and Yugoslav presses," writes Julie Mertus, "Albanian men were declared to be rapists."[1] In fact, there was little evidence to back this up. A 1990 investigation carried out by an independent group of Serbian lawyers found the incidence of rape to be lower in Kosovo than anywhere else in Serbia.[2] The statistics indicated that many rape stories trumpeted by both Serbs and Albanians were inventions.

After my meeting with Shaban, I returned to Rezallë and spoke more with Gjorg. He reminisced about Sofia. He spoke with fear, and reverence, and longing in his voice. The woman he described was open-minded, devoid of hate, generous to the core. She was the good Serb, and the more Gjorg spoke about her, the more I wanted and needed to meet her.

I truly wanted to do this—help Gjorg find Sofia—but I wasn't sure why. I knew it had something to do with the fact that Gjorg had found, or perhaps selected, me. After a year as a reporter in Kosovo, I had met hundreds like Gjorg on both sides of the Ibar—sad, proud, impoverished men who had shared their misfortunes with me. I met them in embattled villages, in refugee camps in northern Albania, in mourning at funerals, and in despair after having lost everything. In almost every case I jotted down notes, filed my dispatch by 8 p.m., washed away the dust of the day with a beer, and barely gave the sufferer a second thought. There was no time to get involved with individuals; the next day's deadline demanded I seek out new sources of misfortune.

But then I found Gjorg. Or more precisely Gjorg found me. Suddenly, I was presented with an opportunity to treat a news source as a human being, to remain in his life for more than a deadline, and provide him with . . . something. If I helped Gjorg reunite with his fiancée would I not be doing both of them a service, and making amends for all those Serbs and Albanians I had interviewed, but never bothered or cared to know?

Crossing that line from being an observer to a participant in someone's life was a difficult step, which was probably why I failed to look up Gjorg on my previous visit to Kosovo. I was doing my best to avoid an entanglement. But Gjorg kept on finding me. As much as I tried, I couldn't convince myself our reunion in June 1999 was an accident. I had interviewed Gjorg once in August 1998. I had forgotten about him, but he found me again ten months later. Amid invading and retreating armies, returning refugees, and generalized chaos, he found me. This was extraordinary, and providence so blatant had to be respected.

I decided that spring I wanted to help Gjorg locate this girl. The question was, could I? In May 1999, I applied for a visa in Yugoslavia. In June 1999 I returned to Kosovo and sized up the lay of the land. Time was running out. Kosovo was becoming more racially polarized by the day. Since the previous summer the lion's share of the Serbs living south of the Ibar River had fled for their lives. Despite the presence of NATO and the UN a reverse ethnic-cleansing was going on. Those Serbs who remained in Kosovo proper lived in ensnared enclaves like Gračanica east of Priština, or north Mitrovica.

I went to see Gjorg at his farm and told him my news. Standing with him on the edge of his cornfield, I told him: "I've applied for a visa for Yugoslavia. I'm going in to do a bit of work. While I'm there I'll find Sofia."

But to do this, I explained, I'd need to know everything—about her, about their past together. Until now Gjorg had related snippets of information that were tantalizing and entertaining, but he had given me little to work on. I offered to come to his farm the next day and carefully go over every detail of Sofia's life to determine where I could find her. Gjorg refused. He wanted to meet me in Priština to discuss Sofia. This soon developed into a rule. We would never discuss Sofia on his farm or in his village. She could be evoked only in neutral territory.

CHAPTER 6

Dying with Gjorg Isufi

Kosovo, March 1999

March 24, 1999, should have been a day of panic and awe. But when twenty-four-year-old Gjorg Isufi saw the first flashes of NATO bombs detonating on Kosovar soil just after dark on that Wednesday evening, he felt relief.

Gjorg was in the village of Turiqevc,[1] which was not his village but was not unlike his village. The community was a collection of houses made of brick and stone set haphazardly on the high and uneven ground at the western edge of the Drenica Valley. Gjorg was a stranger to Turiqevc, but he was not alone. He had arrived that day with his brothers Kadri and Ibrahim, his brother-in-law Hakif, Hakif's son Agim, and Hakif's cousin Migen. The Isufi clan came because they knew war would break out, and as this isolated village had neither Serb police nor UÇK fighters, it was—they surmised—safe from immediate attack.

The men had fled Rezallë under the assumption that as

fighting-age men they would receive no mercy from the Serb *milicija* if captured. They would be arrested and beaten. Women and children, they believed, would be left alone by the Serbs. So the men had dispatched children and women-folk to larger or more isolated towns that were unlikely to be shelled, scattering the family like slivers of shrapnel. Gjorg's mother had gone to Skenderaj. Kadri's wife had found refuge with kin living in Llaushe.

Then the Isufi men fled Rezallë as part of their strategy to avoid Serb forces once war broke out. The Isufis were an odd group. In another time and place, it was unlikely that any of them would be mistaken for rebels. Kadri, the eldest Isufi brother and clan leader, was a chemistry teacher. He exuded the gentility of an academic, and was clearly a man accustomed to having ink and chalk on his fingers, not blood. Well into his forties, Gjorg's brother-in-law Hakif was not only the oldest but also the weakest of the men. A lifetime of smoking had weakened his lungs. For most of the journey to Turiqevc, Hakif had limped far behind the others, supported like a supple cane by his terrified teenage son Agim. And then there was Gjorg's brother Ibrahim, so lean and long he almost looked consumptive. But Ibrahim was not weak. He could walk faster and farther than his fragile frame would suggest. He too was no fighter. Gjorg was the fittest of the lot, but he barely looked older than eighteen-year-old Migen, Hakif's meek and skittish cousin.

The group had set out before dawn and stumbled into Turiqevc by late morning. By evening it became clear that war was on its way. A small transistor radio that Ibrahim carried brought news that NATO fighters had left Aviano air base in Italy. After dark Gjorg and Migen had been washing their feet in preparation to go inside the house where they and a dozen other wanderers had been billeted when Gjorg spotted a flash of light on the eastern horizon. "What's that?" Gorg said.

"Something is happening," Migen said.

They both knew what it was. The flashes were followed by thunderclaps, and then Gjorg heard the roar of jet engines in the sky. Gjorg ran into the house. "Come outside," he said. "It's NATO. They're bombing."

NATO was attacking the Serbs. The West had not forgotten the Kosovars. NATO was joining the fight on their behalf, and Gjorg felt relief. But he also felt despair. For NATO and for Serbs outside Kosovo, this war was just beginning. For Gjorg, the war had started last summer when the Serbs shelled and invaded his home village. That was also the moment Gjorg had first experienced death—his death. Gjorg would always remember the event as the day he died.

It happened seven months before, August 3, 1998, on a hillside just outside of Gjorg's village, almost within sight of his home. Gjorg had been hiding in the hills for most of that day. He had fled his village that morning and desperately wanted to go back home, if home was indeed safe to return to. That was the question: was it clear to go back?

At 5 p.m., just as the sun was on its westward descent, Gjorg crept to the south edge of his village. Hidden in a thicket of brush, he crouched on the summit of a hill of layered shale covered by a thin carpet of soil and topped by bushes and pine trees small enough to grab a foothold in the shallow earth. Gjorg wasn't alone. Four of his cousins, two timid, tired men in their forties and two skittish, silent teenagers, were with him. Gjorg had encountered the others an hour or so before, and they had resolved to see first-hand what was going on. All day long they had heard shelling and gunfire, and they could only imagine the carnage. But as they stared across a small gorge towards their village all looked peaceful. Not a sound echoed from the village—no shots, no voices, not even the rumble of a vehicle. Home seemed so tantalizingly close.

Immediately in front of them was a grassy clearing. A wagon trail traversed it, bouncing down the hill into the gorge and then barrelling up into the verdure on the other side of the chasm. Gjorg knew the trail plodded up the other bank and then rolled, tired and dusty, into his home. All a man had to do was leap on it and the road would carry him home like a mountain stream.

Gjorg was faced with a dilemma. Should he jump on that trail and ride it home, or should he and the others remain in the hills, living hungry and desperate like wild dogs? It was so hard to know what to do. Gjorg had been fretting and reacting for the past four days, ever since a single shell, lobbed by a Serb tank, detonated on the outskirts of the community. Gjorg considered the shell an omen. The next day another shell had landed in the area, but the elders of Gjorg's village had already concluded a Serb attack was imminent and that the townspeople should be evacuated to someplace safe.

Not that any place in the Drenica Valley was necessarily safe. Over the past year Gjorg had watched the violence grow and take shape. In late 1997[2] Drenica resident Halit Gecaj died from a stray bullet during a firefight between Albanian fighters and the Serbian police. Thousands from across Kosovo came to Gecaj's funeral. And then, immediately after Gecaj's death, saviours appeared. At least, Gjorg and most other Drenica Kosovars considered them saviours, even if the Serbs thought of them as terrorists. They wore soldiers' uniforms and great beards, and patches that bore the initials UÇK.

In the beginning it seemed that the UÇK was unstoppable. In early 1998[3] the UÇK fought the Serbs at an oak tree known as the Six Brothers near the village of Likoshan. Gjorg had heard how Adem Jashari, the Great Commander of the UÇK, had stood up to Serbian armour and helicopters. But then, in March, the Serbs came for Jashari. They attacked the

Commander's farm in Prekazi i Poshtem with grenades and big guns, and they killed Jashari and every member of his clan—old and young, women and children. The Serbs took a photo of Jashari in death. People who saw it said the Commander was smiling.[4] Perhaps he understood that his death would only make the UÇK stronger. Perhaps he found a certain peace in a rebel's death, since revolt and insurrection were almost a tradition in the hills of Drenica, now a hotbed of UÇK activity. The fighters took control of a large swath of Kosovo. They claimed villages wherever Albanians lived, which was almost all of the Drenica Valley. Then the Serb *milicija* erected roadblocks and bunkers around these areas, and everyone knew that violence was not far off.

In late May the violence arrived. Gjorg heard that fighting between Serb police and UÇK had broken out near Deçane,[5] where the Serbs had a great monastery. Later, villages were taken by the Serbs. There was the village Bardhi i Madh, and the old city of Rrahovec with its great mosque and narrow streets, and Malisheve. In time the storm settled over Drenica. Gjorg heard that the village of Llapushnik near the big town of Gllogovc had been stormed by the Serbs. Gjorg actually heard the detonations of shells and grenades, and the whispers of townspeople who said how bad it was for the folks there. Before long, more villages fell. Gjorg saw plumes of smoke rising like great exclamation points from these doomed places. And more stories circulated of torching and massacres and endless processions of villagers fleeing their homes in tractors and on foot.

All the while, Rezallë remained eerily quiet. Then the ominous shell landed near the village and it was clear there was no more time. Women filled bags with clothes and food, and loaded essentials—bedding, carpets, tarpaulins—into tractor wagons. Gjorg and his brothers discussed their options. It was decided that the family would go to Bajicë, on the eastern side of the valley, where the uncle of their father lived in a great stone house above the village. Gjorg agreed that Bajicë would provide the perfect sanctuary, but he announced to Kadri he would not be going. "I want to stay," Gjorg said. "I want to keep an eye on the house of our father." Kadri protested at first, but then agreed. The old brick house built by their father was all they had in the world.

On August 2, farm tractors were fired up and the village's innocents departed in a long, sad parade. Women walked, and wept. They rode in wagons that heaved like lifeboats on a swell, and wept. Big kids cried like babies, and little kids waved and laughed at the adventure of it all. Like the Isufis, some of the villagers would seek out family in safer villages. Others would journey to safe areas like Qirez on the east side of the Gllogovc–Skenderaj road. No one was sure when they would be returning.

Gjorg felt hollow as he watched the procession sweep his family away. They were all going—brother Kadri, and Kadri's wife Fatmira, and brother Ibrahim, and his mother Aferdita. Gjorg also said goodbye to cousins and uncles and aunts. They were all descendants of an Isufi, who—Gjorg was not certain how long before—was one of the founders of the village, and watching them leave was painful for Gjorg. His quarter of the village was being bled of forty of its sixty families.

The evacuation came just in time. The next morning Gjorg had scraped together what food he could find and prepared breakfast for the UÇK fighters manning trenches just outside of town. The fighters had set up a defensive line to take on the Serbs should they decide to enter rebel territory. The breakfast wasn't much—sandwiches made from goat cheese and peppers—but Gjorg felt duty bound to help. It was not that he wanted to be a soldier. In Gjorg's estimation a great gulf separated him from the UÇK—the real fighters, not just local men with shoulder patches, but hard men like his older brother Rexhep, who were prepared to be killed and, more importantly, to kill. Gjorg admired these men for their toughness, but he knew he couldn't kill a man, not even a Serb. But he also knew he wasn't a coward.

Gjorg bagged the sandwiches and set off for the front line. He had just left the outskirts of the village, walking gingerly on the road as if the dust were molten hot, when an armed sentry stepped from the bushes.

"What are you doing?" the sentry asked. Gjorg told him. "You can't go there," the sentry said. "The Serbs will attack any time now."

It was beginning. Gjorg ran back to the village and fled southwest into the countryside, the opposite direction from where the Serbs would attack. Once in the hills, he heard shelling and gunfire. What was going on? Were the Serbs storming Rezallë or the neighbouring village? Had the war, which for so long had been faraway plumes of smoke, finally reached his home?

Gjorg wandered the hills for most of the day, until by chance he descended into a small sheltered ravine where he stumbled upon four of his cousins from the village. Like Gjorg, none of them knew what was going on at home. Like Gjorg, they had heard gunfire, but the shooting had stopped hours ago, and they were desperate to learn the fate of their livestock and homes. After sharing sandwiches and gossip, Gjorg and his four cousins discussed the matter. They debated the pros and cons of returning home, and finally decided they would creep to the edge of the village and take a closer look.

Twenty minutes or so later, the five of them were hiding in brush atop a hill. On the next hill to the north lay the northern tip of Rezallë, and from his vantage point Gjorg could almost see his farm. The men scanned the horizon, looking for any sign of danger. Nothing moved. The village looked empty, and Gjorg wondered if the Serbs had ever really invaded. And if they had come, were they now gone?

Gjorg and the others couldn't tell, so all five slipped down the hillside, crossed the base of a grassy gorge, and dashed into the trees on the other side. They were now standing on the last hill leading home, but Gjorg decided he should make sure all was clear before they continued on as a group. There was a bunker nearby, a cave that farsighted villagers had dug in the mountainside. Gjorg told the others to wait there. Continuing on alone, Gjorg worked his way up the trail, completely covered by brush and leaves. Near the top of the hill Gjorg emerged from the trees into a clearing, where he was able to see a meadow above him on the hillside.

The meadow was a natural sentry turret, offering a bird's-eye view of the surrounding territory. Staring into the setting sun, Gjorg could just make out armed fighters loafing there. "It's UÇK," Gjorg said to himself. "The fighters control the village, and tonight I will sleep in the house of my father." Gjorg bounded in the direction of the soldiers. He wanted to enquire about the fighting, and to inform them that he and his cousins in the bunker would be returning to their farms.

After ten hopeful paces, Gjorg glanced up again and stopped in his tracks. Having moved forward just enough to escape the sun's glare, he could now see the meadow through a soft lens of late afternoon light. He could make out the tall grass, and the lazy shapes of the men, and the guns they held loosely at their sides. He couldn't make out their faces, but he was close enough to see their blue uniforms. He was close enough to dying to see that these men were not UÇK; they were Serbian *milicija*.

Gjorg edged backwards, and an instant later he was back in the trees, running down the canopied path to his cousins. Gjorg crawled into the bunker and whispered that they were still in danger. The men, silent and obedient, followed Gjorg across the bottom of the gorge and up a dry creek bed under a cover of brush, to the hilltop where the five had stood minutes before.

Once at the summit Gjorg realized he would not sleep in the house of his father any time soon. He decided it was time to go to Bajicë and find his family. So the cousins exchanged goodbyes, and Gjorg left the brush and headed straight across the small meadow. A few moments later Gjorg was halfway across the meadow when he heard a terrifying noise—the staccato of gunshots. Gjorg turned, looked across the gorge, and realized he had made a terrible mistake. By stepping into the clearing, he had exposed himself to the police on the other side of the gorge. Despite the sun's glare, Gjorg could see the sniper. The cop was standing, staring at Gjorg down the sights of a rifle, and firing. Bullets tore the earth around him and Gjorg fell to the ground.

The four others heard the gunfire and saw Gjorg fall. They crept to the edge of the clearing and stared at Gjorg's body, which lay a few metres away. They saw no blood, but they saw no movement either. Gjorg was as still as a dead man. The cousins lingered for a long while until all hope faded. They eventually slipped away, and headed deeper into Drenica in search of a safe village. On the way they ran into neighbours from home.

"If you see any the sons of Idriz Isufi tell them they must return to find their brother," one of them said. "The police have shot Gjorg Isufi. He is dead."

Death by a bullet was a fitting end for Gjorg Isufi. When Gjorg was born it was traditional in the Kosovo[6] countryside to celebrate the birth of a son by joyously firing a rifle into the air. But if Gjorg hadn't heard gunfire at his birth, he would not have to wait long for this sound to become familiar. In the Drenica Valley violence touched nearly every generation. Life in Kosovo came with a relentless background noise, and this was the crack of a rifle's report. Gjorg's father Idriz Isufi had fought the Serbs in Drenica during the Second World War. The men of Idriz's father's generation fought the Serbs in the first Balkan War of 1912, and again in the First World War. To outsiders, Kosovars who fought Tito's *Partizans* in the Second World War were Nazis, and Kosovars who fought the Serbs and Montenegrins in 1912 were Ottoman collaborators. But to Kosovars like Gjorg these fighters were merely Albanians. Gjorg knew Kosovars needed allies in their wars, but their allegiance was always to themselves, and their enemies were always the Serbs. To Gjorg the war between Serbs and Albanians seemed never-ending. Before Gjorg would turn twenty-five he would hear more shooting than many soldiers hear in a lifetime. Little of it would be joyous rounds celebrating the birth of a boy.

In his own words Gjorg was born "in a poor but honest family." His father was a carpenter. His mother Aferdita was a good wife to Idriz—she bore him more sons than daughters. Aferdita was born in 1932 in a village near Gllogovc. Gjorg's mother must have been relieved to remain in Drenica. Everyone knew that Drenica was special, a place where people held tightly to tradition, more so than in big cities like Priština where Kosovars lived like Serbs, or Prizren where Kosovars spoke Turkish. In Drenica Kosovars lived like Albanians. They cherished their families. They lived according to the Kanun, the ancient laws. Aferdita had been told how the great Albanian lawgiver Lek Dukagjini had set down the Kanun many years before. The Kanun had laws for everything, and the Albanians of Drenica followed them. When Aferdita was young, men in Drenica even took *gjak* or blood, to wash away the dishonour of a killing, crime, or unpardonable insult. The Kanun not only permitted clans to murder to settle disputes over honour, the law demanded it. According to the Kanun, a dishonourable man was a dead man and the *gjak* of his foe was his only means of resurrection. By 1999 there was little enthusiasm in Drenica for the *gyakmaria*[7] or blood feud, although stories circulated in Drenica that there were men seeking blood vengeance in the mountains of Albania, which were so impenetrable that no law could impose order, not even the Turkish Seriat that most lowland Albanians in Kosovo respected during 500 years of Turkish rule.

Gjorg's father died in 1997. While he lived, Idriz Isufi imparted many lessons to his sons. He expected much of them. "He wanted for us to be honourable our whole lives," Gjorg would later say. "Not to steal, not to do bad things." Idriz's sense of honour extended towards Serbs, whom he had fought in the war. There were no Serbs in his village, but there were Serbs elsewhere in Drenica and Kosovo. Idriz told Gjorg and his brothers that they should never forget the Serbs were their enemies. "But you don't need to act against them first," he said to Gjorg. "If you do, you will lose. Don't be loyal to them even if they pay you. They are occupiers."

Now the *milicija* of this people, whom Gjorg and his father considered occupiers, were trying to kill him. But August 3, 1998, would not be Gjorg Isufi's time to die. When he realized that a Serb policeman was firing on him and there was nowhere to take cover, he fell to the ground and feigned death. He did not merely pretend; he assumed death. He did not dare breathe. Then, an hour or two afterwards, when he was sure the Serb police were no longer watching him, he rose from the field and sprinted to the bushes.

When Gjorg arrived at the village of Bajicë, where his mother and brothers had taken refuge, news of his death had preceded him. His sister-in-law was the first to see Gjorg as he sauntered through the great stone gate of the yard. To Gjorg, it was as if Kadri's open-mouthed wide-eyed wife had seen the dead. Moments later Gjorg learned that she had believed she was seeing a ghost. After being embraced by

Ibrahim and Kadri, Gjorg sat before his weeping mother, Aferdita. "They told us the police killed you," she said.

For weeks Gjorg lived like a ghost. Days later the family decided to leave the house of his father's uncle and find sanctuary in Qirez, one of the last corners of Drenica untouched by the offensive. All along the way Gjorg encountered displaced neighbours and cousins who had been told of his death and stared in shock to see him alive. After a while Gjorg began to feel as if he really had died in that clearing and then returned to life. If death was a painless and tranquil place, however, Gjorg did not yet feel any comfort from having assumed the role.

Gjorg felt just as afraid and confused eight months later, on March 24, 1999, as flashes on the dark horizon announced the declaration of hostilities between Yugoslavia and NATO. Standing among a mass of men who reeked of perspiration and panic, Gjorg couldn't help but feel his despair alloyed with elated relief. Something momentous was happening. More momentous events were about to happen. Gjorg was certain that Yugoslavia would surrender to NATO within days. But what would happen then? Would the fighting end forever? Would the hatred disappear? And in a Kosovo without fighting and hatred, what other things would be possible?

Would a life with Sofia be a possibility? Gjorg didn't know yet. He didn't discuss it with the others.

A life with Sofia might someday be possible. But for now and the foreseeable future, she was neither a woman nor a memory. Instead, she may have been the last and best haven Gjorg could retreat to when the shells began to fall.

CHAPTER 7

Two Women

Belgrade, September 18, 2000

After reaching Sofia's cousin by phone, we packed into Zoran's car and sped back to Belgrade. I was elated. We had a phone number for Sofia in Belgrade and knew that Momo had never left Kosovo. Even though I had less than a week remaining on my visa, it seemed perfectly possible I could make contact before having to leave.

But by the next morning—Monday, September 18—everything had changed. Sasha and I stared glumly at each other across a table in the café of the Dom omladine, our unofficial office in the city. (Zoran was spending the day working with another foreign journalist.)

As Sasha lit a cigarette, I tried to make sense of the complication that sat on the tabletop between us like a dirty ashtray. The previous night we had stumbled upon another puzzle piece that completely altered Sofia's portrait. The new information possibly meant we had no Sofia. Or it could mean we had two of them.

The previous day, on the way back to Belgrade, Sasha had phoned Sofia's cousin again, and managed to wrestle out of her the phone number for Sofia's mother. It was an incredible moment I would fully appreciate only much later. After months of dreading and demonizing Momo, he had been reduced to something as tangible and banal as a sequence of digits.

The instant she hung up on the cousin, Sasha declared, "I'm going to call them."

I nodded. A telephone call might be too direct, but I was beginning to realize that only bold steps were getting us anywhere. And we seemed to be on a roll.

Sasha punched the number into her mobile, and put the phone to her ear. I stared at her, and imagined a phone ringing in Sofia's family home. I felt my chest thump, and asked myself again whether this call was the right thing to do at this time. A long moment later Sasha said "*dobar dan*" in a loud, formal telephone voice, and I realized she had made it through. She had made contact. As I watched Sasha I wondered if Momo himself was standing phone in hand on the opposite end of her call. Sasha went on and on. I don't understand Serbian, but I recognized Sofia's last name—Neznanović—mentioned repeatedly. Then Sasha paused. She scribbled something in her notebook. She spoke some more. She hung up, looked up at me, and her face contorted into a question mark.

"I talked to the mother," Sasha said. "I told to her I was Sasha Janković, and I am a friend of Sofia from university, and I am looking for her. I said I know she moved, and I was wondering if she could give me her new address or phone number."

I was both disappointed and relieved Momo hadn't picked up the phone.

"Then she said, 'Who are you looking for?'" Sasha said, "And I said, 'Sofia Neznanović.' And then she asked me to say it again, and I told her 'Sofia, Sofia Neznanović.'" Sasha grimaced ever so slightly as she delivered the bad news.

"She said, 'Our name is Kneznanović. Not Neznanović with an *N* but with a *K. Kneznanović.* You've called the wrong number.' And I said something to her like, 'I know her from university, but I don't know her that well. So maybe I made a mistake with her last name. So can I have her phone number anyway?' She wouldn't do it. But she said she will tell Sofia I called."

Sasha hadn't asked about Momo. And at that moment I didn't care. I remember sitting there catatonic, unsure how to process the new information. We had travelled south, dug hard, met with a bit of luck, and uncovered a direct link to Sofia. I had braced myself for anything—that Sofia was married, living abroad, or dead. I had never expected to find I might have been looking for the wrong person.

"It is not her," Sasha had said.

"Hold on," I had said. "Not necessarily. The name could still be Kneznanović with a K."

Sasha stared at me in silence.

"Look," I said. "This kid, the boyfriend, is Albanian. He's not a Serb, and as far as I know, he only saw her name written down once. Maybe he got the name wrong."

"You mean this Albanian doesn't even know his girlfriend's name?" she said.

I brooded for what seemed like a half hour (it was probably only a minute or two) chewing on the common sense of Sasha's remark. The logic of it was difficult for me to explain, or even understand at times. But it was possible Gjorg did not know her real name. And I knew this was possible for one simple reason: Gjorg had never shared with her his real name or identity.

"Kneznanović has to be her," I said, ignoring Sasha's dumbfounded stare.

It had to be. What were the odds of two girls of almost the same name and age coming from the same place in Kosovo?

The odds of finding two women with the same name would be higher if the surname were common like Nikolić or Ivanović or Marković, but Sofia's surname was rare. Sasha said she had never encountered anyone of this name before in her life.

I flirted with the possibility the Kneznanović distinction was a ruse concocted by Sofia's suspicious mother to mislead us. But I decided this was unlikely. As I went through it over and over again in my mind, I was convinced that Kneznanović was Sofia. We had her last address, and a trail that was only two weeks old and still warm. Now all we had to do was find her.

We left the Dom omladine and made two stops before jumping in the cab en route to Sofia's former apartment in Belgrade. Our first stop was the main post office, just up the street. We went to the desk of the Serbian telecom office and asked for the most recent phone directory for Kosovo.

Sasha thumbed through the warped pages. "It is in here," she said. I peered over her shoulder. There was one listing for Kneznanović, and it was the same number Sasha had called. We now knew the old lady wasn't lying about the family name. As for the man of the household, the book said Kneznanović's given name was Ljubomir.

"It's not Momo, at any rate," I said.

"Momo is a nickname, but it is not common," she said. "It could be for anything."

Still satisfied we were on the right track, I led Sasha from the post office and down the road to my second-floor apartment on Kosovo Street. It was as long and narrow as a mine-shaft. The kitchen was really an extension of the hallway with a stove and sink set into the wall. My only furniture was a musty communist-era sofa that I used as a bed. Sitting in the darkened living room (paranoia still prevented me from opening the curtains) Sasha picked up the heavy receiver of the red phone on the coffee table and dialled the number Sofia's cousin had given us. I had no illusions Sofia would answer. But I did hope this number might reach a new tenant, former roommate, or landlord, someone who might know Sofia's current address.

Sasha sat impassively. I don't know if I heard the unanswered rings or imagined them. "There is no one," she said.

Then Sasha pressed the receiver button with a slender finger, and dialled again. When this call was answered Sasha launched into rapid-fire Serb, and jotted down something in the notebook she had opened on the table. After hanging up Sasha explained she had called directory assistance, and was able to get the address of Sofia's old flat by specifying the phone number. "I know where the flat is," she said inspecting the address. "It's in Banovo Brdo," she said. Banovo Brdo was a outlying district of Belgrade, and according to Sasha "quite far away," so we would have to take a cab. As we made for the street, Sasha added Sofia's phone number was listed under the name 'Lukić, Srdan.' "It is the landlord for sure," Sasha said.

We caught a cab on Terazije, and ten minutes later eased to a stop along an attractive residential street. The taxi driver told Sasha he guessed we were close, but he didn't know which building was the address in question since there were no numbers visible on any of the houses. We got out, and headed up the street. As we scanned facades looking for house numbers, I noticed some signs of prosperity. There was one reasonably new apartment building fronted by a manicured lawn, and a school that echoed with the din of playing children. Most of the other buildings were older. Some were Communist-era block houses. Some were crumbling pre-war palaces. The street was quiet, and not without charm.

Eventually Sasha encountered an old man loitering on a stoop, and questioned him about the address. The man mumbled a few sentences. "The house we were looking for is at the end of the street," Sasha said. We continued. As we approached I started to shiver. We were getting close. I felt her presence like a cold wind. Out of nervousness, I started spewing out instructions.

"There's probably someone living in her flat," I said. "They will know where she lives now. You go in the building alone and talk to them. I'll wait outside. Just knock on the door and say you are looking for your girlfriend. You're both students, right?"

"Yes," Sasha said.

"This guy will have to know," I said. "To send mail. I mean, you always know where the previous tenants are to forward mail."

Sasha agreed.

"She probably left a note," I said, and continued rambling until Sasha threw me a look that said, Shut up. We had come to the end of the street, and looking up I could see the number we were hunting for clearly displayed beside a doorway. Different from many of the buildings we had passed, this structure exuded all the grace of an abandoned bunker. It was an enormous cement box, four storeys high. The front door was open and, from where I stood, the foyer looked like the damp interior of a cave. But people moved in and out of it. In fact, people scurried all around us. Some were passersby. Some were doing business at the kiosk in front of the building that sold magazines and newspapers, or the other kiosk beside it that dealt in fruits and vegetables. Because we didn't want the old ladies buying produce to see that I was a foreigner and become suspicious, Sasha wandered away from me as if I were a stranger, and marched directly into the shadowed entrance of the building. I slipped off to the newspaper stand and pretended to browse.

Two minutes later Sasha appeared. It was too soon. She wandered up to me, and we retreated to the rear of the kiosk.

"No one lives there," she said. "I knocked and knocked, and there was no answer."

"Neighbours?"

"There was a man in the hallway. He told me that no one lives in the flat now."

"Did you ask him if he knew Kneznanović?"

"Yes. I said, 'I have a friend that lived here.' He said he didn't know her. He said it was a student flat and so many people moved in and out and he couldn't keep track of them. I said, because my friend lived here, I wanted to rent this flat if it was free. He said a lady owned the flat, and she lived somewhere nearby, but he didn't know where."

This "lady" had to be Lukić. "We've got to try to find out who this Lukić is," I said. "She'll know where Sofia is."

Sasha could be a tank when she mobilized herself as she did at this moment. A tall old man had sauntered up to the entranceway. Sasha marched up to him. They spoke at length and then disappeared into the building.

Sasha returned five minutes later. She stalked right past me and up to the vegetable kiosk, where she launched into conversation with a plump woman behind the stand, who was wearing an industrial-green apron and a great mane of grey hair.

The kiosk woman heard Sasha out and pointed to a building on the other side of the intersection. Sasha charged across it, dodging oncoming cars, and stopped at the closed gate of a building that looked like a dirty tombstone. The gate was obviously locked, because Sasha lingered at it, talking into an intercom just off to the side. I watched her pressing buttons, and conversing with the console. Finally the gate opened, and Sasha slipped inside.

When she returned to the world again, about five minutes later, she marched back across the street and again right past me. I turned, followed, and did not dare speak until we were a half block away.

I asked her what had just gone on. Sasha told me the tall old man had been helpful. He didn't know Sofia Kneznanović, but he knew the landlady Lukić lived somewhere in the neighbourhood. He was certain someone in the building knew exactly where, so he led Sasha upstairs and they knocked on doors until someone suggested that the old ladies at the kiosk might know. They knew everyone in the neighbourhood. The source had been right. When Sasha queried at the kiosk, the woman behind the counter said the owner of the flat was a Mrs. Lukić (either the wife or daughter of Srdan) who lived right across the intersection. When Sasha stood at that gate she found Lukić's name on the intercom console, and a kind man in her apartment.

But Mrs. Lukić wasn't at home. Her son-in-law was there. He gave Sasha the phone number of their flat and told her she could phone back later.

We walked a few blocks further, found a thoroughfare heavy with traffic, and caught a taxi back to the heart of the capital. We started the day with two Sofias, but by the afternoon's end had solved the mystery. We had discovered that Sofia's real surname was Kneznanović, and identified Mr. Lukić as a contact who could lead us to her current whereabouts.

We seemed to be another step closer.

CHAPTER 8

At War with Boris Postovnik

Belgrade, September 20, 2000

After obtaining the phone number for Mrs. Lukić, I figured that it would only be a matter of hours before Sasha found Lukić at home, or Sofia's Kosovo cousin called us back with Kneznanović's new address.

We had Sofia.

So I turned my attention to Momo, and to the murders that took place in Gjorg's village in April 1999. What did I know about the crime? Not enough. I proceeded on three assumptions: on April 5, 1999, Rezallë was invaded by a combined force of *milicija*,[1] VJ, and paramilitary volunteers; the local women were expelled from the village and the men were shot; and Gjorg had received information that a *milicija* cop or state security (DB) operative or volunteer paramilitary fighter named Momo, father of his Serbian fiancée Sofia, participated in the bloody operation.

While we waited to make contact with Mrs. Lukić, I

asked Sasha to arrange a meeting with Boris. Once again our rendezvous spot was Dom omladine. It was late afternoon on Wednesday, and we were already there, reading wire reports on the election, when Boris lumbered into the café and greeted us with his standard salutation: "Hey guys." Boris was in high spirits after a weekend at home. "I think my sister will now vote for Kostunica," he said triumphantly. "My parents, they are still all for Milošević. But at least my sister will be for DOS."

Ostensibly, the purpose of that day's meeting was to listen to Boris sing. His choir operated out of a building on a quiet street off Terazije, behind the Moskva Hotel. The choir specialized in the liturgy of the Serbian Orthodox faith, in which I had expressed an interest. So Boris invited Sasha and me to sit in on that night's rehearsal.

While we waited, I took Boris aside. "I'm interested in an action that took place in a village in the west Drenica Valley early in the air strikes," I said. "It was VJ and it was MUP [*milicija*] and about eighty people died there."

I paused. "I've heard the Albanian side of what happened," I said. "I want to hear a version from the Serb side."

Boris shrugged. "I was never in Drenica," he said.

"Do you know any veterans who were posted in Drenica?" I asked.

After a few beats of silence Boris summoned a couple of names. But none of the men was available. One guy never spoke of the war and all of the others were in Kraljevo. I reflected a moment as Boris ordered a coffee. An eyewitness to the cleansing of Rezallë hadn't appeared to me, but in Boris I had a man who had served in Kosovo throughout the war. Was there something in his experiences that could shed light on what had happened in Rezallë? During our moving first conversation Boris had shared bits and pieces about the war. He had relayed anecdotes, admitted his fears, and mentioned friends who had returned from the war and others who hadn't.

"I'm wondering if we could talk more about Kosovo," I said. Boris agreed. I opened a notebook, and Boris—after consuming a coffee, and blinking himself back to that time—began to speak. Like the story Gjorg Isufi had recounted months earlier, Boris's story was a simple one, about a life that was altered the day missiles fell on Serbia.

*

March 26, 1999

Two days after the start of the war, Boris Postovnik received a phone call in his room at the student residence in Belgrade. His father was on the line from Boris's hometown of Kraljevo, and the old man had terrible news.

"You have been honoured by an invitation to be defender of your country," Boris's father told him. "You must be proud. You mustn't be afraid. Come home to Kraljevo as soon as you can."

Boris was mute as he struggled to process the news that he, Boris, a twenty-seven-year-old medical student, had been drafted into the Yugoslav army and would soon be going to war in Kosovo. Boris couldn't believe it. But he was getting used to this feeling. He had been bombarded by it almost continuously for the past forty-eight hours. First there was the announcement by NATO Secretary General Javier Solana that NATO would attack Yugoslavia from the skies. Then there were the steady warnings by Serbian TV and radio that "NATO aggression" could commence at any time. But despite the looming catastrophe, on Wednesday, March 24, when it all began, Boris had been oblivious to everything . . . but music.

That day, as the world awaited the start of an air war between NATO and Yugoslavia, Boris was scheduled to fly to

Stockholm for a choir festival. Boris had been anticipating this trip for months. For people who knew Boris, his enthusiasm was not surprising. Boris was a medical student preparing himself for a career as a physician, but a soundtrack had always accompanied his life. He had been born with a booming voice that always seemed greater than the boy, and later the man. As a child, Boris had first heard song used to praise the two things that his family held most dear: Yugoslavia and her great leader, Tito.

Boris remembered the first time he heard his mother sing and how impressed he was by the devotion in her voice.

> *Comrade Tito*
> *We vow to you*
> *That we'll never waver*
> *From your road . . .*

Boris loved remembering these old, patriotic songs. They reminded him of Tito, dead, buried, and mourned. They reminded him of Yugoslavia, the great six-republic federation, also dead, buried, and mourned. Of course, Boris did not sing these songs any more, unless he was drunk at a party and doing a comical turn. There was no real point in singing them; Boris's Yugoslavia ceased to exist after 1995. By that time wars had cut away his beloved Slovenia (Boris's fatherland), Croatia, and Bosnia-Herzegovina from the country. Macedonia had left the federation without a fight. This left a Yugoslavia made up of only Serbia and Montenegro, and Boris considered this a tragedy. But for Boris, there was nothing for it but to study and sing.

After Boris reached adulthood, his taste, talent, and sophistication in music swelled like his body. Boris grew into a Pavarotti of a man. He developed an appetite for food but an even greater desire to express himself through song. He loved spiritual music above all else. By 1999, Boris was a member of a renowned Belgrade choir that specialized in the liturgy of the Serbian Orthodox Church. Because his father had been born in Slovenia, Boris considered himself Roman Catholic, the religion of the Slovenes. But his mother was ethnic-Serb—a member of the Serbian Orthodox Church—so Boris's love of the liturgy of the Serb church came to him honestly. From an early age he perceived a dark, soulful beauty in this music that had been lost to most of Europe since the Great Schism.

On March 24, Boris was set to leave for Sweden. He had a Swedish visa, he had a plane ticket, and he had spending money received that morning from the Ministry of Sport and Youth. He even had sandwiches packed for the long bus trip to Budapest's Ferihegy airport. The bus was scheduled to leave at 9 p.m., and that war might break out before the bus's departure was inconceivable.

At about 6 p.m., a Slovene friend named Robert called and told Boris to flee Serbia in a hurry. "There's going to be air strikes," Robert said, suggesting that Boris use his father's Slovenian birthright to find refuge there.

"You're stupid," Boris said. "This is Europe! There's not going to be air strikes."

For Boris, the thought of war was too bizarre to be believed. It was unthinkable that NATO would attack his country over something as ridiculous as Kosovar insurgency. Boris had attended university in Priština for a year in 1993. And as a boy, Boris—like every child in Serbia—had learned about Kosovo. He learned it in school, and he learned it in songs, and he learned it in stories. He was taught to revere Kosovo as the birthplace of the Serbian people, and the holy home of the Serbian Orthodox Church. He knew that a great battle had occurred there. He knew that Serb princes and knights had fought the Turkish hordes and their Albanian vassals there, and that the Serbs had gone down in valiant defeat. On the eve of the battle, so the story goes, the great Serbian leader, Prince Lazar, had been visited by Saint Elijah who arrived in the form of a grey falcon to give the commander a choice. He could defeat the Turkish armies of Sultan Murat on the field of battle, and win a temporal empire on earth. Or he could be defeated on earth, and win an everlasting kingdom in heaven. As the story went, and as Boris had heard, God-fearing and wise Lazar chose the latter.

The medieval Serbian kingdom had been defeated and conquered by the Turks, and the Serbian people had suffered centuries of cruel occupation as a result. Boris had learned that this war—culminating in 1389 at the Battle of *Kosovo Polje*—was the most important in Serbian history. Turkish rule over the Serbs, which lasted until the nineteenth century, had deprived them of what western Europe experienced as the Renaissance and the Enlightenment. The Turks had cut them off from history. The Turks, Boris knew, allowed Albanians into Kosovo, and were displacing Serbs from their ancient and holy land. Now, 610 years after Prince Lazar's defeat, a familiar enemy was threatening Kosovo. But Boris wasn't prepared to die to preserve Kosovo, and he couldn't believe NATO would risk lives to win it.

"It's impossible," Boris told his roommate, Ivan. "There can't be a war."

When sirens began screaming just after 8 p.m., Boris realized the unthinkable had happened: NATO was attacking Belgrade; yet another war had come to Yugoslavia. Boris lived in Studenski Grad—Student City—a recently renovated state-subsidized housing complex. There were speakers on the street outside the residence buildings, and shortly after the first cycle of sirens and shudders a frightened voice crackled over the speakers.

"Respected colleagues," Boris remembered the voice saying, "NATO aliens have just begun aggression on our country. We ask that you in an orderly and disciplined way go to the bomb shelters. Radio Studenski Grad will inform you of events in the coming hours."

The loudspeakers began pumping out inspirational music like the Communist "Internationale" and patriotic songs celebrating the Yugoslav army and the *Partizans*. They were all songs from the days of Tito.

> *Hey pilots, you are the steel wings of our army,*
> *Go forward and our Commander will lead us,*
> *You are the protectors of our skies.*

Boris's friend Katarina, who lived three floors above him, rushed down as soon as the sirens sounded. She didn't want to be alone. "We're going to die, guys," she told Boris, and handed him the emergency supplies she had collected: a high school graduation gown wrapped in a blanket, dice for game playing, and a loaf of bread.

By this time Boris's girlfriend Jelena had arrived, and all five—Boris, Jelena, Ivan, Katarina, and Boris's pet guinea pig Gizmo—retreated to the shelters.

That night Boris fell into a strange slumber, somewhere between partial consciousness and full sleep. It was filled with ill-defined nightmares, and it offered no rest. Before he drifted off, Boris realized he had stopped fretting about Sweden. He was fated to remain in Yugoslavia.

Then, two days later, his father called.

The draft notice came as no surprise to Boris. That VJ officers had visited his home in Kraljevo to deliver the papers and take him away did not surprise Boris either; door-to-door conscription was standard procedure in a beleaguered nation starving for soldiers. What Boris couldn't accept was that his dad had signed him up.

Most families recognized door-to-door conscription for what it was: kidnapping. Many lodged their sons with distant relatives or friends, and claimed no knowledge of the boys' whereabouts when the army came calling. But Boris's father had not done this. When the VJ officers arrived, he signed the papers on Boris's behalf.

"I can't believe that you did that," Boris shouted into the phone. "Only I can make this decision."

His father said it was Boris's duty to fight and protect the fatherland from the NATO aggressors.

Boris asked if the fatherland was worth the life of his only son. "By doing this, you might be killing me," he said.

His father didn't respond to this remark. "It's your duty to defend Kosovo and Yugoslavia," he said. "You have to protect your sister's children and the old like your mother and myself. Nothing else matters."

At that moment Boris realized it was useless. The war had started and he was going to fight whether he liked it or not. He immediately made plans to go home to Kraljevo to report for duty.

There was an 11 a.m. bus for Kraljevo, and Boris decided to be on it. He didn't travel to the bus station alone. Everyone was leaving. Jelena had decided to return to her home in Požarevac, to be with her family. Katarina was going to Zemun, where she had a boyfriend. And Ivan and Gizmo the guinea pig were setting off for Valjevo.

The four found a riot when they arrived at the bus station. People were lining up, jostling, and panicking to get out of town. The sky was falling on Yugoslavia, and people were desperate to get home and be with their families. Lines as thick and restless as giant snakes extended from the ticket windows and wound out the door of the terminal into the bus yard. Despite the endless queues, Boris and his friends finally secured space on buses leaving for their respective destinations. Boris got a seat on the 2:15 p.m. coach. Jelena would be the first to leave, and so the four retreated from the station so that they could enjoy their final moments together in relative privacy, away from the melee.

The friends sat on the front step of the entrance of a clothing boutique. Boris went over in his mind what he should say to Jelena. He knew he should say something, because he understood the implications of going to Kosovo. He had learned this lesson as a nineteen-year-old during his first war, in Bosnia.

"I don't want to be morbid," Boris said, "but if I don't come back, if I don't see you again, I won't be angry if you find someone else."

Jelena didn't say anything. Ivan strummed the guitar he was carrying. Boris and Ivan began to sing a song they had composed themselves. And when he heard planes flying overhead, Boris sang louder. He was determined that the war would not drown out his voice.

The far and endless vistas forgotten,
The gate to "who knows where,"
Negosava Street, you and I . . .

The mood of the song was right for the moment. But there was nothing melodramatic about Jelena. She was a tough girl, and instead of tears she offered Boris a solution.

"You don't have to go, Boris," Jelena said. "So what if your father signed the papers? Don't go to Kraljevo. Come with me to Požarevac, and hide with my family."

Jelena's offer was sweet, but Boris had to laugh. Jelena's home of Požarevac was also the base of the Milošević family, and as such it was home to more cops, soldiers, state-security agents, gangsters, and informers than any community in Yugoslavia. Taking refuge in Požarevac was like hiding in the warden's back yard after a prison breakout.

Boris loved Jelena for offering. And he knew, as he told

her "*Vidimo se*" and watched her climb onto the coach wearing a helpless expression, that he had lost her. Boris wasn't certain what lay in store for him in Kosovo, but he knew these experiences would alter everything—his life, his relationship with his friends, and especially his affection for Jelena. As Jelena took her seat, Boris sensed a wall going up. He believed when he said goodbye to her that was saying it for the last time and that NATO was tearing his love from him.

Boris then uttered farewells to Katarina and Ivan, and caught the bus. Just under four hours later, he arrived in Kraljevo. Welcome home, he said to himself. Boris walked from the station, lugging his bag on his shoulder, and found his mother home alone. He sensed she would be upset, so he tried to act casual.

"Hey fatty, what are you up to?" Boris said.

The old woman looked sick. "I really didn't know what your father was doing when he signed that paper," she said. "The soldiers came to the door. They gave your father a paper and he signed it. Only after they left did he tell me 'Our son is going to Kosovo.'"

Then she started to weep. Boris tried to console her, and after she calmed down a little, Boris asked about his father.

"He's in the basement," his mother said.

Boris's parents lived on the first floor of a large apartment building, and after the air strikes started, most of the building's inhabitants sought sanctuary in the cellar. When Boris descended the stairs, he found kids playing. They were clearly enjoying their reprieve from school.

"Where are you, old guy?" Boris called out into the dim light. Again he was straining to remain casual, but anger surfaced the moment he spotted his father. "Why did you do this?" Boris demanded. "What are you going to do if I die?"

Boris had surrendered himself to the war before leaving Belgrade but he still hadn't come to terms with his father's decision to send his only son into battle. He hoped a face-to-face explanation from the old man might make it clear.

"Look, son, you have to go," his dad said. "Our country is at war. It doesn't matter if I signed those papers or you signed those papers—you still have to go. Just be careful. You're smart. Take care of yourself and you'll be all right."

When Boris left the basement, he still didn't understand why his father had given him up to the VJ.

Boris did understand others things about his dad. He remembered a trip he and his father took together to Belgrade. Boris was very young, and his dad was taking his little boy to the May 25 Museum to see the *stafeta*—the baton—that he had made in honour of Tito. The *stafeta* was part of a yearly celebration and ritual in Yugoslavia. It happened every May 25 on Dan Mlovosti, or Youth Day. May 25 was Tito's birthday. As part of the ritual a *stafeta* was relayed across Yugoslavia, passed from runner to runner, hand to hand, like an Olympic flame. On May 25—at the celebration's pinnacle—the *stafeta* always arrived in Belgrade and was presented to Tito.

In the weeks leading up to the big day, communities across Yugoslavia got into the act by holding a festival called Slet, in which runners relayed locally made *stafetas*. Factories, police detachments, army battalions, and farming co-operatives made special *stafetas* to honour Tito. One year Boris's father was granted the distinction of being the man who would make the *stafeta* for his army engineering unit. Like all *stafetas,* Boris's father's creation was sent to Belgrade and placed on display in the May 25 Museum. Father and son searched the displays and finally found his *stafeta*. Boris still remembered his father's pride as he gazed upon the baton, forged for Tito by his own hand and now on show in Tito's museum.

Boris remembered too the pride he shared with his dad. Perhaps the Great Man himself had held it and smiled. From an early age Boris had been taught that Tito was not just a great man but the *greatest* of men. He led the Partisans, defeated the Nazis and Chetniks, and defied the Soviet Union. He turned Yugoslavia into a unique country. It wasn't the East; it certainly wasn't the West. Yugoslavia was a world unto itself. Six republics, three religions, innumerable nationalities. And the world revered Yugoslavia as much as Tito did, it was clear. The country had many friends. Yugoslav citizens could travel almost anywhere in western Europe without a visa. Yugoslavs enjoyed the health care and education levels similar to those of western Europe, saw enormous economic growth and enjoyed month-long vacations.

Then, in 1980, Tito died. And Yugoslavia began to die as well. The economy began to ail, and a prosperity that Boris had known his entire life began to slip away. Then the nationalism that Boris had always felt under Yugoslav's smooth surface began to bubble and appear. In the 1980s, long before the troubles in Croatia and Bosnia, Albanians in Kosovo rioted for more power.

Under IMF pressure, the economy began to sag. Unemployment rose. Old nationalisms reappeared. In 1991 war erupted in Slovenia and Croatia. Both republics left Yugoslavia. In 1992 war broke out in Bosnia, and Boris himself was mobilized to fight. By 1999, Boris had long ago resigned himself to the death of his country.

But had Boris's father? Despite everything that had happened, his father seemed locked in another era. Was it possible his father believed that the Yugoslavia Boris would be fighting for was the same Yugoslavia to which he had bequeathed a *stafeta*?

Boris wasn't certain what to think. He felt the world racing, spinning, closing in. He felt a myriad of conflicting emotions. He hated his father, he loved his father. He hated his country, he loved his country. He was a stranger in Yugoslavia, Yugoslavia was his home. He wanted to support the boys of

Kraljevo, to protect his sister Snežana, her children, his mother, and, yes, his father; but he didn't want to die. He would write in his diary:

> I have an incredible feeling in my stomach. Why? Why again? Again? I'm trying to calm myself down without success. Panic is taking over. I try not to show it. I want to escape but where? It is impossible to do it now. I really can't believe the thoughts in my head. There are a million options there, but only one possible solution.

He went over the options: he could go insane, he could kill himself, he could kill somebody else, or he could escape . . . to somewhere. On the verge of killing, dying, collapsing, Boris decided to report for duty.

Boris reported to the HQ of the *Sanitetska Četa,* a mobile army first-aid unit, which was gathering at a school just outside the city. Boris wandered around for a while, found the highest-ranking officer, an implausibly youthful lieutenant named Vlada, and launched right into it, hoping that if Lieutenant Vlada understood the circumstances, he might tell him it was all a mistake and Boris could go home.

In rat-a-tat-tat Kalashnikov delivery, Boris told Vlada about the military police and his father and his upcoming medical exams, and his choir, and that he was supposed to be in Sweden. Boris might have vented for an hour had Lieutenant Vlada not stopped him.

"Hey, shut up," Vlada said. "What's your medical education?"

"High school for nurses," said Boris. "And I'm in my fifth year of med school."

"Excellent," Vlada said. "We're looking for guys like you. Most qualified guys didn't answer the draft."

Lieutenant Vlada officially welcomed Boris to the *četa*. He explained it was a hospital unit only—no soldiers, only nurses, surgeons, and medical technicians, as well as drivers, cooks, and orderlies. Boris wandered around the school. Some of the men were playing soccer. Others were lazing about and smoking. Boris discovered some familiar faces. There was an old school friend named Saša, and Đo, his neighbour, a pharmacist. Boris was allowed to leave the school and go home briefly while the unit awaited orders.

Rumours flew about where the *četa* would be posted. Lieutenant Vlada said they were going "south," and that's all he said. Some of the boys said it might be Raška, which was outside Kosovo. There was even hope the *četa* would remain in Kraljevo.

This would not come to be. On March 31, nine days after Gjorg Isufi had fled Rezallë, eight days after the first missiles fell on Yugoslavia, and four days after Kosovars began streaming into Albanian and Macedonia, the *četa's* motorcade containing personnel, medical supplies, equipment, and food passed the border into Kosovo. For the second time in his life Boris Postovnik was going to war. On the way, he wrote in his diary:

> More than anything I did not want to be in another war. Now we have another war, one unlike any other we've had in the past, one that is very very special.

*

Boris caught sight of the time and stopped abruptly. "Look, guys," he said, "we must go." He was late for rehearsal.

It took us ten minutes to walk to the studio. Boris arrived just in time to sit us in the corner of the rehearsal hall before a choir of healthy and exuberant twenty-somethings assembled. The choir master, a robust middle-aged woman, clapped her hands until the singers grew silent and attentive. She raised her arms above her head, and when she lowered them—almost violently, like a wood cutter swinging an axe—the choir began to sing a piece of Serbian Orthodox liturgy composed by Stevan St. Mokranjac. I recall being amazed by the room's utter transformation. There had been silence, then thirty mouths opened—and the room filled with such intensity you could almost see colours swirling. The sounds were gorgeous, and brooding, and spiritual, expressing rapture, pain, and tremendous desire all at once. But more importantly, it struck me that the competing lyrics and voices that danced in sync at the soprano ceiling and baritone basement of the scale articulated mystery.

Which was what Serbia was to me. Nearly every Serb I had met was the personification of generosity and hospitality. The Serb Sofia Kneznanović was a woman of such beauty and allure that an Albanian boy would pursue her across a landscape of barbed wire and checkpoints for years. But then there was Momo and the murders in Rezallë. I didn't understand any of it. How could a nation that had created this liturgy and people like Boris and Gjorg and Sofia also have involved itself in an orgy of genocide like the Bosnian war, not to mention Kosovo? How could a man like Momo, who created a Sofia, be capable of killing more than eighty people for the high crime of being Muslim and Albanian? Was this question a matter of human nature? I wondered if every nation was capable of the same contradictions. In short, could the same bloody implosion that consumed Yugoslavia in the 1990s happen in Russia, the U.S., or Canada? All our histories are soaked in blood. Could a massacre like the one in Rezallë happen anywhere? Still, I felt there was something tantaliz-ingly unique about Serbia. I had never been to a nation that was quite so enticing, intoxicating and menacing, and I allowed myself to believe that if I found Momo and Sofia I might acquire some vital truth about Serbia itself.

So I was determined to hear Boris out, to go through his wartime experiences and try to understand the conflict from his side. But I still needed to find someone who could testify to what had happened at Rezallë and confirm or deny that Momo Kneznanović had been there.

I phoned Zoran and asked if we could meet.

CHAPTER 9

Momo and the Murders

Belgrade, September 2000

      I met Zoran in the Terazije Avenue McDonald's and, as I nursed a coffee in a white foam cup, asked him if he could help me with some research I was doing on organized crime in Serbia. Hunched over a pastel-coloured plastic table that looked like kiddie furniture under his burly form, Zoran shrugged when I concluded my pitch and said, "I think it is possible."

Zoran was responding to my request that he introduce me to any contacts he might have in Belgrade's criminal underworld. I was withholding information because Zoran still did not know everything about Sofia, and out of respect for her I was still determined to dish out facts sparingly. I didn't tell Zoran I was actually investigating Sofia's father, Momo Kneznanović, nor did I mention I had been developing a theory on Momo's identity that Zoran might be able to substantiate.

If my theory was right, Zoran might also be able to shed light on the real question that was infinitely more important than Momo's identity and Sofia's whereabouts: What happened to the eighty-four men and one boy from Rezallë who vanished in a barrage of gunfire on April 5, 1999? Was Momo Kneznanović involved in this crime that had come to enthrall me?

*

Kosovo, June 1999

By the time I met with Zoran that afternoon I already knew a great deal about the killings in Rezallë. I knew even more about it that I had let on to Gjorg. In late June, soon after my first meeting with Gjorg on his farm I had decided to investigate this ethnic cleansing of Rezallë. At that time the investigation had nothing to do with either Sofia or Momo or Gjorg's search. I was working on an unrelated article, and it would be weeks before I learned of Momo's involvement.

So one afternoon in late June 1999, I hired a translator, a skinny Kosovar kid named Lumi, and set out for Rezallë by taxi. I had wanted my inquiry to be independent of Gjorg. (I wanted the research to be as dispassionate as possible, and I was more than a little reluctant to visit Gjorg given the cool reception I had received days before, when I was last at his farm.) Consequently, when our taxi sputtered into the village, I instructed the driver to bypass Gjorg's farmhouse and head straight for the heart of the community. Gjorg lived in a cluster of ramshackle houses at the northern edge of town. After lumbering along a wide dirt track into the southern and more densely populated side, we stopped at a dusty roundabout that looked like the closest thing Rezallë had to a town centre. There was a long building off to the side that might have been a community hall of some

description. Every other house was a reasonable facsimile
of Gjorg's. At least those homes that were still standing.
Every second or third house was a charcoal shell, torched
and gutted during the war.

Lumi and I climbed out of the taxi. There were no people
about. With the war over for barely a week, most of the village's inhabitants hadn't made it back yet. And if they were in
no hurry to return I could understand why. The area was without food, and since many wells had been contaminated during the war, there was precious little water. What Rezallë had
was mines and booby traps, which might have been anywhere, and a searing heat that pressed down from above and
rose from the ground with the dust. After a bit of exploring,
Lumi finally found a young woman who was busying herself
over a washtub beside a lean-to tent that sagged like a flag at
half mast beside the gutted remains of what had to have been
the family house.

The girl recoiled and called out when she saw us.
Seconds later a stocky middle-aged man, presumably her
father, emerged from the tent. The villager had teeth that
looked too big for his head, and leaned like an old fence post.
Lumi and I chatted with the villager, who became visibly disappointed when he realized I didn't represent the UN, NATO,
or anyone else that could provide him with food or a better
tent. After a bit more banter, I thought of those lonesome
bloated bodies I had seen on the outskirts of town and had
Lumi ask the man if he had heard of any violence towards
civilians during the war. The villager became animated. He
pointed off to the south, and once that arm was in the air he
pumped it repeatedly to emphasize whatever he was saying.
At this point Lumi, enthralled and obviously on to something,
stopped translating. He was sucking up information. Lumi
then grabbed my notebook from my hands, and jotted down
the names of two men on a blank page.

"That man told me where they are buried," Lumi said, on our way to the taxi. "It is just there."

I asked Lumi who exactly "they" were. Were they the brutalized villagers Gjorg had informed me of? Were they another unfortunate lot I hadn't heard about? "That guy said the VJ and police came and killed men from the village," Lumi said. "And that we should go to the other side of the cemetery[1] if we want to see where they are buried." Seconds later we passed the cemetery the villager had mentioned, and came to a stop at a wide turn in the road. At one end of the boomerang-shaped bend was a clump of trees. At the other end, a fence separated the road from farmland that stretched out for kilometres. But between the fence and the road was a large ominous mound of earth. Lumi and I got out, and started to kick around the mound. There was not much visible to suggest violence, except for a massive bone that looked decidedly bovine protruding from the loose earth.

"I think this is it," Lumi said. "I think they buried them here."

I looked at the pile of loose dirt and I thought of Gjorg and Momo. "Did he say how many men were buried here?" I said.

"More than ninety, maybe a hundred," Lumi said. "He said two men didn't die. They lived, and escaped after."

Between ninety and a hundred men! Gjorg had told me there had been a "massacre," but I never imagined it an attempt to wipe out the place. "You mean there are ninety men buried here?" I said.

Lumi shook his head, and looked confused. "No," he said. "They were here. That man said they came with a digging machine and a truck and took away the dead bodies."

I blinked and tried to get it straight. "Ninety men were killed here, but they're not here any more." I said. "Where are they?" Lumi said the man had heard a few stories, but essentially he didn't know. They just weren't there anymore. I remember reeling from the intangibility of the thing, just like I would months in the future when wrestling with Gjorg's affair with Sofia. I was to believe a massacre had happened even though all that was left of it was an incredible story.

Standing under a searing summer sun beside a pretty copse of trees and a meadow, I found this story implausible. Until Lumi gasped, and kicked an object from the grass on the edge of the road into clear view. It was a jaw bone with teeth intact, and it was clearly human.

I wondered where the bodies were, but I knew at least the whereabouts of the two survivors. Their names were inscribed in my notebook. The villager had given Lumi the names of two men (one was a grandfather, the other a mere boy in his teens) who had somehow survived the executions and escaped. Lumi had scribbled both names into my notebook. After asking around a little more, we learned from another local in Rezallë that one of the survivors was living with family in the big town of Skenderaj (which Serbs called Srbica) on the northwestern slip of the Drenica Valley. The man gave Lumi directions to the house, and the next afternoon we found ourselves standing before a wooden gate somewhere on outskirts of Skenderaj.

Lumi called out, and a stout woman appeared in the yard just beyond the fence. "I am looking for Misin Deliu," Lumi said. He identified both of us, and explained that I wanted to talk to Deliu about events in Rezallë. The woman, skittish and more than a little uncertain, called into the house, and unleashed a tornado of activity. There were calls, and footsteps, and within seconds more matronly women and a great brood of children appeared in the yard. The women spoke in urgent tones. The kids scampered like happy puppies, peered curiously at us, and smiled timidly. About two minutes later,

Lumi and I were seated on mattresses on the floor in the *óda,* or men's room of the house, facing the women and all those shyly grinning kids who sat around us as if waiting for a story.

We had been herded to this spot, and I wasn't sure what was going on until Lumi whispered that this house was indeed where Deliu was being billeted. One of the women was his wife, and an indeterminate number of the brood were either his children or grandchildren. We couldn't tell which. Deliu had gone to the market and was expected back any time. Whether someone was sent to fetch him, or whether he happened back on his own volition, Deliu appeared in the doorway five minutes later. He had a tall frame, and long concave cheeks covered by a day's growth of whiskers, which made him look even taller. Although he was only in his mid-sixties, Deliu had the knotted limbs of an old cherry tree, and thick fingers that bent to the side like blades of grass. In a rapid fire exchange with the women, Deliu was told who we were, and the brood made room for him to sit near us.

I felt uncomfortable talking about murder with so many kids around, but we didn't have much time and there wasn't much innocence left in Kosovo. So I got to it.

"I'm investigating what happened when Serb security forces came into Rezallë in April," I said, and Lumi translated. "I was told that you were there. Is that true?"

Deliu took off his shirt, and exposed a scar that grimaced painfully at us. He told us he had received this wound the day Rezallë was invaded by Serb soldiers, police, and paramilitaries in April. He told us he had been shot in a single and sustained volley of fire that killed the majority of the men of his village. He had only been injured, but he feigned death, and eventually slipped away. He confirmed there was only one other survivor besides himself—fifteen-year-old Ismet Rukolli.

"Can you tell me what happened?" I asked.

Misin Deliu did just that.[2] Deliu had spent his life in Rezallë. He was related to one of the town's Albanian founders who had settled on this hilly stretch of Drenica two hundred years earlier. And in many ways life in Rezallë had changed little since then. In 1999 Rezallë did have electricity, and a wide dirt wagon trail that linked the village to the rest of the valley, a development that older folks still marvelled at. But Rezallë had no telephones. Most homes had no indoor plumbing. Families still sustained themselves by farming the land, or herding cows and sheep. Life was simple, and Deliu liked it that way. "You couldn't find a better village," he said. "Nothing ever happened there."

Nothing except war. The village had been attacked in August and again in September 1998. On March 24, 1999, NATO launched air strikes against Yugoslavia, and thirteen days later—April 5—gunfire erupted on the outskirts of the village.

Both Rukolli and Deliu were awakened by the shooting that began around 5 a.m. Both knew that Serb security forces had occupied the northern edge of the village (where Gjorg's home was located) on April 2. But they had no way of knowing that two hundred Yugoslav troops had mobilized that morning, and with the support of tanks and armoured personnel carriers planned to seize the the village.

Neither man could have realized that by nightfall they would be the only men of Rezallë left alive.

Young Rukolli, hiding with his mother and sister, understood only that he was in grave danger. The bullets seemed perilously close—as if they "were flying everywhere." Everyone in the house cowered well away from the windows for fear they would be shot.

Old Deliu, on the other hand, went to the window, and spotted houses burning on the northern edge of village. He realized that the Serbs were coming, and was waiting for them at 9 a.m. when the main body of the invasion force rolled into the centre of the village. When he heard the rumble of armour through the walls of his house, and saw the invaders from his window, he stepped outside with hands held high. For Deliu the scene was nightmarish. His Kosovo may well have been a province of Serbia, but he couldn't recall the last time he had seen more than two Serbs (cops, that is) in the village at any one time. Now there were armed Serb troops everywhere. They stood on the road, and in yards of houses. There were VJ troops in green camouflage, and combat police in their distinctive blue camouflage, and wild-looking men in mixed martial attire Deliu knew could only be paramilitaries, or Četniks, as Kosovars called these irregular combatants. (First used in reference to the Serbian royalist militiamen of the Second World War, Četnik, is derived from četa.)

Deliu was immediately approached by a pair of VJ, and he greeted them in Serbian, a language Deliu had learned while serving a compulsory stint in the Yugoslav Army. The soldiers must have been impressed by his language skills. They conscripted Deliu as an interpreter, and had him go with them from house to house, and tell the people to leave their houses immediately and stand in their gardens.

Over the next hour, Deliu's neighbours heard the message he was relaying, and nervously left their houses. The soldiers came to the house where Rukolli was staying at about 10 a.m., and ordered everyone out. When Rukolli and his mother and sister, and the members of his extended family, tentatively stepped outside, the entire village was already outside, standing quiet and still from fright. They stood in their yards and waited, but for what no one knew.

It seemed for a while even the soldiers didn't know. As morning became afternoon, a soldier chatted with Deliu. He gave him cigarettes, and they traded sad stories. They talked about how awful life was. That was something a Serb and

Albanian could agree on. Deliu told the Serb about his two young nephews who had fallen into a well and drowned.

The soldier's eyes welled up. "I have two children," he said. "And I don't know if I'll ever see them again. We're shooting at you, but NATO is shooting at us."

Late in the afternoon the dreadful inertia was broken. The soldiers told the villagers, still standing in their gardens like scarecrows, that it was time to move out. Farm tractors the size of riding lawn mowers were commandeered, and fired up, and those unable to walk—the very young, the very old, and the sickly—were loaded onto the rear wagons. The rest of the town, as many as two hundred people, was ordered to march beside the wagons while soldiers shepherded the villagers on the road that passed through the village like a river. In the minutes that the people had to prepare, many women, assuming this to be the beginning of a long exile, packed whatever provisions they could gather (blankets, warm clothing, diapers,) into bags that they toted on their shoulders on their way out of town.

Some of the villagers must have wondered where they were going. If the soldiers had driven them north, they could have assumed the men were to be arrested, and placed in the jail in Skenderaj, where the *milicija* had a headquarters. But the Serbs were driving them south, into UÇK territory. Perhaps they would skirt the rebel lines and end up in Gllogovc, which also had a *milicija* HQ?

But no one wondered for long. The Serbs stopped the procession on the outskirts of the village, just beyond the graveyard at a wide bend in the road. Tractor engines were reined to an idle, and then turned off. The people shuffled, but said little and asked the soldiers nothing. Everyone was very afraid.

Then gunfire erupted. The shots came from far off, perhaps echoing from a skirmish between Serbs and UÇK elsewhere in the Drenica Valley. But the soldiers immediately became incensed.

"Look!" one of them screamed to Deliu. "Your army is killing us."

Rukolli grew fearful as the agitated soldiers began beating villagers. One soldier spotted young, able-bodied Rukolli in the group and tried to pull him from the lineup to beat him as well. But Rukolli was supporting his father's eighty-year-old uncle, Jonuz Rukolli. He and the old man were clutching each other, and the soldier—unable to wrestle the boy free from the old man—gave up in disgust and turned his fists elsewhere.

The firing soon died away. The soldiers settled down and drove the villagers to a barn just off the road. They lined them up. Then one of the soldiers shouted out that the women were to surrender any belongings they had brought with them. And as the women stepped forward and piled their clothes and bedding in a growing mountain of dirty laundry, the men were told to hand over any weapons. Then the soldiers began searching the men one by one.

"If I find a single knife on any man here," Deliu heard one of the soldiers shout, "I'll kill him with it."

Men were frisked from head to foot. One older man had been stripped almost naked in the search for weapons. If the soldiers found anything resembling a weapon, they took it. Of course, if they found money, they took that too.

After everyone had been searched, a soldier made an announcement. "I want all the men to move to the left," he ordered. "Women, children, and those who are sick are to move to the right."

The men were being singled out, and some understood how dangerous this was and what it might mean. Misin Deliu had an aged aunt in a wheelchair. A man was needed to push her, and Deliu's fifty-five-year-old brother Ibush leapt forward and took the job, gripping the handles of the old woman's wheelchair as if it were the edge of the precipice he was dangling from.

Others who could have stepped to the right stayed with the men. Burim Zabeli was only twelve years old, and even the soldiers considered him a boy. But he went with the men so he could hold the hand of his blind fifty-two-year-old father, Xhemajl Zabeli. When the men were told to leave the group, Ismet Rukolli's mother seized her son and dragged him to the right with all the force and fear of motherhood. But a soldier saw her, and would have none of it. He tore the boy from his mother's embrace. Ismet's mother wept and pleaded and begged.

"He's just a child," she said. "He belongs with the women." But Rukolli, strapping and healthy, looked manly enough to the soldier, who thrust him to the right.

"Look for your father," Ismet's mother called to him.

Ismet knew what she meant. Ismet's family lived on the north side of the village. Just before the Serbs had rolled in on April 2, Ismet, his mother, and sister had sought safety with relatives on the other side of town. But his father had stayed behind to keep an eye on the house and their possessions. He was now likely in Serb custody, and Ismet's mother hoped they would be taken to the same place. In a strange way, her instincts were correct. Although she had no way of knowing it, her husband was already dead. He had been shot, killed, and interred in a shallow grave as soon as security forces had occupied their town. His son Ismet was on his way to the same fate.

Minutes later the soldiers spurred the women and children with rifle muzzles and shouts, and started driving them down the road. The women moved slowly. They were frantic at having to leave their husbands, and fathers, and sons behind. They wailed and cried and called back to them. But the soldiers kept them moving. Only minutes down that road, Gjulferie Deliu[3] heard truck and tractor engines start. And moments later she heard gunfire that neither engine roar nor the screams of the women could drown out.

Soon after the women were marched away, soldiers ordered the men back across the road to an open area near a fence and a copse of trees. When the men crossed over, they were herded into a rough semicircle directly in front of the tractors and army transports that had been parked in the centre of the road. The soldiers prodded the men to stand in a line, but the trembling men bunched together like sheep on the right end of the line, perhaps seeking both to hide and protect themselves in the flock.

Neither Deliu nor Rukolli had any idea what would happen next. They—like everyone else—hoped for the best, and refused to fathom the worst. But the wisest in the group know the worst was about to happen. As he jostled in the line, Ismet Rukolli heard old men praying under their breath. He and some others started praying as well.

Then the engines were fired up and the soldiers took cover behind the vehicles. There was a brief moment when Albanian villagers and Serb soldiers faced each other. They stood only fifteen paces apart. But the chasm that divided them was much greater. The boundary between the two groups divided the living from the dead.

Ismet Rukolli knew. He just knew he was about to die. Despite the roar of the tractors fifteen-year-old Rukolli was overwhelmed by a sense of calm. He would later remember those final deafening moments as somehow silent. He stared into the faces of the men who were about to kill him, and noted how young they were. He noticed from their uniforms that most were also VJ, regular army soldiers. Everyone knew that VJ were the "softest" of the Serb soldiers fighting in Kosovo. The *milicija* were much harder, and paramilitaries— the private soldiers—were men to be despised and dreaded. For a moment these youthful human faces, perhaps because they reflected weakness and uncertainty and remorse, made Ismet Rukolli believe there was a chance.

But Ismet's hope was killed by a bullet. An instant later, the soldiers opened fire on the men. They shot from the tractors and the trucks. A bearded Serb fired with a heavy machine gun from a house twenty metres or so away.

Amid the bullets, engine screams, and thunder of gunfire, the men of Rezallë began to die. The child Burim Zabeli died. Misin Deliu remembers seeing him fall, still holding his father's hand. Aziz Deliu, fifty-six, died. He was a factory employee and Misin Deliu's brother. Demir Deliu, sixty, died. He was a construction worker. Jsuf Rukolli, forty-two, died. He was a teacher. Rexhep Rukolli, seventy-five, died. He was a janitor. The mound of bodies that collected on the grass also included Shet Zabeli, eighty-seven; and Mehe Zabeli, eighty-three; and Sadri Zabeli, sixty-six; and Sadik Malaj, sixty-eight. They were all farmers. Hetem Deliu, fifty-three, was an ambitious man who had worked in Ljubljana, Slovenia. He died. The dead also included the brothers Jahë Aruqi, forty-four, and Isuf Aruqi, forty-seven.

When the shooting began Ismet Rukolli fell to the ground immediately. His father's uncle Jonuz Rukolli, whom young Ismet had been helping, fell over the boy's body and covered him like a sack. Jonuz died that very moment, and Ismet would forever wonder whether the old man had tried to shield him or had simply fallen. The ground provided better cover than standing. Bodies stopped bullets like warm sandbags.

A bullet grazed Ismet's face. He felt a burning sensation but no pain. Then a bullet bored into his arm, and still he felt no great pain. Then he felt a bullet strike his back. Ismet worried his spine was severed. So he moved his feet just to ensure that he could. He felt the burns of two more bullets that tore his clothing, but only scraped his skin.

The shooting stopped. Ismet, bleeding from cheek, arm, and back, kept still. Still as a corpse.

When the tractors fired up and the shooting began, Misin Deliu had been standing to the left of the semicircle, away from the thick concentration of men. He felt a sharp pain under his armpit and threw himself to the ground, and stayed there as bullets flew and dying men moaned and the dead continued to fall. When the shooting stopped, Misin lay deadly still.

At this moment young Ismet and old Misin were still alive, but they weren't out of danger. Soldiers walked up to the bleeding, groaning heap, and sprayed the bodies with bullets. Deliu could feel that the soldiers were concentrating their bursts on the dense pile of men to the right. With his eyes barely open, Rukolli could see one soldier coming towards him. He was moving along the line, methodically shooting every man. It's hopeless, Rukolli thought. I'm going to die. These executioners are too thorough. But just as this efficient killer was about to reach Rukolli's spot in line, he ran out of ammunition. Rukolli heard him reload and resume his methodical firing. But somehow in the reloading he had bypassed Rukolli's body.

Soon after that the shooting stopped for good, and when it did eighty-four men—the lion's share of the manhood of Rezallë—lay on the ground, most of them warm and dead.

Rukolli had no idea where the soldiers were, and he remained as quiet as old Jonuz who lay on top of him, warm, perfectly still, and very dead. Then Rukolli heard voices. Two men who had survived the volley were whispering to one another. Rukolli waited. When no Serbs stepped forward to end the conversation, the young Kosovar realized the soldiers had likely all left.

One of the voices Rukolli heard may have belonged to Pajazit Kelmendi, who was mortally wounded, and lying beside his old neighbour Misin Deliu. Pajazit had touched Deliu's leg and whispered his name and then apparently died.

At this, Misin simply rose like a spirit from the horde of corpses and slipped into the nearby woods. He crept off so quietly that Ismet Rukolli did not hear. But not long afterwards he too realized it was safe to move. So he wriggled out from under Jonuz's limp body and crept to the bushes a short distance away, where he hid.

But Ismet's movements did not go unnoticed. Pajazit Kelmendi had not died beside Misin Deliu as Deliu believed. Kelmendi had fallen unconscious, and awoke to see Ismet Rukolli creep into the trees. Kelmendi crawled after the boy and pulled himself into the bushes after him. Ismet did his best to make the old man comfortable. Kelmendi had at least two bullet wounds in his back.

"I think I should go to Tushilë," Ismet said.

Kelmendi still had his wits about him. "No," he said. "There are probably Serbs in Tushilë."

Rukolli saw more movement among the bodies. Another injured man struggled to his feet and stumbled to the nearby fence that separated the road from the fields. The man was climbing the fence when a red Mitsubishi approached. Rukolli recognized the car. It had belonged to a friend of his. But now it was obviously a military vehicle. The car stopped. Serb soldiers got out and shot the man as he tried to mount the wire. Then the soldiers, seemingly satisfied everyone else was dead, climbed back into the Mitsubishi and continued on their way.

Rukolli waited with old Kelmendi in the trees until night fell and then around midnight, certain there were no soldiers near, he said goodbye to the old man and promised to send help. As Rukolli rose and passed the jumble of dead bodies for the last time, he heard another voice.

"Who are you?" the voice said. It came from the man who had been shot trying to climb the fence.

Rukolli crept up to the man, who was now lying on his

back, and identified himself. "You're my cousin," the man said. And Ismet Rukolli realized it was true. "Help me," he said. Ismet tried to make him more comfortable, but there was not much he could do. He slipped into the night, found safety, and survived his wounds and the war.

But old Pajazit did not survive. He either slipped away into death lying in the bushes, or he was discovered by soldiers and finished off. He, like his eighty-three neighbours, was buried at the site. A day or so later UÇK guerrillas hiding in the woods reportedly watched as earthmovers arrived, dug a pit, and bulldozed the bodies into a mass grave.

The women were spared. They were marched to Gllogovc to begin a long, miserable exile. But some of the men who escaped with them were not so fortunate. Ibush Deliu, Misin's brother who was spirited away with the women clutching his aunt's wheelchair, was pulled from the throng somewhere on the road to Gllogovc. He was never seen again.

*

With that Misin fell silent, and—after a few moments of silence that echoed like a tribute to the lost men of Rezallë— I told the old man that Lumi and I had visited the spot where he and others say the executions took place.

"There are no bodies there," I said. And I left the question that naturally flowed from it unsaid, and that question was: If eighty-four men were killed there on April 5, why aren't they still there?

Deliu shrugged, and said the men remained there until sometime in mid-May, when a digger and dump truck rumbled to the site. He said the truck carried the rotting carcasses of cows and horses in its bucket. He said the digger extracted the bodies and filled the grave with the dead livestock. He said witnesses saw the truck lumber out of the area with the dead men. No one knew where they ended up.

Deliu seemed sincere. But I couldn't shake a feeling of uneasiness. We left Skenderaj and I returned with Lumi to the scene of the alleged execution to try to put everything into perspective. The crime was proving frustratingly intangible. Deliu, Gjorg, and others in Rezallë would have me believe that a mass murder had occurred on this spot, but almost nothing remained of the victims or the event. Just as Sofia had vanished without a trace, all these men had been swallowed up by the war.

But maybe not all traces were lost. One thing did remain in abundance. As Lumi and I were kicking around the site, an old man limped up. He wore a dirty white skullcap on his head, and probed the earth with a knotted cane he held in his hand. When the old man discovered the partial jawbone we had found on our previous visit, he picked it up and held it close to his face so that his weak eyes could examine it. Lumi walked over and asked the old man what he was up to.

"I'm looking for my son's gold tooth," he said. The old man was a seventy-nine-year-old named Rexhep Arugi. His two sons Jahë and Isuf had been in the village on April 5. He had been told they were taken from their homes, marched to this spot, and shot. "I'm very worried about the bodies of my boys," he said. "I don't know where they are." So there were no physical remains left at Rezallë. But there was unfathomable grief.

*

When I looked into the murders at Rezallë in June 1999, I found no reference to anyone named Kneznanović. But Momo already cast a shadow over the crime scene. Sometime between my first encounter with Gjorg at the end of the war and my visit to his farm when he had given up on Sofia, a human rights investigator had come to the area to interview villagers about the events during the war. Because he was the only Kosovar within kilometres who spoke English, Gjorg had been conscripted as a translator in interviews with locals who had been at home on the day of the invasion. He had heard from them that the force that invaded Rezallë was made up of VJ and *milicija*. But Gjorg learned more. Some of the locals reported soldiers wearing the mismatched fatigues of the *Četniks*. One villager recognized Russian being spoken, which suggested that Russian soldiers or volunteers numbered among the combatants. A woman described the man she considered the leader. He was stocky like a water barrel, and he wore a great beard and a helmet on his head, and the irregular uniform of the paramilitary. She confided she was struck by the man's green eyes. Gjorg questioned his neighbour at length, and decided this man could only be Momo Kneznanović.

Gjorg was horrified by the news, so horrified he had told me he wanted to forget about the woman he considered his fiancée. His resentment of Sofia soon disappeared, but he felt nothing but dread and hatred for Momo. I heard it in his voice when he first told me about his theory that Momo had been an executioner or conspirator at the massacre. Later on, I called him on it. "Are you sure that paramilitary was Momo?" I said. "There are a lot of short green-eyed men in the world."

"My neighbour did describe him," Gjorg said. "And I know it was Momo. Momo was a very specific man."

Given what I knew about Momo Kneznanović, the question was: Was Gjorg's profile of Momo consistent? If Momo was a state-security operative, as Gjorg claimed, could he have been in the force that invaded Gjorg's Rezallë on April 5?

To find some sort of answer I needed Zoran to find contacts who could give me insight into the Serbian underworld, the strange synergy that seemed to exist between organized crime and the state security apparatus, and the bloody times and short life of the Serbian warlord Željko Ražnatović, better known as Arkan. In my mind, all three factors were connected.

Zoran told me it was "possible" to dig up information on Serbian organized crime. And then, a moment later, he smiled as if an idea had occurred to him and added: "I know somebody you can meet. His name is Dragan. He's a crazy bastard."

CHAPTER 10

The First Long Night

Kosovo, March and April 1999

On the first full day of NATO air strikes, while Serbian Boris Postovnik languished in Belgrade, Kosovar Albanian Gjorg Isufi took refuge in a basement in the village of Obri e Úlët, and listened to the howl and explosion of Serb shells all around him.

Gjorg and the others had come to Obri that morning thinking it a clever decision. Obri was rebel territory, rife with UÇK fighters. Yesterday it was prudent to be in a neutral spot like Turiqevc. Today they had decided it was best to be surrounded by bodyguards. Their plan was to stay alive just a few more days. Now that NATO was fighting for them, everyone believed the Serbs would surrender Kosovo. It would take only days for this to happen, three or four at most. Which meant that Gjorg and the others had to remain alive for four more days.

The six men left Turiqevc before dawn, trudged through the hills, travelling under a cloak of frigid darkness, and

arrived at the UÇK sanctuary of Obri e Úlët just in time for a
Serb bombardment. No sooner had they set foot in this unremarkable Drenica village than mortars and tank shells began
to explode around them. But they didn't seem to mind.
Unbeknownst to any of them, waiting in Obri at the house of
one of Hakif's relatives was a woman who began to tear with
relief the moment she saw them. This woman was Shota, sister to Gjorg, Kadri, and Ibrahim, wife to Hakif, and mother to
Agim. Shota was there with her daughters. She had come
impulsively the day before, looking for her son and husband.
She had stayed because the war had broken out the night
before, and now she was rewarded with a reunion with her
husband, son, and brothers, whom she hadn't seen for days.

The reunion was short-lived. Almost immediately upon
their arrival, Gjorg and the others realized they had blundered
by coming to Obri e Úlët. Shelling meant that an invasion
would follow, and when the Serbs came, they would spare
only women and children; the men were a different story. So
all agreed they had to continue running. They had to stay
alive four more days.

Running was an easy decision for Gjorg to make. He had fled
his home the day the Serb police invaded the previous summer, and he had been fleeing ever since. In fact, Gjorg had
spent most of his life searching for sanctuary. As an eleven-
year-old he used to walk two kilometres to school every day in
shoes that did not match, dressed in bulky frayed clothes
inherited from his brothers. The schoolteacher was a quiet
middle-aged scholar named Gani who was determined to arm
young Kosovars with knowledge.

Gani took a special interest in Gjorg, and Gjorg responded
with enthusiasm. Students came to class equipped with
blank scribblers for taking notes. Albanian-language textbooks,
carted across the border from Albania, were not plentiful, and

Gani had only one copy of some titles. So students took turns reading aloud from a text in class while the others copied the lesson into their scribblers. Sometimes Gjorg was too poor to bring a scribbler to school. Instead, he would absorb every word uttered in class and then, at recess, borrow a page from a classmate's exercise book and copy out the lesson for himself.

Gani was so impressed by Gjorg's hunger—both physical and intellectual—that he took the boy aside one day after school and gave him five thousand dinars. "I give you this because you are the best, just for that," Gjorg recalled him saying. Gjorg used the money to buy two litres of oil, sugar, and salt for the family.

Gjorg brought his studies back home every afternoon. He had obtained a battered English textbook. Some evenings he walked to the end of the cornfield where the family cow grazed. The cow kept Gjorg company while he studied English. He sounded the English words out as best he could, and pronounced them to the cow, who chewed approvingly. When they lost the cow, Gjorg's oldest brother, Kadri, asked, "What are you going to do now, Gjorg? Your English teacher just died."

While his English teacher lived, Gjorg forced himself to learn many words. One was the word "highness." This is what Gjorg aspired to have. This is what his family had achieved. *Highness*. His father was poor, but he had fought the Serbs in the war, and he was honest, and had worked hard when his body was younger and stronger. He had highness, and the people of his village looked up to him.

But having highness wasn't the same as having a life. Gjorg secretly wanted to leave Kosovo. Once, he had seen images of America on his cousin's television, and he fantasized that he lived there with a family. The family was made up of two boys and a girl, all of whom were younger than Gjorg. The parents recognized highness in Gjorg and asked him to stay with them. They gave him a job and treated him with kindness.

This fantasy was not Gjorg's only refuge. He also escaped into words. Gjorg loved to write as much as he loved to read, and he explored the meaning of words as if they were the woods outside his village. Life was confusing, and Gjorg struggled to find words—in any language—to make sense of things. He began writing poems. One of his first compositions was written in 1989. Gjorg wrote that Albanians were slaves, and he compared Kosovo to impoverished Ethiopia, which he had seen images of on his cousin's TV. Gjorg eventually showed the poem to one of his brothers, who told him to be careful. "A poem like this is dangerous for you and us," he told Gjorg.

Huddled together in the cellar, Gjorg, Kadri, Hakif, and Ibrahim discussed the situation as explosions echoed outside. They had tried fleeing to the neutral territory of Turiqevc, and found it unsafe. They had come to Obri e Úlët because it was rebel territory, and it offered no better protection. They decided now to go somewhere out of reach of the war. Someone mentioned Tushilë, and everyone liked the idea. Situated in the high country between Turiqevc and Likovc, the men reasoned that Tushilë was too far away from army positions to be shelled and too isolated to be overrun by soldiers.

When the bombardment stopped later in the day, the men ventured outside and discovered that other refugees had the same idea. A cavalcade of tractors was heading in the direction of Tushilë, and they found one wagon that had room for all of them. With the skies over Kosovo beginning to dim, the Isufi men bade goodbye to Shota and the girls, climbed into the wagon, and rode it out of town.

The men were on the road and in the open, but they felt safe. They realized that night—when NATO fighters cruised the dark skies and Serb soldiers hid in bunkers—was the best time to travel. Gjorg knew that they could still die from a NATO bomb, but he and the others had decided there was no better way for an Albanian to die than by a missile intended for the enemy.

As the tractors rumbled on, the sky grew darker and Gjorg could see nothing but the road ahead. Every now and then the tractor passed people. Gjorg saw men carrying bags, and men supporting other men, and men walking alone. The wanderers would be visible for only a moment before dissolving back into the night.

About an hour or so after the commencement of their journey, silhouettes of men with guns appeared ahead. The armed men weren't Serbs, as some in the group feared. They were UÇK fighters. They asked the men where the caravan was going, and when the men answered, the fighters told them Tushilë was not safe.

"It is surrounded by Serbs," a fighter said, "and will soon be attacked."

The guerrillas said the only safe place to be was the other side of the Gllogovc-Skenderaj road. Gjorg, Kadri, Hakif, and the others listened to the fighters, whispered among themselves, and decided to believe them. The tractor drivers didn't. So the men climbed down from the wagon, and headed out on foot along a road as dark as a tunnel. As the UÇK had suggested, their destination was the main road, which cut the Drenica Valley east from west. They couldn't know that only half the group would make it there.

Within an hour, Gjorg, Kadri, and Migen—young, robust men—drew ahead of Hakif, Ibrahim, and Agim, who stayed close to his father. Once again Hakif had trouble walking. His legs and his lungs just couldn't carry him the way they once had. His boy Agim helped him along, and Ibrahim encouraged them to keep moving; the going was painful. Hakif was forced to stop and rest from time to time. All three wondered about the others, but they assumed they were just up ahead.

But they weren't. When Gjorg, Kadri, and Migen arrived at the darkened crossing thirty minutes or so before Hakif, Ibrahim, and Agim, they were as stumped as the others would soon be. They had lost their bearings in the night. They weren't sure where they were, and had no idea which fork would take them to the road.

Gjorg stared at the crossing. The fork gave few clues as to the direction to take. This dilemma was not new to Gjorg. Last August, when he was alone in the hills above his village, he found himself making decisions minute by minute. Should he take this route or the other? Was it better to travel through trees that offered shelter or over open ground that provided visibility? Gjorg knew that it was safest to avoid paths and roads altogether, and to cross fields and meadows where there was no chance of encountering *milicija* or soldiers. But he had rejected this idea from the beginning. As scared as he was of death itself, he was more fearful of dying someplace where his body would never be found. This was not a religious concern. It was a personal fear. If Gjorg were to be killed by a sniper's bullet in a faraway field, there he would lie forever. He would decay secretly and seep into the hard earth of Drenica. Even if he were eventually found, swollen and rotting, no one would ever identify him as Gjorg Isufi.

So he decided he would move over well-travelled paths. But then he was faced with another question: what was the safest route to take? On his way to Bajicë, having been left for dead by Serb police, he had wondered, should I pass through Likovc or steer clear of it? Should I follow this wagon trail or that cow path? After a while Gjorg found that the least maddening tactic was to let the way choose him. He learned to close his mind and surrender himself to whatever route felt like his destiny.

Now, staring at the fork, Gjorg wondered what the road was telling him. He stared, reflected, and decided that the route to the right was the one they should take. Gjorg told Kadri his hunch. If they assumed they were still heading north, a shift to the right would place them on an easterly bearing, which was the direction they wanted.

"All right," Kadri said. "We go to the right."

Migen also agreed. Young and passive with fear, Migen was content to go along with whatever the older men decided. There was still the matter of the others. Gjorg and Kadri didn't want to pass the crossing without Hakif, Ibrahim, and Agim, so they sat down and waited for them to catch up. Gjorg's shoes were already soaked from the mud of the road, and his feet ached. Sitting still put him at the mercy of the damp and the cold that attacked him like insects as soon as he stopped moving. The darkness that hid him from his enemies was slipping away with every passing second. He and the others shivered from the cold, and from the fearsome prospect that a Serb patrol might find them before the others did. Gjorg and Kadri knew they were running out of time. They had to make it to the main road, and cross it, and hike to Qirez, where they had friends and were assured of shelter. And they had to do all of this before dawn. If the light of morning came and they were still on the open road, they would be in terrible trouble.

So Gjorg and Kadri made the agonizing decision to take the crossroads and continue on without the others. They tried to ease the pain by telling themselves that their kinsmen, close on their heels, would take the same fork and eventually catch up. Whether or not they really believed this didn't matter. Their worry for the others was overwhelmed by the reality of their predicament. The three stood at a crossroads as the night slowly slipped into morning. A conflict so colossal they could barely fathom it raged above them. They wanted to live, and from where they stood they could stay alive only by pressing on, and reaching Qirez before morning. To wait any longer or turn back to search for the stragglers drastically reduced their chances of reaching their destination, which lay close by. The real goal was to be still alive by this time the next night.

So Gjorg, Kadri, and Migen got up and headed down the right fork. About two hours later they passed through a silent farmyard, crept down a lane, and stood a short distance from the asphalt ribbon that had been their destination all night long: the Gllogovc–Skenderaj road.

Kadri feared the *milicija* was somewhere nearby, and he wanted to spot them before being spotted. Leaving Migen in the shadows, Kadri and Gjorg crept to the roadside. In their hands they carried sticks like guns. If sighted, they wanted the Serbs to think they were armed. Crouching on the shoulder of the pockmarked two-lane road, they stared in one direction and then the other, but saw nothing but darkness.

Kadri stood up and walked to the centre of the road. He held himself straight and high, and gazed one way and then the other. Kadri wanted to be sure he reconnoitred properly, but he was also making a statement, and that statement was that he, Kadri Isufi, with nothing but a stick in his hand, commanded this stretch of road in Drenica. But any confidence Kadri felt disappeared an instant later when figures jumped from the darkness, surrounded them, and overwhelmed them with a terrible noise.

*

Gjorg couldn't have been surprised by the attack. Or the war, and the threat of violence he had lived with most of his life. Violence was a fact of life in Kosovo. Gjorg knew this very well. He knew this from the stories he had heard as a child.

They were stories of the first Kosovars—two brothers named Muja and Halil. They were not like Gjorg and Kadri, or any other Kosovar who lived these days. They were giants, and they lived long ago, before the time of the Turks, before the time of heroes like Skenderbeg. They lived in ancient times when giants walked the earth.

Muja and Halil came to Kosovo from Bosnia. They had been born simple boys, but they became great and powerful through the supernatural strength they received as a divine gift. Gjorg's grandmother had told him how it happened. Once, when young Muja and Halil were exploring the forests of Kosovo, they heard the cries of children. They followed the noise and found a brood of infants in a crib made of twigs and leaves. They soothed the babies with kind words. They couldn't know the children belonged to the forest goddess Zanat. But they learned this lesson suddenly when Zanat fell upon them, just like the attackers who had ambushed and surrounded Kadri and Gjorg on the road north of Gllogovc. Zanat could have killed the young brothers, but she recognized that Muja and Halil had cared for her children. And she recognized that Muja and Halil were hungry. So she took out her breasts and allowed Muja and Halil to drink her divine milk. Zanat's milk did more than soothe the brothers' hunger. It had magical qualities that transformed them. It gave them great strength, and changed them into giants.

Gjorg knew this to be true because he had seen the evidence of their deeds. Near his farm there are two boulders that lie in a meadow on the edge of town. When Gjorg was a child, his grandmother told the story of those stones. The brothers were in the Çiçavicë Mountains far to the northwest. After arguing which brother was the strongest, they decided to see who could throw a boulder the furthest. Halil picked up a stone that was more than three hundred kilograms in weight and heaved it with all his might. The stone not only left Çiçavicë, it sailed halfway across Drenica and landed on the spot that, far in the future, would be Gjorg's village. Muja threw a stone of the same size and weight, and it sailed across Drenica and landed beside Halil's stone—proof that the powers of Muja and Halil were tremendous but exactly equal.

Gjorg knew that Muja and Halil were great warriors. When the Serbs and Montenegrins came to Kosovo, Muja and Halil fought them, like true heroes, with great swords. They faced their enemies like men—bravely, and honourably. And they were always victorious. No Serb nor Montenegrin nor Turk could beat them. Still, despite their prowess and power, they were overwhelmed. But Gjorg knew that Muja and Halil were not defeated. He knew they left Kosovo and the world by choice. They were driven away by the same sadness that propelled Gjorg, Kadri, Migen, and the others in their endless flight.

*

When the forms leapt at them from the shadows Gjorg believed he and Kadri had been ambushed by Serb *milicija* and would die then and there in the middle of this road. But an instant later Gjorg realized their attackers were not Serbs. Nor were they Albanians. He had anticipated bullets but he was assailed with howls and snarls. Gjorg and Kadri were being attacked by wild dogs. The dogs barked hysterically, and circled them trying desperately to attack from behind. If they lunged at them the dogs might have been as dangerous as the police. If they kept on barking, Gjorg realized, they might summon the police if there was a bunker or patrol nearby. Gjorg dug his arm deep into his bag, pulled out a stale piece of bread, and threw it on the road. As he had hoped, the nearest dogs went for the food and the others followed, and Kadri and Gjorg were able to slip away. They gathered Migen and dashed across the road into eastern Drenica, slipping back into the dark and comfortable countryside like turtles into the surf. They had crossed the Gllogovc–Skenderaj road, but there would be no safety until they reached Qirez.

The first village they encountered was Gllobar, literally only a few paces away. This cluster of gently sleeping houses was safe. But Kadri wasn't sure about the other villages they would need to pass on their way to Qirez. Were these villagers *milicija*-controlled? Were they safe to pass through? The three approached a farmhouse on the edge of the village. The home was obviously Albanian, and Kadri told Gjorg that he would knock on the door, awaken any inhabitants, and find out if there were police garrisons or bunkers between there and Qirez.

Kadri was the eldest Isufi and clan leader. But despite Kadri's good judgment, Gjorg told him it was a bad idea to awaken the farm house.

"We have to find out where the Serbs are," said Kadri. "We have to ask someone." Gjorg couldn't deny that he was right. They were now in east Drenica, an area they knew barely at all. They had heard that Qirez was safe, but they didn't know this for certain, and common sense dictated they should speak to a local Kosovar before going on. Still Gjorg would not relent. He did not want Kadri to go to this house, and Kadri eventually yielded. He was under no obligation to listen to his younger brother, but Gjorg's fear had spooked him.

So they headed north to Qirez. The night was heavy and the countryside quiet, but Gjorg knew the security of the night was deceiving. It was slipping away. He didn't know what time it was, but he knew they had to reach Qirez as soon as possible because morning would eventually dawn hard and fast. About thirty minutes later, the group arrived at the village of Vrboc. No one knew whether this village was safe or not. But they soon found out. As they approached the first farm house on the edge of the tiny community Gjorg saw a shadow shift, and a man take shape—a man holding a rifle. Fearing they had blundered into a police checkpoint, Migen ran, but had only sprinted a few paces when Gjorg and Kadri called out to him. "Stop, stop," Gjorg said. "It's not Serbs."

Despite the darkness, Gjorg saw something in the shadow's posture and manner that told him he was UÇK. Kadri called out and identified the three of them.

The gunman told them to come forward. "You're safe here," he said. "Don't worry." The rebel sentry said the Serbs hadn't invaded Vrboc, or any of the other nearby villages. The area was all UÇK controlled.

The men then told the sentry they had just come from Gllobar.

"You are lucky," he said. "There are Serb police in Gllobar." Then he described how the Serbs had commandeered a farmhouse just outside the town. The sentry described the command post, and Gjorg and Kadri realized it was the same homestead that Kadri had wanted to awaken for directions.

Gllobar had been another junction. How many more would they encounter? The wanderers said goodbye to the sentry and continued on. They stumbled wet, cold, and weak into Qirez just before dawn. They found the home of Kadri's school friend, and he welcomed them to stay as long as they liked.

Dawn fell on Kosovo like a bomber's payload. Now safe, the travellers felt time slow down. A day later Gjorg could only assume that Hakif, Ibrahim, and Agim had not taken their route, and he wondered whether they had parted ways forever. He might have felt grief for leaving them on the road if there had not been so many others to grieve for. He thought of his mother in hiding in Skenderaj, and he wondered if he would see her again. He thought of his brother Rexhep in the UÇK, and his sisters, and cousins. When he wondered how many of his family might die before the war ended he understood the myth of Muja and Halil, and why they had abandoned Kosovo and its people to enemies like the Serbs.

Standing in a village under the long shadow of the Çiçavicë Mountains, where Muja and Halil once revelled, competed, rejoiced, and in the end brooded, Gjorg could not forget the fate of the first Kosovar brothers. Because their fate was his fate now.

*

"Muja and Halil were the greatest warriors in the Balkans," Gjorg was told by his grandmother. "No one could match them with a sword. No one could throw a stone farther. They battled and defeated Kosovo's enemies, and would have done so indefinitely. But one day they happened upon a band of cow herders. One herder carried a curious weapon that he had obtained from abroad. It was long and slender like the trunk of a willow. Muja and Halil asked what the weapon was, and they were told it was a gun.

"'A gun? How does it work?' they asked.

"The herders explained what a marvellous weapon it was. You simply point it at your enemy, and pull a switch, and the rod kills by hurling fire and metal. With such a weapon you could kill an enemy at a great distance, and kill better than with a bow and arrow. With such a weapon you need never face your enemy again, and taste his blood and sweat in battle. Muja and Halil could hardly believe their ears. A weapon that kills by spitting hot metal, and kills better than a sword or arrow, and kills from afar?

"'Shoot my hand,' said Muja. 'Show me how this weapon can harm a man.'"

The herder fired into Muja's hand, and Muja raised his limb in wonder and inspected the torn flesh and flowing blood. The gun's wound did not really injure Muja, but the prospect of the gun—the violence it promised —caused both brothers searing pain. They brooded over the arrival of this weapon and came to a conclusion. "We do not want to be alive in the world with a weapon like this," they said. "This is no longer our time."

Muja and Halil returned to the forest and sought out Zanat, and when they found the goddess who had given them strength and life they beseeched her to release them from this world. They asked to be turned to stone. Zanat must have understood how Kosovo was changing with the advent of this new weapon, because she granted their wish. She summoned her powers, and transformed the brothers into a stoic outcrop of rock. Their dread was well founded. After their departure guns spread across Kosovo. In time almost every Albanian man would have guns. They would kill Serbs with them, but they'd also kill Albanians—in error, in anger, and in bloody vengeance. The Turks would use guns to rule Kosovo, and the Serbs would use guns to win Kosovo, and the dead would be innumerable, and Muja and Halil understood all of this only too well.

At least, this was how Gjorg's grandmother told it. Others said that after being shown the guns of the cowherds, the Albanian brothers simply wandered off in sadness and confusion, and disappeared. Gjorg understood the similarity between the first Kosovars and today's. Muja and Halil were defeated by guns and violence. The violence hadn't killed them. It simply made it impossible to live a decent life.

And Gjorg couldn't help but wonder: When was the long violent night that sent Muja and Halil in dark despair to end their lives? When the air strikes began Gjorg truly believed the Serbs would soon surrender, and a new Kosovo would emerge, perhaps like the old one, a place where men were free to play games and roam the countryside without fear. But by his first night in Qirez, Gjorg no longer held any illusions that this would be a short war. Gjorg now knew the fighting would go on and on. The only question was whether he and his family would live to see the end.

CHAPTER 11

Crazy Bastards

Belgrade, September 2000

I was seated under an umbrella on the patio of the
Sports Café the next evening when Zoran marched up with
Dragan, his underworld contact.

The Sports Café was a popular restaurant in downtown
Belgrade. Zoran had called me that morning and told me to
be there at 7 p.m. if I wanted to meet Dragan. He told me a
little about Dragan, and I had to agree—he was worth meeting. I didn't think there was much of a chance Dragan knew
Sofia's father personally. But I was developing a theory on
Momo's profile and, if I was right, Dragan might be able to
provide some useful information.

I arrived early at the Sports Café and took a seat on the
empty patio. I sat outside so I wouldn't miss my contacts'
arrival. I spotted them the moment they appeared at the end
of the alley that led up to the terrace and the café entrance.
Both men moved with the swashbuckling assurance of gangsters. Their swaggers were different. Zoran heaved from side
to side when he walked, and his powerful arms never touched
his body. Dragan had the defiance of a strutting rooster.

At a glance he was as different from Zoran as a knife is from a pistol. Zoran was built like a boxer. Dragan, on the other hand, was tall and gangly like a high-school basketball centre. Still, you wouldn't mistake him for an athlete, although he would later tell me being a footballer had been his greatest dream. Maybe it was the troubling cocksure strut, or maybe it was a violent quality in his asymmetrical baby face. But the closer Dragan got, the clearer it became he was no boy scout.

Zoran recognized me from the alley. He strode onto the patio and up to my table. "This is Dragan," he said, "my friend I tell you about."

Dragan and I shook hands. I said *"Dobar dan,"* but Dragan said absolutely nothing, and we all settled into plastic patio chairs as if we were slipping into a cold Jacuzzi.

I was about to call a waiter and offer Dragan a drink. I could see he was troubled. There was no one else on the patio, but Dragan scowled and peered about like a hunted man. Zoran glanced at his friend and suggested we get a table inside.

We made our way across the sleek metallic dining room, amid the strategically placed television sets blaring sports contests. It was early evening and business was booming. At almost every table there were women with high Slavic cheekbones and hair that was either wheatfield blond or oil-slick black. They held cigarettes close to their faces or over ashtrays, and flicked as they talked. In almost every instance their male escorts wore tight designer T-shirts and had closely cropped hair. They looked like thugs. Most, of course, were not. Despite the black marketeering the average Serb had to do to make ends meet in those days of sanctions, isolation and unemployment, I had no doubt that most of the young men in this bar were upstanding citizens. But even if you weren't a gangster it was still cool to appropriate the look—crew cuts, gold chains, shirtsleeves that covered biceps like paint.

Zoran led us to a table at the back of the room. His back to the wall, lost in a crowd of beautiful big-haired women and tough-looking men, Dragan appeared infinitely more relaxed. While we waited for our meals (both Zoran and Dragan ordered heavy plates of grilled meat and fries), I asked Dragan where he was from in an effort to ease into a rapport with him and to establish his credentials.

"I grew up in Voždovac,"[1] he said, "where everyone wants to be a criminal."

Dragan had got what he wished for. He was twenty-four years old, and he ran a medium-sized car fencing ring that boasted links with Germany, Hungary, and Austria. Cars were stolen abroad and smuggled into Yugoslavia for sale. Of course he was always on the lookout for cars to steal at home as well. Business was brisk. Thanks to trade sanctions, relatively new used cars in Yugoslavia were available only on the black market. Prices reflected demand. An old model Mercedes usually got him 30,000 Deutschemarks. A new Mercedes went for as much as 100,000. Demand fluctuated. "Sometimes I can't sell anything for two weeks," he said. "Then, bam! I have a sale."

Dragan said he sold one or two cars a week, and only occasionally did it happen that a potential buyer would try to make off with the merchandise. Once when he was trying to sell a stolen motorcycle, the buyer tried to bolt. He gave me a wounded look of childlike innocence when I asked him if he had ever had to kill or maim someone to protect his goods.

"You can get into a lot of trouble these days if the police catch you carrying a gun," he said.

But when Dragan went to the toilet, Zoran leaned over to me. "My friend did not tell the truth," he said. "When that guy tried to steal that motorcycle, Dragan shot him." Zoran assured me that Dragan had only wounded the guy, and when he smiled I could tell what he was thinking.

What did I tell you? his smile said. Dragan is a crazy bastard.

*

What I couldn't understand about Dragan was that he seemed to be merely getting by, when he should have been prospering.

He did have a cottage thirty kilometres outside of Belgrade that he retreated to on weekends with his girlfriend. But he lived in an eighty-square-metre flat in the outskirts of the city, was dressed almost shabbily, and seemed to be happy with his lot. At first this didn't make sense. But I had only to look around at all the ostentatious would-be gangsters in the restaurant to understand. When Dragan said every boy in Voždovac grew up with dreams of becoming a "criminal," he wasn't boasting or being facetious. I was certain that youngsters in Voždovac and across Serbia were as well-intentioned, hopeful, and confused as youngsters anywhere. But Serbia was different from most places. It was a place where crime was a fixture of everyday life. Most Serbs may have decried this fact, but few could deny that crime was the surest route to fame, wealth, and women in the beleaguered Yugoslavia of 2000. It had been that way ever since Slobodan Milošević became the leader of Serbia.

After Milošević took control of Serbia in 1989 he initiated a revolution that altered the federation's power structure. Ultimately his changes transformed Serbia into a criminal oligarchy. The breakdown of law and order didn't happen overnight. The rot spread gradually, exacerbated by the wars that began in 1991 and the punishing UN-imposed trade sanctions that followed. The UN embargo triggered an economic upheaval that enriched an underclass by choking off legitimate forms of trade. The sanctions made moguls out of bottom-feeders—thugs, petty thieves, and political toadies—who became financial giants when the smuggling of precious goods like tobacco and oil became the nation's economic mainstays. These mandarins used political connections to turn smuggling rings and state concessions into lucrative monopolies, which were often nothing more than state-sanctioned criminal syndicates.

The moguls of this para-economy went to the streets and raised an army of poor, young, ruthless thugs to serve as their foot soldiers: men like Aleksandar 'Knele' Knežević, Radojica Nikčević, and Goran Vuković. They were paid well for their services as killers, bodyguards, and heavies. Different from the discreet tycoons whom they served, these youthful gangsters made no secret of their power and wealth. They wore Rolexes and Gucci shirts unbuttoned to expose muscled abdomens, and each hung enough gold around his neck to sink a corpse. You could see them on the river boats or in *de rigueur* restaurants. They lived hard and lavishly, drove fast cars, and adorned themselves with beautiful women. Of course, ordinary people recognized them for what they were—uncommon criminals. But even a well-adjusted young man might have trouble suppressing a little envy for the outlaw gentry. You could see this grudging mimicry in the gangster aesthetic on display in the restaurant where we were sitting.

But this wasn't Dragan's style. With his dirty running shoes and jeans, he was the only young man in the room who wasn't dressed like a gangster.

"Don't you want to make more money?" I asked.

Dragan shook his head. "When you work hard and make money you have enemies," he said.

Dragan said he fenced stolen cars in harmony with four or five other gangs, who were careful not to step on each other's toes for the sake of peace and their livelihoods. "I could easily make more money," he said. "I could traffic heroin. There's a fortune in that."

The drugs came to Serbia from Turkey, Bulgaria, and Albania; Serbia is the gateway to the west. But trafficking makes you rich and famous in certain circles, and fame and riches were what Dragan did not want. "Money makes enemies," he said. What Dragan yearned for was invisibility—sweet and complete anonymity. Because money not only made you enemies, it got you killed.

Then the conversation swung like the barrel of a gun to Željko "Arkan" Ražnatović, a figure who was on my mind at that moment as much as Sofia's father. Until January 15, Arkan had been the most visible and arguably the richest underworld figure in Serbia. Arkan was better known internationally as a war criminal, secretly indicted by the UN in 1997 for crimes committed in Croatia and Bosnia.

Both Zoran and Dragan got misty-eyed when I mentioned Arkan. "Arkan was 100 percent cool," Dragan said. "He was a big patriot. He wanted to unite the Serbs." I already knew where Zoran stood on the matter. We had already argued over Arkan.

"Arkan, he was very good to his men," Zoran had told me earlier. "They say he always led the way into battle. He always went first." When I suggested that Arkan was a killer who had gone first into defenceless villages where he and his men savaged innocents, Zoran guffawed. "Arkan had money, women," he said. "If I could trade my life for Arkan's I would. In a minute." He said that knowing full well that on January 15, 2000, Arkan had been assassinated in the lobby of Belgrade's luxurious Intercontinental Hotel.

Arkan had probably taken to spending his time at the Intercontinental for security reasons. On that day, four men dressed in track suits had approached Arkan's entourage and asked whether the hotel's fitness centre was open. Arkan said no. He shook hands with the men. Then one pulled out a Heckler and Koch machine gun, and sprayed nine-millimetre fire into his face. One bullet entered his brain by way of his left eye, another smashed through his mouth, and yet another bore a hole into his temple. He was dead before he reached the hospital.

The gunfire that killed Arkan sounded around the world. CNN carried the story. Obituaries appeared over the Associated Press, the *New York Times,* and scores of western dailies. Martin Bell, British MP and former BBC journalist, shocked the UK when he called Arkan "a friend," and noted his "raw military courage." Madeleine Albright expressed disappointment he would never stand trial for war crimes. At home, the police made arrests, alleging that the actual killer was twenty-three-year-old Dobrosav Gavrić, and that his accomplices included former cops Dejan Pitulić and Vujadin Krstić. All three may have been trigger men. But the question everyone was still asking was this: Who had ordered the killing?

*

It was some nights later before I got a straight answer. I was again out with Zoran, who had offered to take me to the promenade along the Sava River where huge boats are anchored to the bank. Each is a floating night club or restaurant, and on weekends they are the epicentre of the city's night life. In a highly charged city like Belgrade that was a distinction. When Zoran and I started out it was still early—no later than 8 p.m. But as we drove downtown along Bulevar Revolucije and onto Moše Pijade, there were a lot of cars on the street and I could already see people in the windows of the cafés and restaurants we sped by. Belgrade, it seemed, was that type of city. It stood to be engulfed in a civil war in only a matter of days, yet it remained a place you could drink, dance, and eat all night long if you wanted. It was not that Belgrade never slept. But it was certainly awake when most cities weren't. I thought about the conversation we had had with Dragan the other night.

"What do you think? I asked. "Who killed Arkan?"

By this time we were cruising down Bulevar Mira. I was staring at the green of Hajd Park when Zoran pointed to a wreath of flowers on the edge of the asphalt. "That scandal which you see, this is Mirko Bosnjan," he said.

According to Zoran, "Mirko the Bosnian" was the nickname for a hoodlum who had died in a hail of Kalashnikov fire at that spot as he waited at a traffic light.

Zoran paused and immediately corrected himself. "No, not a Kalashnikov," Zoran said. "It is always a nine-millimetre machine gun. That's the favourite of the killers. It's a good one, and it's easy to hide."

"Bosnjan was the biggest face here in town for stolen cars. He had connections with the West, and he co-operated with other West groups who stole and smuggled the cars. But he died because he was also connected with the assassination of three Mafia faces from Belgrade."

"They know he killed them because when the three guys died Bosnjan was the last guy they saw alive. He would call a meeting, meet with them, and then five minutes later the guys were killed. So they killed Mirko there. This happened six months ago. His mom comes every day from Novi Beograd to leave flowers."

We pulled into the parking lot at the promenade near the river. I could smell the water the moment I opened the door. The floating clubs were in plain view: the Monza Racing Café and Club Rio, the Bibis Pub, the Amsterdam, and the Acapulco. There were beefy, bald-headed security guards on the gangplanks. There was a lot of action, even though it was only a Thursday. Beautiful girls in short dresses were lined up at the planks waiting to climb aboard. There were young men, some in leather, more than a few of whom resembled Zoran, which is to say they looked like young gangsters. Others looked more like footballers.

"That's Mirko's boat," Zoran said, pointing at one of floating clubs. "That's the club he owns." Zoran used the present tense as if the wreath on Bulevar Mira and his mother's grief kept "Mirko the Bosnian" anchored to the living world like these boats to the bank.

The atmosphere inside the Monza was calm. Pretty girls huddled around a nearby table. There were couples at other tables and single guys at the bar. Music blared, but no one danced. As soon as we sat down, Zoran shifted his attention to the girls. Before he started chatting one up, I brought up Arkan again.

"Tell me, what do you think about Dragan's story?" I asked. "Who was it he mentioned?"

"He was this guy Skole," Zoran said.

It had taken some prodding, but the other night at the Sports Café, Dragan had told me who he really thought was responsible for Arkan's death. I was surprised because Dragan's information differed from any I had heard. There were two common theories about Arkan's death. According to one, he was killed by Marko Milošević, because it was believed the president's son was one of the few men powerful enough to move against a figure as awesome as Arkan. According to the other, Arkan knew too much about Milošević's role in the bloodletting in Croatia and Bosnia, and consequently had been silenced by agents of the regime on the orders of the president himself. But Dragan's story was different, and seemingly implausible.

"Skole was his name?" I prodded Zoran.

"Not his real name," said Zoran. "It's what they call him. His real name is Zoran Uskoković.

"Anyway, Skole, he came from Rakovica. This is an area of Belgrade. He played judo for a lot of years, and I heard he was good. Then later on he started with criminal activities. He killed one guy in a disco club on the Sava River. The police was looking for him for a few years. He finally gave himself up, and told them how he done it. But my friends say he never co-operated with the police. And he's only criminal in Belgrade who never co-operated with police.

"Later, Skole started with drugs business. He didn't deal here. He sent the action to the West. He made a lot of money. He bought a hotel in Spain. He bought restaurants in Sweden. He opened a few companies in South Africa just to wash the money. And then he started business with Arkan. They bought the young football players and sold them for a lot of money."

"And?"

"It's like my friend say to you—one of Skole's boys, he killed Arkan," said Zoran.

"But why?"

"Skole, he wants to be the number one, that's why," said Zoran. "He wants to get all power. He wants to be number one in drugs and rackets. He wants to control Belgrade and Serbia."

"So does he?"

"No." said Zoran. "Skole, he's dead maybe three months after Arkan."

Then Zoran told me how Skole died, and his story shone a foglight on power politics in Serbia, and Momo.

*

Arkan was an intriguing character for obvious reasons. In the firmament of hard men who had risen to ascendency in

Serbia in the 1990s, Arkan was a superstar. He had been a key player in the events contributing to the bloody historic rupture of Yugoslavia. But more importantly to me in September 2000, eight months after his assassination, his life and its termination dovetailed with a theory I was developing about the identity of Momo Kneznanović.

Arkan was born Željko Ražnatović in Slovenia in 1952. By most accounts, he was a precocious criminal. Zoran had shared a few Arkan myths with me. How young Željko stole cars on the streets of Sarajevo while still a boy. How he made forays into Italy as a teenager, and made serious cash as a thief, smuggler, and enforcer. How even as a lad he lived fast and well. These tales may have been apocryphal. But Arkan was no doubt a handful for his parents. Arkan's father—an air force officer—reportedly asked contacts in the Secretariat for Internal Affairs (SSUP) to help straighten the boy out.[2] Clearly, agents at state security saw that young Željko was crooked. He was bent like a crowbar and they quickly surmised it would be useless to try to bend him back. And a terrible waste. So internal affairs did what any thug would do with a crowbar in hand. They swung it. They put Arkan to work. They dispatched him to western Europe to murder émigré Yugoslavian dissidents. Arkan's criminal apprenticeship proved invaluable in his new job as a spy and assassin and accounts for much of his folk popularity. He robbed banks. He broke out of jails in Belgium, Holland, and Germany, and shot his way out of a Swedish courtroom. He acquired the nickname Arkan from one of his many false passports.

By the late 1980s Arkan was back in Belgrade, his days as a state-security spy seemingly behind him. He became the high-profile president of the Belgrade Red Star football club fan association and ran a pastry shop. The football fans called themselves the Warriors. Around the same time,

Arkan had been tapped by the regime to assist in the efforts of Serbian state security office (SDB) to arm and organize Serbian enclaves in Croatia and Bosnia. The SDB became an instrument of Milošević's determination to control as much Serb-owned territory beyond Serbia's existing borders as possible.

Arkan's skills as a murderer made him the SDB's most lethal weapon. War broke out in Croatia in 1991. But as early as 1990 Arkan helped organize the Serbian Volunteer Guard, better known as Arkan's Tigers. The Tigers received the best weapons, tools, and supplies the SDB and interior ministry could supply, and Arkan manned the guard's ranks with convicts, street thugs, a few true believers, and hooligans from the Red Star fan club. The football thugs proved excellent storm troopers. Yugoslav football hooliganism over the past generation had exhibited a violence and jingoism that might have spooked even the more brutish fans of Manchester United. One football chant conjures up the tenor of the times:

> *The emblem on my beret*
> *is shaking, shaking*
> *we will murder, we will kill*
> *all who are not with the Star* [3]

During the Croatian war that began in 1991 and the Bosnian war that followed a year later, the Tigers operated from Erdut in Serb-controlled eastern Croatia, and added a new dimension to the phrase "ethnic cleansing." They are accused of killing 250 Croatian patients and medical staff in Vukovar.[4] They are accused of killing as many as 1,400 local Muslims "in various ways" in Foca, Bosnia, beginning in April 1992.[5] They are accused of spreading terror on behalf of a regime that couldn't entrust the Yugoslav People's Army (JNA) with such bloody work. The accusations of rape, torture, murder, and looting against them would fill volumes. And Arkan and his Tigers weren't the only ones. In 1994 the UN reported that eighty-three paramilitary groups (i.e., private volunteer armies) were raising hell in Croatia and Bosnia. Fifty-six were Serbian, and included the Grey Wolves (led by Slobodan Miljković), and the White Eagles (sponsored by radical nationalist politician Vojislav Šešelj). Fourteen paramilitary armies were Croatian, and thirteen were Bosnian.[6]

In 1992 Arkan used his wartime fame to launch a career in business and politics. First he was elected to the Yugoslavian parliament as an independent candidate from Priština. In 1993 he founded the unsuccessful Serbian Unity Party (SUS), but failed to win a seat for himself. He married the Serbian pop star Ceca, had two children, and lived in a pink villa with a glass elevator in the Dedinje suburb of Belgrade. Arkan made a fortune from state oil and gas concessions, and by dabbling in football and other, more nefarious, enterprises. He wore expensive suits, travelled in a cavalcade of blue SUVs, and fifteen days into the new millennium he was shot dead in the lobby of the Intercontinental Hotel.

Zoran's story—identical to Dragan's the other night—was that Skole's boys had murdered Arkan. I told Zoran I didn't believe it.

I thought what most people thought: that the regime itself had ordered Arkan's death for the crime of knowing too much. The proof was all the other paramilitary commanders who had been silenced in recent years. In September 1996, the body of White Eagle general Miodrag "Johnny" Đorđić was pulled from the Morava River. He had a nine-millimetre round in his head. Shortly before his death Đorđić had told a foreign reporter that Serbian state security had been the chief supplier of the Eagles and other paramilitary groups. In April 1997, Radovan "Badža" Stojičić, Minister of the Interior and

Public Safety, was gunned down in a restaurant. Badža was believed to have been Arkan's interior ministry contact during the wars in Croatia and Bosnia, and to have helped mastermind the ethnic cleansing of Bosnia and Croatia, possibly serving as the link between front-line killers like Arkan and Milošević himself. On August 7, 1998, Lugar, the *nom de guerre* of Slobodan Miljković, head of the Grey Wolves, was murdered in Kragujevac, Serbia. Lugar's lawyer declared that he had been assassinated by the Ministry of the Interior at the behest of Milošević because of what Lugar knew.

"Arkan knew too much about Slobo's role in the war," I suggested. "And Serbian state security killed him."

"No way," said Zoran.

"Why?"

"Because Arkan *was* state security," he said.

According to Zoran, Arkan's relationship with the SDB had never been broken. In fact, a state-security officer had been sitting with Arkan the night he died. And after Arkan's death, state-security assassins went after Skole with a vengeance.

"They hunt down and kill them all," Zoran said of Skole's boys. "They got Skole after this long car chase. They chase him all over Belgrade, and then they drive Skole's car off the road. When the state-security guy goes up to the car wreck to finish Skole off, there is a cop in the seat beside him. The cop was his bodyguard."

Zoran paused as if to say, *And that was that.* I would later find some of this on the record. On Thursday, April 27, a car containing Zoran "Skole" Uskoković, policeman Milos Stevanović (classified as "away on sick leave") and a driver was forced from the road after a spectacular chase. Uskoković and the cop were killed.

"They kill Skole, and they kill off his gang for Arkan," Zoran said. "Right now only three of Skole's boys are alive.

One is the guy who planned the assassination of Arkan. He is in Germany hiding."

Dragan had tried to tell me much of this the other night, but his message was not that state security had obliterated Skole and his men out of vengeance for killing Arkan, one of their own. Dragan believed that state security had destroyed Skole because he had become too powerful.

"Gangsters don't live long in Belgrade," he had said. "State security eventually gets them." According to Dragan, state security had become a regulatory body in Serbia's outlaw society. If an underworld figure became too powerful, he was eliminated. This was the real reason Dragan yearned for invisibility. This was why he had said, "When you work hard and make money you have enemies."

Dragan may have had a point. In addition to the unsolved killings of paramilitary leaders like "Johnny" Đorđić, Stojičić, and Miljković, most of the gangland princes that rose to such dizzying heights in the early 1990s were murdered, violently and decisively, by persons unknown. "Knele" Knežević was killed in Room 331 of the Belgrade Hyatt in March 1993. Branislav "Beli" Matić was shot twenty-seven times in front of his home while his wife and children looked on. Radojica Nikčević was executed by an assailant in a blue coat in front of his Belgrade office. Before Voždovac crime boss Goran Vuković was murdered, he told Belgrade reporters that state security was organizing execution squads.

The question of course was: How did any of this increase my understanding of Momo Kneznanović? I had two clues about Momo's identity: Gjorg's assertion that he had committed murder in his village, and that he had been a member of the Uprava Drzavne Bezbednosti (UDB), or state security. Before meeting up with Zoran and Dragan I had asked myself if these two vocations fit. Arkan's career was the most high-profile testament to the synergy between state security and the private paramilitary armies that the regime dispatched in its ethnic wars to make mayhem in disputed territories like Kosovo.

The answer was yes. If Momo had been a state security officer it was possible (and even likely) he had fought in Kosovo as a paramilitary fighter. The only problem with Gjorg's story was that the branch of state security he claimed Momo worked for didn't exist. Gjorg said he once glimpsed Momo's identification papers, which revealed him to be a member of the UDB. I later learned the UDB was created in 1948 under the auspices of the Minister of Interior. Its first chief was *Partizan* leader and Tito loyalist Aleksandar Ranković, a steel truncheon of a cop who cracked down hard on Kosovo in the late 1940s and 1950s. Ranković's supporters said he was squashing the ethnic-Albanian insurgency that had allied itself with the Nazis to push the Serbs out of Kosovo and still threatened the government. Critics said his iron-fisted rule really stemmed from a Stalin-like paranoia, ardent nationalism, and a distaste for Albanians.

Perhaps both were right. In any event, Ranković's heavy-handedness made the UDB infamous in Kosovo. By the time I visited the province in 1998, Kosovars often mentioned Ranković and the UDB even though the latter had been dismantled in the 1960s after Ranković was accused of plotting against Tito. By 1999 the SDB was Serbia's central state security agency, which raised the question: How could Gjorg have seen identification in Momo's possession for an agency that hadn't existed for over thirty years?

After much thought I decided that Gjorg must have seen "SDB" on Kneznanović's ID. Perhaps because it was written in Serbian he translated the information into a form he was more familiar with, "UDB". I didn't pick up on the UDB/SDB complication until I had entered Serbia. So I was unable to question him about it. But the more I delved into the lives of figures such as Arkan, Lugar, and Badža, the more convinced I was that Gjorg was right on both counts: Momo was state security, and Momo was in his village on April 5. This also meant that Momo was an extremely dangerous man.

That was all the information I was able to get from Dragan and Zoran. I had surmised that Momo had parlayed his state-security and paramilitary war record into a career in the underworld. But if Momo was a gangster, Dragan claimed that he had never heard of him. Zoran made more enquires about Momo in Belgrade's mafia netherworld, and also came up empty. As convinced as I was of Momo's general profile, I realized I wouldn't find Momo or information about the Rezallë massacre in Belgrade.

I would have to go back to Kosovo.

CHAPTER 12

Shots to the Heart

Kosovo, April 1999

While the Albanian Gjorg Isufi was seeking sanctuary in the hills of Drenica, the Serb Boris Postovnik waited in Kraljevo to go to war. The wait ended on March 31, one week after NATO had begun raining bombs on Serbia. On that drizzly morning the *Sanitetska Četa* of the Yugoslav army assembled itself into a cavalcade of trucks, cars, and APCs. The military convoy left Kraljevo and headed due south, towards Kosovo. For Boris this was a momentous day, and not just because the NATO bombardment had entered its eighth day, or because a western journalist would report that thirteen thousand Kosovar civilians had been driven across the border to Albania over the past forty-eight hours, or because on that day Serb forces would capture three U.S. servicemen on patrol along the Macedonian border.

The day was momentous for Boris Postovnik because at the age of twenty-seven he was about to embark on his second war.

Boris had been deposited in the rear of an old ambulance. The ambulance had no windows, but it carried a huge stockpile of food. Seeing Boris off, Lieutenant Vlada must have glanced at Boris's waistline as he watched him get ready to leave.

"Hey, remember," Lieutenant Vlada said, "this food is for everybody."

Boris nodded. But only a few kilometres out of Kraljevo, Boris broke into the bread. He was terrified and anxious. Soon they would pass the border into Kosovo, and Boris imagined legions of Albanian terrorists everywhere in Kosovo—in hills, in villages, behind trees, waiting for the convoy to pass. He envisioned NATO warplanes in the air, circling and ready to attack. There was nothing Boris could do about it, except spread canned meat on bread and listen for the howl of fighters.

Boris jotted notes in his diary: "I can imagine that dangers really come from every dimension—the land, sky." But Boris heard no warplanes, only the patter of rain on the roof and the swish of tires on asphalt. Boris thought of a saying: Three things follow soldiers into battle—*kučiči, kurve,* and *kiše.* Dogs, whores, and rain.

At about 10 a.m. the convoy passed the village of Lešak and stopped for a rest. Boris realized he was in Kosovo, for the first time since 1993. Then he was a student; now he was a soldier. Yugoslavia was at war. And it was raining.

Boris had not known where he and the convoy were going, but during the brief and nervous rest stop in Lesak, he learned that the next stop would be Priština and after that Klina, a godforsaken city somewhere to the west. Boris had never been to Klina, but he had lived in Priština. Rumbling towards the capital, Boris thought of the past—his own and Kosovo's. Their shared history. "So Boris you have the honour of returning to the Serbian Holy Land," he wrote in his diary. "At that moment I remembered when I started my school in

Priština in 1993. Then I had never been to Kosovo before. Kosovo was a New World to me—full of mysticism, the Orient. It was an exotic place."

This appreciation of Kosovo's past made its present shocking to Boris when he went to study in Kosovo in 1993. He had always believed that Kosovo was the heart of the Serbian people, so he was astonished to see that Serbs had become a minority and that Albanians were the majority. Officially, 80 percent of Kosovo was Albanian. Some whispered that the percentage was even higher, over 90 percent.

Boris had heard various explanations for the Albanian domination of Kosovo. Most Serbs blamed the Germans and Italians, and the Albanian who collaborated with them. They had driven Serbs from Kosovo during the Second World War.

Others blamed Marshal Tito, Yugoslavia's Communist-era leader, who was part Croat, and in the minds of many Serbs worked long and diligently in his thirty-five-year reign to undermine Serbia. According to some, Tito was responsible for Kosovo's porous border with Albania, which allowed tens if not hundreds of thousands of Albanians to slip into Kosovo and take up residence. Others claimed Tito encouraged Kosovar Albanians in their tradition of large families. While a Kosovar Serb family had two children, Albanian women bore ten or more, Boris heard. With every generation there were more Albanians and fewer Serbs, and a six hundred-year war was being lost in the womb.

It seemed to Boris and many others that many Kosovars believed Kosovo to be part of Albania and not Serbia. Boris knew well that no matter how many rights Albanians enjoyed in Kosovo, they always agitated for more. Boris recalled how Albanians in Kosovo began rioting in the early 1980s, driving as many as 20,000 Serbs out of the province long before the arrival of Milošević and the troubles of the 1990s. Some people tried to say that these riots were a product of the economic problems beginning to grip Yugoslavia or represented the emergence of a new Albanian nationalism in Kosovo. But many Serbs argued that Albanians would not be content until every Serb had been driven from Kosovo.

Nevertheless, Boris was charmed by Kosovo in the beginning. For Boris, Albanian Kosovars—their Islamic faith,[1] their walled gardens, their non-Slavic language, their bazaars—conjured up the glamour of the East. But Boris's fascination with Albanian Kosovo eventually gave way to alienation.

He sensed it in the unreadable faces of passing Kosovars, who always kept their distance. Although they occupied the same Kosovo as Slavs like Boris, they resided in another universe. They did not ignore the Serbs, because Serbia under Slobodan Milošević would not be ignored. But Albanians—*Šiptars,* as Serbs called them[2]—kept to themselves. And this bothered Boris. It was contrary to the conviviality of Yugoslavia, or at least pre-1991 Yugoslavia and its ideal of cosmopolitanism.

One day Boris had had enough. He walked up to a group of Albanian Kosovars playing basketball in Priština and asked to join the game. The boys froze and said nothing. Then they glanced around, exchanged a few words, and agreed to play with him. Boris was delighted. "OK, let's make it Kosovo against Serbia," he said.

Ultimately, Kosovo won. After the match was over, the Kosovars quietly said goodbye and left Boris standing there. He was disappointed. There had been no backslapping or jokes or invitations for coffee. These are strange, strange people, he told himself after the players walked off.

Boris did remember some gentle moments with Albanians. He used to go to the old bazaar near the mosques downtown, where the kindly Albanian sellers, who understood he was a poor student, gave him apples as gifts. They smiled sweetly, but Boris would later admit he was never convinced that the same kindly sellers would not attack him given the opportunity. War was being waged in Kosovo in 1993. It was not like the war in 1999, but it was a battle nevertheless. I was at war with them, he thought then. But I haven't been introduced to them. I don't understand them.

Boris was glad when the convoy arrived at Priština. He felt nostalgia for the city, which had hardly changed in the past six years. Above his head, houses clung to the hillsides of Dragodan and Taslixhe, and minarets soared. Beneath his feet, the streets were muddy. It was the Priština he remembered. Boris saw few signs that a war was going on until the convoy resumed its journey south.

As the *četa* neared Lipjan, Boris heard the war for the first time—the crack of gunshots, the rumble of faraway explosions. Then Boris saw the war, or at least the aftermath of it. Staring out the rear doors, he spied charred skeletons that had once been Albanian homes. Passing ruin after ruin, Boris realized that terrible violence had taken place here, and that Kosovo had been a scene of conflict for some time. He wrote in his diary:

> We are passing through villages. Lonely villages. Black. Without smell and sound. The wind is bringing us the morning fog coloured by the sun. Hungry dogs are barking at our convoy, and eating the meat of dead animals left on the side of the road to rot in their innocence. Finally, I understand the war here continued many months before our arrival. We have been invited for the final Ball.

At 4 p.m. the convoy arrived at its destination, Klina. Boris was home. He wasn't sure what to make of Klina. It wasn't a village, but he considered it too small for a town. "This place has stopped on the road without a wish for a future," Boris wrote in his diary.

Situated due west of the Drenica Valley, and just off the main Komoran-Peć road, the old community of Klina was potentially dangerous. Every soldier knew there were terrorists in Drenica, to the east, and in the mountains beyond Peć, to the west. This made Klina a precarious place, seemingly safe but surrounded by the enemy. Boris saw right away that Klina was home to a lot of VJ and many Serb civilians. The Serbs appeared to feel secure, and they looked on Boris and the new arrivals with curiosity.

The *Sanitetska Četa* moved into an abandoned clinic on the outskirts of town. The new posting immediately disheartened Boris. The structure was a banal grey concrete blockhouse erected in the Tito era, identical to many other hastily built structures across Yugoslavia. Comprised of two storeys and a basement, the building was large enough to accommodate the unit, but the clinic, soon to be a hospital, was startlingly squalid and most of its rooms were unusable. Windows were broken. The basement was a sewer, flooded with urine and feces. The *milicija* who had bivouacked there must have used the cellar as a latrine, and for good reason: Boris found there was no toilet in the building, except for an outhouse in the back.

That night, Boris was assigned his sleeping quarters. He shared the large, dark room with three others. Two of the men were young enough to be his brothers. There was Aleks, a school friend from Kraljevo who was in his late twenties, and Milan, a technician in his early thirties. The third man was Ljuba. Somewhere in his late fifties, Ljuba was a carpenter who had been conscripted into the medical unit because he had served a stint as a nurse thirty years before. Ljuba was the first to admit that thirty years is a long time.

"Look," he said right away, "I don't know anything about medicine any more. I'll do everything else."

Ljuba led the effort to make their filthy room inhabitable. The four drummed up a pail and water and detergent. They scrubbed the floor, and walls, and windows, and washed away most of the stench. Uncle Ljuba, as they called him, scoured the area and returned with a table and four chairs. Within a short time Boris, Aleks, Milan, and Uncle Ljuba created a comfortable lair—a sanctuary, clean and quiet.

Boris understood the importance of having an ordered place to retreat to, but he knew this room would offer no escape. Boris had only to gaze out the window to see disturbing things. In Klina he noticed groups of silent *Šiptars* in the street, dressed as civilians and guarded by *milicija* with automatic rifles.

That day, his first of many in Kosovo, Boris scanned Klina from the refuge of his room and jotted notes in his diary. "As I write I look from my window and I see smoke which changes colour from black to white. Someone has burned another house. Who could do this?"

Boris wondered if fleeing Albanians were burning their own homes to prevent Serbs from taking up residence. But he saw other things. He had noticed Serb children running into empty Albanian houses and carting away everything they could carry. In some instances the *Šiptar* owners of the looted possessions watched the thievery take place from where they had been corralled on the street. "Children run on the street and steal everything they can carry from Albanian houses," Boris wrote. "Older people help out. They are taking TVs, refrigerators, satellite dishes, computers. Some owners are looking on, and watching what their neighbours are taking away."

Graffiti adorned the walls. The words were like shrapnel marks from a procession of grenades. An Albanian had written, *Death to Serbs*. A Serb had crossed it out and written *Death to Albanians*. There was *UÇK* and beside it, *Četnik*. The scribbles were shouts and arguments over who possessed

Kosovo. Boris nodded off to sleep to the sound of gunfire, and felt the vibration of every volley.

The next morning the unit began the task of transforming the Klina clinic into a hospital. Leading this work was the *četa*'s most influential physician, a surgeon and specialist in abdominal injuries named Dr. Zvonimir. Lieutenant Vlada ran the unit on the army side, but Zvonimir was the real leader. On that first day he took Boris aside.

"You are studying to be a doctor, but you're not a doctor yet," he said. "What do you want to do here?" Boris said he wanted to be a technician. "Boris, we have enough technicians. We need doctors. Can you do it? Do you have the balls to be a doctor?"

He was sussing out Boris's mettle. In the bloody crises ahead, with fragile lives at stake, the elder doctor would need him to shoulder responsibilites for which he was not yet qualified. He would accept Boris as a doctor and treat him as such, but he had to know first whether this young man had the will to be one.

"Yes, I'll do it," Boris said. "I have the balls. But I need help. You'll have to help me."

Boris was eased into his responsibilities. His first assignment was to inspect the sick and wounded in Emergency, diagnose them, and identify those patients who needed to go to surgery. This was a Serb military hospital, but almost from the beginning Albanians came to their door. At first Boris was surprised, given the looting and burnings and evictions he had witnessed during the first days of his deployment, that there were Albanians who dared to remain in Klina. And still more surprised that they would turn to the Serbian military for help.

Early on, an Albanian man arrived at the clinic with his pregnant wife. The wife was about to deliver, and the man asked for help. While Boris's colleague Zvonko, a gynecologist, cared for the woman, Boris asked the Albanian why he had opted to stay. The answer was a revelation.

"I'm Catholic," the Albanian said. "There are a lot of Catholics in Klina." He told Boris Catholic Albanians had stayed because they had no quarrel with Serbs. It was Muslim Albanians who were at odds with them.

This story touched Boris. He confided to the man that they shared a common heritage. "I'm half Catholic," Boris explained.

Now it was the Albanian's turn to look surprised. By 1999 everyone understood the political and historical baggage that religion carried in this region. Catholicism was the religion of the Croats, who fought the Serbs in 1991 and cleansed the Serbs from the Krajina region of Croatia in 1995. Catholicism was the religion of the fascist pro-Nazi Croat forces who murdered thousands upon thousands of Serbs during the Second World War. The same distinctions existed in Kosovo. Just as an angry Serb might call a Muslim Albanian a *Šiptar,* he would call a Catholic Albanian an *Ustaša* after the Croat paramilitaries that sided with the Nazis.

"You're welcome to come to our church," the Albanian told Boris. "You might have trouble understanding the sermon, but you're welcome any time."

Boris thanked him, and later marvelled at the episode. Boris had never before had a conversation like this with a *Šiptar.* In fact, he had never before had a conversation with a *Šiptar,* period.

His perceptions of Albanians were influenced by the conduct of some of the Serbs in Klina. The looting of empty Albanian homes continued. During those early days Boris even spotted a woman carting away plastic bags. The home had been stripped, so the woman took away the only items she could find there—plastic bags. Boris found this episode so troubling that he recorded it in his diary: "The fact that I'm remaining silent is making me an accessory to this."

Other strange things occurred. A mob of Albanians passed through town. It started at about 2 p.m. one day. First a handful of *Šiptars* arrived at Klina under police escort, and passed right by the clinic. Then more poured through the streets. Boris watched from a window upstairs. Some Albanians staggered along on foot—women in long dresses and coloured headscarves shepherding children, old men with white hats hobbling on canes—hurried on by police in blue camouflage. Other Albanians—women, kids, and old men—arrived in tractor-pulled wagons and horse-drawn carts. The mob passed through in the direction of Peć.

Boris watched the parade with puzzlement. He saw Serb civilians line the road to curse and spit and throw stones at the Albanians, who ignored it all and trudged on to wherever they were going. Some of the men from the *četa* gathered outside the building. Some harried the Albanians with insults. Others, obviously as perplexed as Boris, asked questions among themselves: Why are they leaving? What are they running from? Where are they going?

Boris shared these questions He had heard rumours of cleansings of Albanian villages, of Serb security forces driving out civilians en masse. Boris had noticed the disappearance of Albanians from Klina but had never really wondered where they had gone or why. Now he did. Instead of an answer, he whispered a prayer. "Thank you, God, I am not them."

Boris's first task as a wartime doctor had been to help bring an Albanian baby into the world, but it would not be long before real casualties arrived. Like a bomb from a high-flying warplane or gunshots from a guerrilla in the woods, Boris's first exposure to blood surprised and shook him. It began in the early morning of April 2 when Aleks woke Boris and the others in their room. He had heard something, he said. It sounded like an explosion. Nearby. No one else had heard anything.

"It's nothing," somebody said.

"It was an explosion," Aleks insisted.

"Shut up and go to sleep," Boris said.

But Aleks knew what he had heard. "Boys, we're going to have work to do soon."

A few wounded soldiers arrived at the clinic that morning, but they were immediately transferred to the hospital in Peć. Wearing a helmet and holding a rifle, as regulations demanded, Boris rode along in the ambulance that transferred the injured men. He had feared leaving Klina and the clinic, but the trip was uneventful. He saw nothing along the road, and Peć was a welcome novelty.

When Boris got back to the unit at 4 p.m., the war still seemed abstract and far away, like the explosion the night before that he had slept through. But no sooner had Boris arrived back than he heard the alarm sound. He ran to the emergency room, where any wounded would be delivered. Boris's eyes immediately zeroed in on his friend Zvonko from Kraljevo, the gynecologist who had delivered the Albanian baby on their first day in Klina. Zvonko was always cheerful and goofing off. Now he was agitated, and so was everyone else. The emergency room was filled with dying and mutilated men.

Boris had no sense of how many there were. There were simply too many. Nor could he imagine the scale of the violence that might have created this havoc. The mutilations were unbelievable. One man had no jaw. Another was without a left leg, and a man beside him lay with his intestines exposed, coiled on his lap like a sleeping snake. A legless man had brought his severed limb in the hope that it could be rejoined. It lay not far away, and its owner, when not delirious with pain and shock, considered his limb in stunned horror. There were others less seriously wounded. Some moaned to themselves. Some called out for help. A few shrieked.

Boris and the others set to work. An orderly went to each casualty and cut away any clothing around the wound so that the doctors could get a good look. A surgeon went from stretcher to stretcher and decided who would get treated first and who would go to the OR.

Boris and Zvonko worked at the side of the doctors. They searched for veins. When they found one, they penetrated it with a needle and began pouring in blood. In some instances the wounded men had lost so much blood that the veins were almost impossible to find. But they always found one. They squeezed and tightened tourniquets until a slender purple line appeared.

Boris was rapidly learning a valuable lesson about doctoring. He decided that a patient—even a horrifically injured one—had a 90 percent better chance of survival if the attending physician could stop the bleeding and find a vein. He would later decide that the other 10 percent of the life equation depended on the man's fortitude and how much he wanted to stay alive.

Starting that afternoon Boris began to recognize the distinction in the eyes of the wounded men—the winners and the losers, the ones who survived and the ones who didn't. Some eyes blazed, and he realized these were the fighters—the men who determined not to die no matter how bad their situation appeared. In other eyes he saw a fading light, and he soon realized that these men were giving up. If Boris saw eyes flicker, fade, and surrender, he would shake the dying man and with his booming tenor voice bully him back.

"Breathe," he would shout. "Open your eyes, talk to me." If a man didn't respond, Boris would remind him of a reason to stay alive. "Do you have a woman?" he asked one man. Boris's question immediately caused a light to reignite in the wounded man's eyes. "Yes, I have a wife and kid," he mumbled. Then the man fought on.

Boris was introduced to many things that day, but the theme, the symbol, the overriding metaphor for the experience was *blood*. Blood was everywhere. Bodies pumped it and uniforms became drenched with it. As a stretcher was carried in, blood dripped from the canvas like water from a bag. Every doctor and nurse and stretcher-carrier was covered with it.

The blood flowed so heavily that its odour filled the air. For the first time in his life as a soldier and medical student, Boris became conscious of its smell. The odour was potent. It hung in the air like it pooled on the floor. Once the scent got inside your head, it stayed there. The reek of blood was bad enough, but combined with the stench of sweat, burned skin, and singed hair, the air in the emergency room became unbearable. After a while some of the younger technicians in the unit started gagging when they entered the ER.

That day brought other lessons. He learned that men who shouted were the least in need. He learned that the quiet and pale ones were actually calling the loudest and needed immediate attention. Once Boris found himself telling a complainer to shut up while efforts were being made to keep alive the silent man beside him.

Boris had no idea how long he had been working. Normally he would have measured time by the passage of patients out of the emergency room and into the operating room or the clinic or ambulances bound for Peć. But for every wounded man that left the ER, stretcher-carriers brought in more. So Boris was not sure how long he had been working when he found himself face to face with Željko, an old classmate who was wandering the emergency room in shock. Boris was glad to find his old school friend, because Željko was a field medic assigned to the VJ group that had been attacked.

He told Boris what had happened. An infantry unit—his unit—had been assigned to protect a group of tanks deployed in a meadow. NATO fighters must have spotted the men and armour, because suddenly the sky began to rain down deadly cluster bombs. These murderous weapons are dropped in large canisters that open in mid-air and release hundreds of individual bomblets, which fall to the earth pulling small parachutes. For soldiers on the ground, a well-targeted cluster-bomb attack can bring suffering and destruction like the darkest verses from the Book of Revelations. The bomblets are incendiary weapons, able to generate heat so intense that they can penetrate a tank's armour and detonate its fuel and munitions. Bomblets are also man-killers. Each detonation emits a lethal spray of shrapnel. The shrapnel is designed to kill soldiers, but just as often the airborne shards sever, disembowel, and disfigure. Because a high percentage of bomblets don't detonate, they hide and wait like land-mines, killing indescriminantly days, months, and sometimes years after raining to earth.

Today, Boris was wearing the blood of such casualties. Before now, such mutilations had been unimaginable to him. Anyone could fathom a broken leg or the familiar injuries of peace-time, but who could imagine losing a jaw or holding your intestines in your hands or contemplating the toes of your severed leg? One of the worst moments came when Boris kneeled over a dead man who had been reduced to a charred hulk. The man had a head, torso, arms, and legs, but his face had melted away, so that his humanity appeared very distant, like the mummified remains in a museum exhibit. Maybe because the man's injuries had rendered him so anonymous, Boris glanced at his name tag. He did not recognize the man, but he knew the name. This man had grown up with Boris in Kraljevo, and as an adult lived next door to Boris's sister Snežana. Boris did not know him well. His sister's neighbour was just a guy—an unremarkable part of Kraljevo's backdrop. Now this war had distinguished him by mutilating him beyond recognition and belief. How many others like him would be similarly distinguished before this all ended? How many more Serbian boys would NATO kill on behalf of the Albanians?

The *Sanitetska Četa* plodded through the army of casualties. They covered wounds and stabilized vital signs. They treated for shock. They resuscitated. They operated. They bandaged the lightly wounded and sent them back to their unit. They bedded down the moderately wounded in Klina and transferred the serious cases to Peć. Eventually the stretcher-carriers stopped coming with bodies, and the emergency room cleared. Only the blood remained on the ground, and the orderlies mopped this up.

When it was all over, Boris and Zvonko sat together and spoke quietly about what had just happened. They were lit by a dim and dancing candle flame, since it was after 7 p.m. and electricity in Klina had been switched off, either to conserve power or to enforce the blackout. Boris and Zvonko didn't say much. They did not need to. They had shared this life-altering experience as soldiers and doctors, and what more could a man say about it?

Suddenly, sirens wailed and from the darkness of the clinic someone whispered, "Not again." Minutes later an officer marched into the ER. He was from the same VJ unit that had been attacked earlier that day. The officer announced that he had not come with wounded—only dead. "One of our guys killed himself," he said.

The officer talked as the dead man was carried in. He was a boy, really—twenty years old. According to the officer, he had been here, in the clinic, only a couple of hours before. He hadn't been physically wounded, or if he had, his wounds weren't serious. He was afraid, though. And traumatized. He had told a psychologist in the clinic that he couldn't take it any more. Boris didn't need to be told what it was that the boy could endure no longer. It was the fear, and the depression, and the loneliness, and the dread of mutilation or death. The soldier told the psychologist he didn't want to go back to his unit. If he was sent back, he would kill himself. But the psychologist tried to soothe him, and then sent him back to fight.

The boy followed orders. He returned to his unit in the field. He was also true to his word. Once back, he took a white handkerchief from his possessions and scribbled a brief note on it—four simple words. Then the soldier pinned the handkerchief over his heart as if it were a medal, and shot it—and himself—with his sidearm.

The officer placed the handkerchief on a table. "See what he wrote," he said.

The message read: *Pray for my soul.*

Boris wondered how such a thing could happen in this world? How could such a thing happen in Kosovo—Serbia's Holy Land? The first Serbs who had fought and died at Kosovo Polje, 610 years before, were defenders of the faith. This was what Serbs today were told. Now the fight was continuing, but Boris had to ask himself: How could the horror of war ever be holy?

A little later a few VJ soldiers came to the hospital to load up on medicine to fight diarrhea. Boris overheard them.

"My grandfather told me to kill two Albanians for him," one young soldier said. "So far I've killed eleven. Even Granddad is going to be surprised. Even Granddad is going to think this is a bit over the top."

Boris wrote in his diary that he was beginning to doubt: "I don't doubt my people and our personal motivations. But I have my doubts about being here at all. Do we have a right to be here?"

But that wasn't Boris's greatest doubt. He finally came to this conclusion when Uncle Ljuba announced, "OK, boys, it's Easter today. Easter! Let's celebrate. Let's have an Easter dinner."

Easter? It was Sunday, April 11, but Boris had completely forgotten that this day was Orthodox Easter. Why would he remember? The pilots who bombed them nightly were not observing it despite the Pope's pleas for a paschal ceasefire. The Serbian fighters who six days before had rolled into Rezallë and murdered eighty-four civilians were not observing it. The world seemed oblivious to any commemoration of Christ's suffering. The war raged on. The air strikes had entered their nineteenth day. The deportation of Kosovars continued, and at that moment over fifty thousand Albanian refugees languished in Montenegro, over 100,000 in Macedonia, and over 300,000 in Albania in homes, camps, tents, and makeshift shelters. In Albania the refugees would soon be joined by a NATO force of eight thousand soldiers, who had been ordered to serve, according to some, as the vanguard of an invasion force.

The war raged on. But on Easter Boris and his roommates fought to push it from their thoughts. Uncle Ljuba dug up a bottle of *rakija*. Someone else got hold of some beans. Boris, for his part, did the impossible: he obtained three steaming loaves of bread from the last functioning bakery in Klina. That evening the four roommates—Boris, Aleks, Milan, and Uncle Ljuba—sat down to a feast. But before they broke bread, Ljuba bowed his head and delivered a prayer.

"OK, God," he said. "If you can hear us, save us." And then Ljuba made the sign of the cross on his chest.

At that moment Boris understood the fear that had been nagging at him ever since he arrived in Kosovo. It wasn't that he and his comrades had forgotten God and the holiness of Kosovo through their actions. No—it was that Boris sometimes felt so lonely and isolated in this far-flung place, which seemed so distant from family, friends, and his former life, that he feared *God* had forgotten *him*. For the longest time Boris had thought this was only his fear, but clearly he wasn't alone.

After Uncle Ljuba's appeal, Boris, Aleks, and Milan crossed themselves on this, the holiest day of the Orthodox Year, and began to eat.

CHAPTER 13

Election Day

Belgrade, September 21, 2000

By the time I had given up on finding Momo in Belgrade, the date was Thursday, September 21. The election was three days away. My visa expired in four.

I now had mere days to make contact with Sofia, and for the first time I was beginning to worry. That morning I sat with Sasha in the café off Dom omladine. As she sipped her ritual cup of cappuccino, she briefed me on the status on both Lukić and the cousin.

Sasha said she had been phoning the landlady repeatedly over the last week, but with no success. "That lady Lukić is never at home," she said. "I leave my number, but she don't call me back."

Fucking hell, I thought. I was being stymied because a landlady was not returning her phone calls. "And the cousin?" I asked.

Sasha frowned. The last time Sasha had called, she still hadn't heard from Sofia. She had promised to call Sasha the moment Sofia contacted her. But she had not called Sasha back, and there was no indication when she would. What if it took weeks for Sofia to get around to sending her current address to her cousin?

Sasha and I discussed both contacts. We decided Sasha would give the cousin a little more time before calling to pester her for Sofia's change of address. In the meantime she would keep after Lukić. I was convinced she was the simplest and best route to Sofia. Lukić had to know where Sofia Kneznanović could be found, and because Lukić's relationship with Kneznanović was strictly business, there was no reason why she wouldn't divulge the information. "You have to talk to this woman," I told Sasha.

It didn't surprise me that Lukić wasn't returning Sasha's calls. Lukić could have been preoccupied with a business or personal matter, but I suspected she was as distracted by the election as everyone else. With the day of decision less than a week away, people seemed to be hunkering down, securing their lives waiting for the election to hit as if it were an approaching hurricane.

Over the past few days I had noticed that everyone was tense. Outwardly, Belgrade hummed along. Idle men loitered in smoky cafés. Working people marched off to their jobs every day. Old people could be seen on the street, walking their dogs and going to market. But as normal as life looked, the very air of Belgrade was imbued with maddening tension. Everyone was focused on September 25—the day after the election. Some people were wary. Others were fatalistic. Everyone was paranoid.

Even taxi drivers. Late one night I delivered Sasha by taxi to her mother's flat. I did this most nights that we worked late. Rarely did I notice the taxi driver, but on this night I did. He was inescapable. He was a monster of a man. He had a head like a lion, and sat so high in his seat that he looked like a normal-sized man pumping the steering wheel of a kiddie ride. No sooner did Sasha step from the cab than the giant at the wheel addressed me in flawless English.

"Where are you from?" he asked. I lied. I told him I was American. (I was so unnerved by the guy I was afraid to tell him anything about myself.) He grunted and drove on. We passed few cars, it was that late. Not only was there no traffic, there were no lights in the massive projects of Novi Beograd. As we drove along an almost deserted highway, the dark apartment blocks stood off to the side like a massive Stonehenge. Finally I worked up the courage to ask him about the election. He said he had no intention of voting.

"What's the point?" he said. "For our entire history the destiny of the Serbs has been decided by foreign powers—Washington or Moscow. Don't you agree? The JUL party make good points in their propaganda." This was the Yugoslav United Left party of Milošević's wife Marković. "They say Macedonia is independent, and what has it got them? Their ministers are being killed like dogs every week. America is occupying them.

"And Hungary is shit," he added, turning from Serbia's southern border to its northern one. "Do you know that seven thousand prostitutes in Hungary make more money than the economic product? That's what I mean. If I'm going to get fucked, I'd rather be fucked by the Serbs."

Despite all the surrounding tension, I toyed with the idea of returning to Mrs. Lukić's apartment and waiting at the entrance for her to either come out or return. But I found myself inclined to do what everyone else in Serbia appeared to be doing—sit back, and nervously await the election and its aftermath. However, I didn't have time for that either. And I had a job to do—people to interview and news stories to write. Which was instructive as well. I knew that if we didn't make contact with Sofia Kneznanović by September 24, whatever transpired on that day would alter the future of Gjorg's search.

Zoran tended to think that nothing would change. People would do what Milošević told them to do. But there were dissenting voices. Just before the vote, Sasha and I had a coffee with a member of the Otpor ("Resistance") movement in a café on the Knez Milhailova pedestrian street. The activist, Vukasin Petrović, looked like a revolutionary, but more in the old European Trotsky mould. His hair was wild, the frames of his glasses wire-thin. I asked Petrović about Otpor. It was a unique organization if only because it was operating so successfully right under the nose of the police.

Petrović answered that Otpor was such an effective organization during the Milošević era for the simple reason that it wasn't—an organization, that is. "We don't have a structure. We don't have a president, a vice-president, members. We just have responsibility for our jobs."

Otpor grew from the failed student-driven protests of 1996/97. After the protests the regime cleaned house at the universities. It fired intransigent professors, and installed pro-government faculties and administrations. New laws were passed forbidding meetings and gatherings within the university. Student protestors became targets of the police. They were harassed and arrested. So fifteen innovative students created Otpor.

"It is a people's movement. We have more than 800,000 members. We have branches in 136 towns and cities in Serbia. We have been in operation for the last two years. We have two main goals. The first is to put away from our lives Mr. Milošević. The long-term aim is to improve our society."

As Sasha stared at Petrović through a cloud of cigarette smoke and I wrote notes, it occurred to me that this was Darwinism at its purest. Milošević had turned Serbia's political environment into the Sahara Desert. Nothing political could survive except the regime. But evolution had manufactured a new species—Otpor. And it was thriving. Moreover, it was omnipresent. Otpor posters and graffiti were everywhere in the city, particularly its *Gotov Je* slogan, which means "He's Over" and was a clear reference to Milošević and his era. Even Belgrade's wisest marvelled at the genius of it. Marija Bogdanović, a leading Belgrade academic, had told me during my first days in Belgrade how invincible Otpor was. "Those children have created something Milošević can never beat," she said. "How do you kill a snake that has no head?"

Clearly, one positive by-product of the regime was the creation of a highly sophisticated and committed generation of activists. The student protests of 1996 and 1997 were impressive campaigns. The protestors' disciplined use of nonviolence all but neutralised the police, and their stamina and relentlessness drove Milošević to distraction and drink.[1] Otpor was a continuation of this finely developed culture of protest.

"They have a problem with us," said Petrović, "because we are not a movement of people. We are a movement of an idea. For the first two years we spread the idea of resistance. You can fight against people. You can arrest them. You can kill them. But you can't kill an idea."

"That is all well and good, but what will happen on September 25?" I asked.

"We have different plans for Monday. Right now it depends on Mr. Milošević." With that thought he stopped smiling, and I understood why. Now, as it had been for the past thirteen years, and as it might well be for years to come, everything depended on Mr. Milošević.

There it was. As the election approached, Serbia was awash in paranoia and fatalism and hope, hardly the ideal moment to act as Gjorg's emissary. Four days before the vote,

Sasha and I discussed my future in her country. I was faced with several possible courses of action. I could try to get my current visa extended without leaving the country. This could be risky. I had been working as a journalist without a proper visa. I worried that if the police were on to me I could implicate Sasha if we marched into the station house together to apply for more time. I could just stay put in Serbia without a visa and see what happened. But if I got caught and deported, I could be banned from Serbia for years. Lastly, I could go the lawful route: leave the country when my visa expired and immediately begin the process of getting another one. After much thought I opted for the last option.

"You'll be here on Monday morning," Zoran said, referring to the day after the vote. "By that time you'll know whether we will be free or not."

Sunday. Election day. Sasha and I spent the morning visiting voting stations. We loitered near the entrance of the station near her apartment in Novi Beograd. Rumours flew that opposition election monitors were being barred from stations, but Sasha said she had seen no signs of cheating when she voted there that morning. There were five major political parties, and she was obliged to show her voter registration to a total of six monitors—officials of each party and an independent observer.

While we lingered at the station's door, a smart-looking twenty-seven-year-old voter emerged and claimed he had had no problems. "I don't know if it was fair," he said. "We will have to see. They've stolen from us before. They can do it again."

At 3 p.m., Sasha insisted we go to Sveti Marko church in downtown Belgrade. We had been in this church the morning I met Boris for the first time. As Sasha stood a yellow candle in a bed of grey sand, I thought about Boris. He had told me he would return home to Kraljevo to cast his vote. I suspected he wanted to be at home with his family if the worst occurred—if there was war or unrest or a violent crackdown. Everyone seemed to expect the worst, though it was unclear exactly what the worst would be. The Belgrade-based election watchdog CeSID[2] had pointed out that Milošević's SPS party had regularly used voter fraud in past elections to win. CeSID director Marko Blagojević told me that a favourite trick was to stuff empty ballot boxes in the province of Serbia where Kosovars have been boycotting votes for years as part of a campaign of passive resistance.[3] Blagojević said he suspected Milošević would again try to stuff boxes in both Kosovo and Montenegro, which was also boycotting the upcoming vote in a puzzling show of protest.

Open theft of the election threatened to trigger unrest among the population, which would tempt Milošević to use the *milicija* and VJ to put down any demonstrations. There was simply a feeling in the air that Milošević and the opposition were two locomotives barrelling towards each other on a single track—a collision was inevitable.

"What are you lighting candles for?" I asked. Sasha lit candles in every church we entered, and often it was for a relative or friend who had passed away.

"For the election," she said. Sasha crossed herself with a flourish and we retreated to the rear of the church. Sasha mentioned the mood of Belgrade, and I suspected she brought it up because the city seemed as cavernous as this old church. There was no one on the streets. This worried me. Belgrade did not seem like the capital of a nation about to usher in dynamic and historic changes.

"People are at home for their Sunday lunch," Sasha said. "It's quiet, but I like the air. It's calm like before a storm. But I think it feels positive."

That evening we stuck close to Republika Square. If there were to be problems, it would be there, I guessed. The SPS party had set up a sound system for an election-night folk rally. Opposition supporters congregated on Terazije Avenue, on the edge of the square, for their own celebration. Riot police appeared, and Sasha and I expected trouble. But the police, donning helmets and holding shields, simply isolated the two Serbias. They formed a cordon between the competing rallies and made it impossible to pass from the square to Terazije.

Clearly, the night was building towards something, but it was not bloodshed. No one, even the cops, seemed to have the stomach for it. But there was defiance, and a venting of the anger I had been sensing for weeks. On the street, opposition supporters attacked posters of Milošević and tore them from building facades and bus shelters. Such acts were more defiant and heroic than they sound. Only days before, the public desecration of a Milošević election placard could trigger a beating if it was done in front of a cop or a pro-regime ruffian. Otpor and DOS posters could be defaced in plain view, but Milošević posters had to be molested with caution.

At 10 p.m., Sasha and I went to the conference room of the press centre to see if results were being reported. Polling stations had long since closed, and partial returns were coming in. CeSID announced that ten out of a total of sixty-two polling stations in Požarevac had been counted. Opposition leader Kostunica had earned 52 percent of the vote. There was a cheer in the room. Something big was happening. Požarevac was just one city, but because it was Milošević's hometown, the base of his gangster son Marko, and a viper's nest of state-security agents and cops, it was arguably one of the most fearsome dots on the map. It was a place where Marko had been known to beat enemies on the street. Yet Požarevac citizens were marching to polling stations and voting their hometown tyrant out of office. An analyst told the room that the Požarevac result together with other results showed that a trend was taking shape, and if it continued, Milošević would be defeated in the first round. There was another cheer, but this one rang of incredulity.

Later that night, with the pro-opposition trend continuing and results indicating a Milošević defeat, the government suddenly stopped counting votes. Government spokesmen disappeared and refused to make statements. If the administration was hoping to fend off the opposition by leaving ballots in boxes, they would be disappointed. By the next morning DOS election monitors reported their own findings: Kostunica had won 55 percent of the vote. They declared him the first-round victor. Independent observers like CeSID endorsed the DOS count.

The regime countered by posting its own figures, which were endorsed by no one except the regime. The state Election Commission said that Kostunica had won only 48 percent, and that Milošević had culled 40 percent. This meant that no candidate had secured a clear majority, and a runoff election was required. The Commission scheduled the second-round vote for October 8. In the face of the DOS declaration of victory the government's strategy seemed clear enough. It wouldn't try to fudge the results enough to give Milošević an outright victory. They would cheat just enough to keep Milošević alive for another two weeks. This would give the regime time to come up with another idea.

On Monday, Sasha and I lingered in Belgrade, but the mass demonstrations we anticipated never happened. People roamed the streets and protested either for DOS or for the government. The cataclysm everyone had been talking about hadn't materialized. Would it come? The streets were eerily calm, but politically the barometric pressure felt hurricane-low. Early Tuesday morning, with only hours left on my visa, I climbed on board a train bound north, for the border. I got off at Subotica and took a taxi to the frontier. By noon I was standing on Hungarian soil. I had been in Serbia for almost a month, but I had not discovered the whereabouts or the identity of either Sofia or her father.

Not long after I reached Budapest, my phone rang. I could tell by the cavernous echo on the phone line whom I was speaking to.

"John," a voice said. "I am Gjorg. I call to hear if you are all right," he said. He didn't mention Sofia by name, but I knew Gjorg. I could tell by his hollow voice that he was growing impatient. He was asking me if I had found her. And if not, why not?

In coded language, the indirect way in which we always spoke of Sofia and Momo, I gave Gjorg a status report. I told him that I was very close to finding Sofia. I couldn't give him the details over the phone; the line was too stormy and Gjorg's English was too limited. But before I boarded that train, Sasha had promised to pursue Mrs. Lukić and the cousin and find Sofia's address. Because the election was over and violence had been averted, there was no reason for either of them not to cooperate.

"I'll have something to tell you very soon," I said.

PART III

Giving Up

CHAPTER 14

Going Back In

October 2000

When I spoke to Gjorg I really believed that Milošević had succeeded in hanging on to power in Yugoslavia. I didn't think he would endure indefinitely. But I assumed that he would remain for the foreseeable future, and little would change in Serbia. I would be able to return and continue the search in much the same way I had before the vote. I was wrong.

Events that I never anticipated began to unfold. When the Election Commission announced the October 8 runoff vote, the opposition demanded an audit of the results. The regime refused, and opposition forces announced a campaign of civil disobedience. Workers and students across the country started to walk off the job. Bus drivers turned off their ignitions. People barricaded themselves in factories. Every day, I watched the images on CNN and the BBC. The opposition escalated the protest from civil disobedience to a general strike on October 2. Nearly 4,500 miners went on strike at Kolubara, the largest coal mine in Serbia, which provided up to 50 percent of the nation's supply and kept the country's electrical turbines spinning.

I phoned Sasha. "What's the mood in Belgrade?" I asked. I wondered if a momentum of anger and defiance was building.

"It's quiet," she said. "It's almost normal."

When Sasha told me this, I really doubted whether the Serbs had it in them to seize their election. I doubted on October 2, when Milošević addressed the nation and accused the opposition of being agents of NATO. I doubted until October 5, when I got a call from my Serb friend Đorđe while I was walking downtown. "Are you watching it, are you watching it?" he said. "It's beautiful, man. Fucking beautiful. They're attacking the parliament. I watching 'em on TV. They're burning it down."

I ran home, and turned on the TV. He was right. An opposition rally had been called for Belgrade. Protestors from across the country had descended on the city by bus and car that morning. By late afternoon, smoke was pouring out of the parliament. The assembly had fallen to the people.

The next day, Friday, October 6, Slobodan Milošević appeared on TV. He was pale and hangdog. He announced that he was conceding the elections and stepping down. The most reviled European strongman since Stalin looked like a man with a broken heart. I was stunned. When Milošević fell I had anticipated an upheaval of Biblical proportions. After the wars, the migrations, the appalling carnage, and the enduring hate, a calamitous and sensational end seemed only natural. But Milošević went out with barely a whimper after a single day of vigorous but bloodless demonstrations and a raucous afternoon of cathartic vandalism. I felt giddy that the election and the street revolt had been so surprisingly successful. I also felt sad. If discarding Milošević was so easy, why wasn't it done years ago?

The next day I boarded a train. The borders had momentarily collapsed. Hacks were flooding into the country. I

rumbled into Belgrade at 10 p.m., and walked from the station
to a downtown café, where Sasha and a friend were waiting.
A two-day street party was winding down as I marched
through the city. Torn posters and broken bottles—the flot-
sam of the post-revolt Mardi Gras—were everywhere.

The revolt had been brief, but you could see the results.
A perfume shop next door to the Terazije McDonald's had
been broken into and looted clean. The store, I was later
reminded, had been owned by Milošević's son Marko. I
swung by the parliament buildings and inspected the broken
windows and the grey shells of incinerated cars. I walked
along my old neighbourhood on Kosovo Street and admired
the cold skeleton of a torched police van directly in front of
the building where I had lived.

I didn't have to see the garbage and read the news to
know that Milošević was gone. The tension, fear, and paranoia
that I had lived with during my last long stay in Serbia was
gone. Sasha was exuberant and relaxed, and ready to work.
She too understood how things had changed in the span of an
afternoon. "My boyfriend was so depressed the other night,"
she told me. "He said, 'We have our elections, but what do we
do now? We have no one to fight.'"

Now I was back in Belgrade, I felt some urgency to get on
with the search. The next day Sasha and I returned to Sofia's
old apartment in Banovo Brdo. Like all of Belgrade, the street
looked deflated and sleepy. While I remained out of sight,
Sasha asked more neighbours about Sofia. No one had heard
anything new. Sasha still hadn't been able to reach Mrs.
Lukić.

That afternoon I came up with another route to Sofia.
Her cousin in Kosovo had mentioned that Sofia was an art
student. So, on Monday we visited the academy of applied
arts in the plush Dedinje suburb, where the deposed tyrant
Milošević was living under army guard—or house arrest. The

academy building was shiny and postmodern. I waited outside while Sasha went in to charm the clerks in the registrar's office. She came out twenty minutes later. The registrar's office was closed, but she had met an instructor in the hallway. The faculty was small, and he had never heard of Sofia. He even checked some class lists but found no Neznanović or Kneznanović.

For reasons I can't recall, Sasha and I walked to the back of the college. The scene looked like a bus wreck. Plaster torsos and limbs—all discarded school projects—lay on the ground. Among the sculptured body parts was the bust of a woman. The face was smooth as porcelain—no lines, no illusion of hair, just curved feminine cheeks, a small nose, and long blank eyes that were almost smiling.

"We found her," said Sasha, staring down at the face. "That's Sofia."

She later told me the generic statue reminded her of Sofia because that was what Sofia was to her—featureless and naked. But I had to wonder: Were we giving her attributes based on the best available facts, or were we manufacturing her? I would know soon enough.

Not long afterwards, Sasha began an ordinary morning at the Dom omladine with news.

"I found Mrs. Lukić," she said. "I talked to her about Sofia."

CHAPTER 15

Lost Souls

Kosovo, April 1999

Gjorg, Kadri, and Migen left Qirez when Serb armour massed on the outskirts of the village and an invasion looked imminent. Leaving was painful. They had waited for the others to catch up with them. They had waited for NATO to beat the Serbs into submission. Neither thing had happened.

When they arrived at their next destination, the village of Terstenik, they were forced to say goodbye to Migen. "I want to stay here," he said. Terstenik was Migen's home, and this teenager was tired of running, even if staying put was a risk.

Gjorg and Kadri believed it was safer to keep moving, but they didn't leave Terstenik that night for the sake of perpetual motion only. They had personal reasons. They had to find out what had happened to Ibrahim, Agim, and Hakif. The task wasn't as difficult as it might have seemed. They knew that if Ibrahim was alive and able to travel, there was one place he was certain to go.

After leaving Terstenik, they turned south and headed for Bajicë, the village of their father's uncle. They stumbled into the village at 11 p.m. Bajicë was dark and quiet. There were no lights in windows, and if anyone was outdoors, they took care to hide. Bajicë might have been a dreamscape—a place of fear and shadows. To get to the farmhouse they had to creep along a road that skirted an old graveyard, and the tombstones loomed like bad omens.

They arrived safely at the farm of their father's uncle, and were embraced by him when they knocked tentatively at the door of the main house. After a brief reunion their uncle led the two to the nearby *óda*, or men's room, housed in a separate building. Built thirty-seven years before, this *óda* was perhaps the finest in Drenica. Red-and-yellow shutters covered the windows, red carpet softened the floor, and the ceiling was made of varnished wood. The cushions of the *óda* bore a tiger-skin design. Coincidence or not, the uncle's son was a member of an elite corps of UÇK fighters called the Tigers. When the Tigers fought in this area, some of the men slept here. Last summer, when Gjorg and his family had taken refuge here, Gjorg had cleaned their guns.

This memory was vivid as Gjorg entered the dimly lit room. But it was immediately forgotten when Gjorg's eyes adjusted to the light and he recognized the shadow of a man standing before them. Long-lost Ibrahim.

The three brothers embraced. Then Gjorg took a measure of Ibrahim. He was thinner than he remembered. He was so lean, it looked as if his broad smile was too heavy for his bony frame and the weight of his teeth might topple him over.

How wonderful it was to see Ibrahim alive. But the euphoria of seeing him would immediately flicker out like the flame of a candle. Ibrahim was alone in Bajicë, and the words that came from this stout smile brought bad news.

In fact, Ibrahim's news was more worrying than bad. It was about Gjorg's brother-in-law Hakif and his nephew Agim. Ibrahim did not know for sure that they were dead, but he didn't know for sure that they were alive. The troubles began the night at the junction when the group had been separated. Ibrahim explained how he, weary Hakif, and trembling Agim had decided to take the left fork of the road. It was not until they reached Tushilë that they realized their mistake. They had come to the very place the UÇK had warned them to avoid.

They had been warned away for good reason. The Serbs were poised on the periphery of Tushilë, and it was obvious to all that they would attack. At least, it was obvious to Ibrahim. "We have to leave here now," he told Hakif. "The Serbs will be here any time."

But getting out would not be easy. They'd have to take to the hills and fields, and Hakif was not up to it. He had limped into town, and he simply didn't have the strength or agility or will to flee into the hills. And who really knew if and when the Serbs would attack? It was the same dilemma all the wanderers wrestled with. Was running more dangerous than staying in one place? How could you know? But Ibrahim knew. He felt in the marrow of his brittle bones that Tushilë was no sanctuary. So he parted ways with Hakif and Agim.

Ibrahim took to the hills. He wandered around west Drenica before getting his bearings and making his way to Bajicë where he had come to find Gjorg and Kadri, but on his way he had run into a troop of UÇK fighters who delivered some bad news it pained him to repeat. The UÇK fighters said that Tushilë had been attacked and overrun by the Serbs, and all the men had been marched away. If Hakif and Agim had survived the shelling and then the invasion, then it was certain they were now prisoners.

Gjorg fretted over the fate of Hakif and Agim, but worrying about others was an extravagance you couldn't indulge for long. There was enough misfortune to go around. In fact, misfortune had been waiting for them in Bajicë. Gjorg and Kadri had arrived just as the Serbs were about to attack. And the problem was, there was no place left to run.

The situation was critical. Serb armour was said to be on the outskirts of town. So the next morning the entire family—Gjorg and his two brothers, and the women and children of his father's uncle—crept out of the farm before dawn. They spent the day dozing in an old house on the outskirts of town, and returned at night. They did this for four days.

On the fifth day the inevitable happened. The sound of weapon fire cracked the air. Shells exploded a short distance away. The attack came so early that the Isufis were still in the village. Instead of readying themselves for another day in the house outside the town, Gjorg, Kadri, and Ibrahim packed their meagre belongings and prepared to run. The family of their father's uncle also packed up. The uncle's family moved in a daze, unable to fathom how quickly their circumstances had changed. In the time it took for a shell to explode, they had gone from being hosts to homeless. They were now about to pile onto the roadway with what little clothes, bedding, and food they could marshal, flee their village, and join Kosovo's swollen population of the dispossessed.

As they passed under the great gate and left the farm, the men discussed where to go next. Kadri argued for the mountains. Gjorg said no, they would be isolated and alone in the mountains. In the end the boys simply followed where others led.

When they descended the hill into Bajicë proper, the two families joined a crowd that had gathered on the street. Small farm tractors, baying like frightened cattle, lined the road. With urgency that bordered on panic, the remaining men of Bajicë were preparing their escape. Gjorg raced up and down the line, and found a partially empty wagon. The tractor's owner told Gjorg he was going to Qikatovë, due east. He invited Gjorg and his brothers to ride along with him. Their hosts, the family of his father's uncle, had already found spots in other wagons.

They were going to Qikatovë whether they liked it or not. Kadri may have felt like laughing. Why didn't they just surrender themselves to the Serbs now? Qikatovë was right outside the big town of Gllogovc. It was a place the Serbs called Glogovac, and there was a *milicija* headquarters there and cops everywhere. But the explosions that shook the ground and tore the air made Gjorg want to stay with the convoy. "I'd rather be shelled with these people than die alone in the mountains," he said. Kadri agreed.

The Bajicë convoy did not have far to travel. By powering due east, the tractors arrived at Qikatovë e Re, or New Qikatovë later that morning. New Qikatovë was really an extension of Gllogovc, although it lay on the west side of the Gllogovc–Skenderaj road. Gllogovc itself was situated on the east side of the road, and Qikatovë e Vjetër, or Old Qikatovë, was a half-hour's walk east from there.

As soon as they wandered into the town, Gjorg realized they were now living in a refugee city that somehow existed under the very nose of the *milicija*. New Qikatovë and all of Gllogovc were overrun with displaced, homeless, and harried Kosovars—all lost souls like himself. Gjorg would calculate that as many as forty thousand displaced people had found sanctuary in greater Gllogovc—all living side by side with the dreaded *milicija*. In the countryside, particularly rebel territory, Gjorg and the others had lived in fear of encountering the *milicija*, believing it would lead to arrest, beating, or death. But in towns like New Qikatovë a strange truce seemed to exist. It was as if big towns, undeniably in *milicija* hands and out of the reach of UÇK, were neutral territory. But no Kosovar took this for granted. Especially Kosovar men who knew that they were now at war with the *milicija* and that violence could come at any time. So men lurked in doorways and were glimpsed at windows. Children, the least likely to be harmed, took air in the gardens. Women roamed the streets. Some were clearly foraging for food. Others carried containers sloshing with water. Everyone scurried. Everyone had a destination. Every face was taut and hungry. You could smell fear; it was the pungent odour of rotting garbage and decaying animals and soiled, terrified bodies.

Gjorg, Kadri, and Ibrahim had no direct family in Qikatovë, but Hakif had a cousin by marriage in the town, and they headed for his house. There, they found more than a welcome. Once again they were reunited with their sister Shota and the three girls. Once again Shota wept when her lost brothers set foot in the house. But she wasn't weeping out of joy or relief that her brothers were alive; she was distraught, and her eyes shone with fear. Standing beside Shota was Hakif, whom Gjorg and Kadri had not seen since that muddy night at the beginning of the war when the men had been separated.

Hakif was alone.

"Where is Agim?" Gjorg asked. Shota looked like she might collapse.

After they settled in, Hakif huddled with the Isufi brothers and told them what had happened. He repeated Ibrahim's story of how he, Agim, and Ibrahim had gone to Tushilë, and how Ibrahim had parted company with them. Hakif confirmed what Ibrahim had heard from the Drenica fighter: soon after Ibrahim's departure the VJ and *milicija* invaded the village. Hakif and Agim were hiding in the cellar of a house with a large group of men, women, and children when the troops moved in.

The Serbs ordered people from all the houses. They separated the men from the women and children, and marched them out of the village. In a long parade, the men tramped from the high country and descended to the Gllogovc –Skenderaj road, the same ribbon of pavement that Hakif, Agim, and Ibrahim had failed to find that first long night. The prisoners were then marched north to Skenderaj. Along the way they passed checkpoints of VJ soldiers and scruffy para-militaries. Dead Kosovars lay face down on the roadside here and there. Finally the prisoners limped into town and were crowded into jail cells at the large police facility in the city centre.

The police took the names of all the men. They checked them for weapons, money, and ID papers. And then, unex-pectedly, the entire group was released the next day. "You're free to go home," they were told.

Hakif and Agim—father and son—trudged out of town, reeling from their unexpected good fortune. When they set foot in their home and were greeted by Shota and the three girls, it was an incredible feeling—to think you took the wrong road at a crucial junction only to find it had been the right one all along.

That night Hakif and Agim slept in their own beds. For the first time in over a week they felt safe. Because the VJ and police had already invaded this small corner of Drenica, they seemed unlikely to return. Hakif and Agim might be able to live out the remainder of the war at home.

When the *milicija* appeared at their door the next day, Hakif was dumbfounded. He had left the house to look for food in some abandoned farmhouses nearby. Hakif was maybe a hundred metres away when he saw combat *milicija* approach the house, where his wife and children were hiding. Hakif yelled. He wanted the family to bolt out the door and disappear into the trees that surrounded the farm. A scream escaped his chest, but it was too late. The cops heard him and fired. Hakif ran into the trees and hid.

Shota, who had been sitting off to the side, continued the story. It was the same one Gjorg had heard again and again. Other families were flushed from their houses and herded into a single frightened mass near Hakif's farm. The cops separated the men, and chased the women and children out of town, shouting "You're going to Albania." Shota and her three daughters left with the other women, but they had not marched far when she heard gunfire—a long, terrifying report of automatic weapons. Hakif said he heard the shooting as well, but he had been too afraid to investigate. He escaped into the hills and made his way to Qikatovë, where Shota and his daughters eventually ended up.

When Gjorg heard how the story ended, he felt empty.

"What do you think?" Shota asked Gjorg. "Agim has been arrested by the police, yes? He's safe now in jail. He is much safer than we are."

"Yes," Gjorg said. "Agim is safe in jail."

It is likely that Shota's affection for Gjorg was never greater than at that moment. Gjorg was her younger brother, he had lied to her at a crucial moment, and she could only love him for it.

Within a short time Gjorg realized that Qikatovë was no easier to survive in than the wilderness. The problem was finding something to eat. The forty thousand who were billeted in the area devoured food like swarms of ants. Every night, Gjorg left Qikatovë for Gllogovc to forage. On one visit he found something totally unexpected—a friend, a young woman, a girl really, whom he had not seen since the previous summer. Her name was Floria. Gjorg had met her in August when he was hiding in Qirez, after Rezallë had been attacked for the first time, and he had arrived as a ghost—a man everyone believed had died.

Floria was twenty-two-years old when she was hiding in
Qirez with her family. She was originally from Pejë, the city
the Serbs called Peć. She had found sanctuary in the cluster
of farmhouses in the meadow that belonged to Kadri's school
friend. Gjorg had noticed her when she was serving tea to the
men. At the time, Gjorg was planning, secretly, to steal into
Mitrovica to find Sofia. While he was thinking of Sofia, he
noticed Floria. She was so different from Sofia. Where Sofia
was bold and troubled and fascinating and inquisitive, Floria
was timid. She behaved like an Albanian woman. She
laboured silently, and served men, and obeyed older women.

Gjorg was happy to see her in New Qikatovë. Floria, it
turned out, was also living near Gllogovc, with her sister-in-
law and father. At night Floria and Gjorg would meet and
scrounge for food. They searched empty houses. Supplies like
tins of meat, bread, and potatoes had long ago been carted
off, so they searched for dustings of flour at the bottom of sacks.
Sometimes they struck it rich and found a cache of beans or
rice. Usually they found nothing.

Floria began to venture to nearby towns to collect food. As
a girlish young woman, Floria found she could move about the
Gllogovc area with greater ease and security than a man like
Gjorg. As a potential UÇK fighter every able-bodied man was
at risk if he encountered the *milicija,* even in a quiet village
like Qikatovë. Even mature women, who were rarely accused
of rebel collusion, faced dangers.[1] But Floria had the soft and
coy features of a young girl, and she knew how to be self-
effacing in the presence of police. She acted the same way
she did in the presence of Albanian men; she was silent and
contrite. She stormed checkpoints like a virginal guerrilla.
She marched in tiny steps, head down. She tossed the cops
gentle and penitent words, and they always let her pass.
Floria would cross the main road into Gllogovc and search for
food there. If none was to be found, she would walk the extra

half-hour to Old Qikatovë, and then come back. And it was checkpoints all the way.

It was frightening. On one scavenger hunt in New Qikatovë, Gjorg and Floria came across a dead body in the yard of an abandoned house. Dead for weeks, it loitered in the living world like inconsolable grief. Seeing that dead man reminded Gjorg how was easy it was to die these days.

Corpses weren't the only reminder of danger. One day the police burst into the house where Gjorg was living. Some of the cops wore black masks over their faces. Several carried rifles. One carried an axe. He fell on Ibrahim, threw him to the floor, and held the axe blade to his neck. "Give us money," he shouted. "Give us money or I'll cut his head off."

"How much money?" someone asked.

"All of it," the cop replied. He told them to hurry, and repeated the threat.

Fortunately, the people of the house had money. Families hoarded and hid their savings, or what was left of them. Everyone understood the power of the Deutschmark. If a family was driven from Kosovo—and according to satellite TV, thousands were being ejected every day—the Deutschmark would be vital. People also knew that cash helped purchase commodities other than food. Deutschmarks could buy a life—like Ibrahim's.

The men pulled banknotes from hiding places—the lining of jackets, shoes, the seams of sacks—and gave them all to the police. Most of the money was handed over in blue one-hundred-Deutschmark notes. When the blue was flashed, the cop with the axe rose to collect the bills. Then the cops left, and the women wept with relief, and Ibrahim rose, no doubt reeling. He might have viewed his survival a gift from God, but Gjorg saw it as an omen.

This terrifying episode convinced him that Qikatovë would soon be attacked. The police were paying attention to the displaced and lost who had insinuated themselves in and around Gllogovc. The Isufi men decided they had to move on. Gjorg said goodbye to his friend Floria. He wished her luck and wondered if he would ever see her again. He hoped he would. He had grown fond of Floria. She was quiet, dignified, and hardworking. She was devoted to her family. He would say she had the "highness," he so admired. God willing, they would meet again. But for that to happen Gjorg would have to continue with the difficult business of keeping a step ahead of the *milicija* and staying alive. To this end, late one evening, with the Serb cops, soldiers, and paramilitaries of Gllogovc sequestered in their bunkers, and with NATO jets cruising the skies, Gjorg, Kadri, and Ibrahim once again set out. They were going to the last place in Kosovo that might offer safety—the mountains, the high village of Berishë.

The war had been going on for so long that Gjorg had almost stopped wondering when it would end. NATO bombed relentlessly. The Serbs shelled relentlessly. Kosovars fled, wandered, and died relentlessly. But for Gjorg all of this was about to end. The war would go on, Gjorg's debilitating fear of dying, and the dread and worry he felt daily, would cease. Gjorg was on the verge of something he hadn't experienced since the days in Mitrovica when he was in the company of the Serb girl Sofia.

CHAPTER 16

The Landlady

Belgrade, October 2000

I had almost forgotten about Sofia's landlady when Sasha sat down at my table at the Dom omladine, and said, "This lady Lukić called me."

"And . . ." I said, blinking.

At first the news barely registered. Sasha had been trying to reach this woman for weeks without success, and as a result I had begun to lose interest and focus on other elements of the project, like identifying Momo. But Sasha hadn't given up on Sofia's landlady. Since before the elections she had phoned Mrs. Lukić tirelessly. Often there was no answer. When someone did pick up, usually Lukić's son-in-law, Sasha requested a call back and left the same message. "I'm a student and I want to rent the flat that my old friend Sofia Kneznanović rented," she would say. "And by the way, could you tell me Sofia's current address? I seem to have lost touch with her."

Lukić didn't call back, and I understood why. Most of Sasha's calls occurred during the run-up to the election, and I knew that the high anxiety of those days had been a distraction. Sure enough, after the October 5 revolt and Milošević's peaceful retirement, Lukić called her.

"She said, 'I heard you tried to call me about the flat,'" Sasha told me.

Finally, I thought.

"Then she said, 'I want to tell you that you are mistaken,' She said, 'I never rented that flat. No one lived there. It wasn't for rent before, and it's not for rent now.'"

"I don't get it," I said. "We know she rented out that flat. If she didn't the son-in-law would have said so. And we know Sofia lived there. Why would Lukić lie to us?"

Sasha's voice fell an octave. She took on the look of a doctor about to give bad news. "I think Lukić knows Sofia," Sasha said. "I think this Lukić told to Sofia that I was asking questions about her, and Sofia told her to say she don't know us."

"You're telling me that Sofia knows we are looking for her and has instructed Lukić to try to mislead us?" I said. Sasha nodded, and I had an urge to throw a chair through a window.

Now we were fighting Sofia. And the fault was mine. I had screwed up royally. Lukić had received Sasha's messages about the apartment and Sofia. She had told Sofia that a stranger was looking for her, and at the same time Sofia was getting reports about us from her cousin. She was spooked and I didn't blame her. How could she know we were trying to get a message to her from Gjorg? Sofia had been so close, but I had been clumsy. The task now was to come up with another strategy.

CHAPTER 17

Losing Hope

Kosovo, April 1999

After the bloody attack on the VJ brigade, news reached Boris that he would be descending deeper into Kosovo, and into the war. The news was that orders had come down transferring the *četa* to a city in the south. The orders first reached Boris as a rumour. This was nothing new; rumour was a currency more valuable than Deutschmarks and more common than bullets. Some of the stories Boris heard over meals, around candles, and through the mist of cigarette smoke terrified him.

Rumour had it that NATO was about to drop bombs so powerful that they sucked oxygen and suffocated every living thing within the blast zone. Rumour had it that NATO planned to carpet bomb and pulverize every inch of Serbia, and then occupy it like the Germans once had. These stories sapped morale like those mythical NATO "Daisy Cutters" sucked air. The invasion from Hungary never came to pass, but one rumour did come true—the story Boris first heard on April 9 that their unit would leave Klina and relocate in Orahovac.[1]

Where's Orahovac? Boris wondered. He went to a map and saw that Orahovac was due south of Klina, and terrifyingly close to Albania. Boris was overwhelmed by the sense that he was being drawn deeper into Albanian Kosovo. He was falling, and the question was, how far would he fall before it was impossible to return?

Boris got the answer the day he awoke to the sound of footfalls, and voices issuing orders, and the rumble of engines. He dressed and ventured out into the cold, wet morning with the last of his belongings. A convoy was preparing to head south to Orahovac, and Boris would be travelling with it. As the trucks were loaded with the last of the supplies, Boris took one final look around. Already nostalgic for Klina, Boris marvelled at the Prokletije mountains[2] in the distance, the range that swells from Albania into Montenegro, and bulges into the northwest corner of Kosovo. The clouds that sat like a halo on the summits of the range were sometimes white, but more often than not they were blue-grey. Boris had often asked Klina people, "Are the Prokletije clouds always that colour?"

Boris was once again wondering about the clouds when he was told the convoy was ready to go. Boris was assigned a Vartburg, an East German car larger than but similar to a Trabant. Boris sat in the back, clutching his rusty AP 70 rifle and wearing a helmet. He was pleased. Even with four in the car he would be more comfortable in the Vartburg than in a truck.

As they drove south, Boris glanced out the window and noticed the detritus left by the recent flood of Albanian refugees who had passed this way. Blankets and clothes littered the ground. A child's doll was crumpled on the roadside like a corpse, and near it an old Albanian woman lay outstretched like a doll. Some minutes later Boris's car passed a *milicija* checkpoint near a railway crossing. A military procession had been hit by a NATO strike, probably the night before. Charred vehicles and mangled bodies were sprawled on the tarmac and roadside.

An unexploded bomb of some description rested on the asphalt. The cops were directing the vehicles around it one at a time, and Boris's car rumbled to a stop in the middle of the carnage—the crumpled and melted machinery, the dead soldiers—to await its turn to pass through. The scene at the crossing was grisly—bodies with no heads, limbs and organs stuck to the asphalt. But when Boris looked out the window, he saw something else that would stay with him perpetually, a sight that for reasons he was never able to explain would trigger a catharsis.

Boris saw four dead horses.

Two of the horses were white and two were brown. One lay on the asphalt, while the other three were stretched on the grass between the road and the railway line, which approached at an angle. The horses presumably died in the same attack that destroyed the men and machines.

The eyes of all four were open, and when Boris first spotted them, his gaze connected like a laser with a pair of big brown eyes. Boris saw in those huge eyes, as deep and shiny as gemstones, all the pain of the world. He had only to look into them to connect with this sorrow and suffering and feel it cut him like shrapnel. Boris never understood why, but those butchered horses with the haunting eyes affected him more than the sight of the dead soldiers or the dead Albanian woman.

Boris later recorded the incident in his diary. "If they weren't lying in their own blood, I would say they were playing and stopped to rest," he wrote. "I expect to hear them whinny like a person would talk . . . We forget the death of people too quickly. The deaths of animals are never remembered. I can't remember how many deaths I've forgotten, and how many will I forget."

"Guy, are you OK?" Boris would later ask himself. "Those horses left a bigger impact on you than real people." He would later decide that his sympathy for these beasts was linked to the civilians who died shortly afterwards under a hail of NATO bombs.

Minutes after Boris's vehicle resumed its journey, the convoy passed a caravan of Kosovar Albanian civilians. It was still early, and the Albanians were just preparing to embark on a journey. Women worked over fires, and men packed tractors and trailers that were parked along the road. If Boris had reflected, he might have decided that this throng was destined for exile in northern Albania. But Boris felt nothing. These people were victims, but the big wet eyes of the horses had drained him of all empathy.

The convoy arrived at Orahovac, pulling up in front of the Dom Zdravlja, literally the Building of Health, a relatively new complex that looked about fifteen years old, which served as the city's hospital. Boris's safe arrival almost made him forget about the horses and their death stare, until a neurologist from his unit, a guy named Đuka, rolled up, trembling, and told the story of the attack.

Đuka had left Klina with Boris's convoy, but his vehicle had broken down in the midst of the Albanian refugee column. Đuka described how NATO fighters appeared in the sky above the civilians and attacked them like hawks. Tractors and trailers received direct hits and were engulfed in flames. Women and children were immolated. It was butchery. Đuka wasn't certain how many *Šiptars* had been killed, but he assumed a lot. Đuka told the boys how lucky they were. "It was close," he said. "If our convoy had been a few minutes late, we would have been hit too."

Then a thought, horrifying and painful, occurred to Boris: Đuka had it backwards. It was not that the *četa* had been lucky to pass through the area fifteen minutes before; the caravan had been *unlucky* to be on the road their military convoy had just travelled. He felt certain the missiles that devastated the refugee caravan had been meant for his convoy. NATO surveillance planes or satellites had probably spotted the military vehicles, and had called in warplanes, which found the civilian caravan and mistakenly attacked it.

Boris felt complicit in the deaths of all those Kosovars, but still he felt no sadness. This changed on April 17 when mail arrived from Kraljevo. Boris received a letter from his mom and father and one from his sister Snežana. When Boris opened Snežana's letter, a folded sheet of paper fell out. It was a drawing by Milena, Snežana's eight-year-old daughter. When Boris laid eyes on it, he was overwhelmed by shock. The drawing was of a horse in a field near a railway track. The horse reared happily, and beneath the sketch Milena had written the words: *Be careful uncle. He will jump over you.*

Boris thought immediately of the dead horses and the catharsis their stare had generated. How could Milena have known? Of course, she couldn't know. But why, out of all the images in her young imagination, had she chosen to draw a horse? In a meadow? Near a railway track?

Out of the violence and the suspension of civilization's norms grows a war-time mysticism. Boris concluded that there was an umbilical cord linking his present life in Kosovo with his past in Kraljevo. There was a connection, and the child Milena had illuminated it. There was also a connection between his *četa* that escaped the NATO bombardment and the refugees who died in it. Boris realized that the rail crossing where the dead horse lay had become a crossroads in his life. He would never see war the same way again. There was a link between his home and Kosovo, between the people he left behind and the people he encountered. There was a link between victims and survivors. There was a link between Boris and the *Šiptars* in the Drim River valley whom he passed on the road that day. He was linked with the Albanian refugees who lived and the refugees who died.

For the first time, he felt sincere sadness for them all.

*

The brothers Gjorg, Kadri, and Ibrahim Isufi eventually encountered a UÇK patrol on their way up to the mountain village of Berishë, the last place in Kosovo they believed they could find sanctuary. By the time the UÇK appeared, just outside Obri e Epërme, the Isufis were not alone. They had become part of a horde of desperate civilians who were attempting to make the ascent, and the fighters offered to guide the group.

"We'll lead you into the mountains," one of the fighters said. "But don't smoke or speak. Be very quiet." They would be passing precariously close to VJ outposts and patrols.

It was fully night by this time, and the group wound into the high country like a dying snake with the rebel fighters as the head. At one point the fighters in the front discovered a thin wire crossing the path in front of them. It was a Yugoslav military communication line. One of the fighters held the line aloft like a telephone wire and shepherded the displaced underneath it, one or two at a time.

"Be careful, don't break it," the UÇK fighter said. "If you break it, they'll check to see where the line has been broken, and start shooting."

The entire group eventually skirted under the line and continued their silent march. They walked all night. It was too much for some of the men. Older and younger ones fell asleep at rest breaks, and had to be shaken awake when it was time to push on. Even the fittest men like Gjorg stumbled and staggered from fatigue. The group climbed higher and higher along the trail, and some wondered whether their ascent would ever end. The ones who were exhausted to the point of delirium might have wondered if they were still living, breathing men. Or was this how the Kosovar dead left the living world, guided upwards by dirty bearded angels carrying guns?

For Gjorg, such metaphysical illusions would soon make perfect sense. Berishë would indeed be the end of a journey for him, a place where he would face fate, mortality, and God, and come to terms with them. His journey had begun the previous August, when *milicija* sentries fired on him and the world left him for dead on the outskirts of his village. The sentries hadn't killed him, but so many had died, so many were feared dead. Would they, like Gjorg, defy the worst fears of their loved ones, and miraculously appear one day? What about the men of his village? After leaving Qikatovë, Gjorg and his brothers had encountered a neighbour from their quarter of Rezallë, who passed on a terrible rumour. He said that the Serb military had invaded in early April. They had ejected most of the women but killed the men—shot them, and buried them. The villager listed the names of some of those rumoured to be dead. Each name that he uttered conjured up a face in Gjorg's mind and a stinging pain deep inside his stomach. It didn't sound as if there was much chance that Serb bullets had missed these men, that they would rise en masse once their would-be executioners had departed, and rejoin their women in havens like Bajicë. No, it sounded as if all these men and boys—cousins, neighbours, old familiar faces—were dead. They hadn't survived the war, and it was unlikely that Gjorg would either, because the Serbs seemed relentless, their bullets innumerable, and the war never-ending. Would the war endure until these bullets had killed every Kosovar Albanian, including himself?

Gjorg, his brothers, and the weary horde of displaced

Kosovars finally staggered into Berishë. He would soon have nothing to fear. That realization came to him after it began to rain. The men lay on the ground shivering, trying to rest after the ascent. Then the skies opened up and rain pelted down, and the droplets were so cold it was painful. Gjorg and the others immediately got up and looked for shelter.

They were not alone. There were so many in Berishë, and not only the group that Gjorg, Kadri, and Ibrahim had journeyed with. There were already scores of refugees living in Berishë and on the surrounding slopes. They lived under lean-to plastic tents. They huddled under trees. Gjorg and his brothers had no tent, so they crowded into a school building. But there were so many of them in there that everyone was forced to stand shoulder to shoulder. Gjorg was so cold his bones ached. He was wet. He was tired. But more than that, he was *weary*. He was weary of running. Above all he was weary of clinging to life, of living every moment with the fear that a Serb bullet would find him as arbitrarily and easily as all the others had missed him before. This will never end, he thought.

And then Gjorg's world changed. Somehow, inexplicably, for no reason, it changed. At that moment Gjorg, crowded into a dark building on a desolate summit, cold, inhaling the stench of damp bodies, mindful of all his neighbours who had died in Rezallë—at that moment he realized his worst fear would never happen. A Serb soldier or policeman would never kill him. *Never*.

Only God can take my life, he decided. He gave me life, and he'll take my life.

It was a simple conclusion. It wasn't original, but it was a thought that had never occurred to Gjorg Isufi before in his long, fearful life. In some ways the wave of acceptance experienced by the Albanian Gjorg on the summit of Berishë was similar to the catharsis of grief experienced by the Serb Boris

Postovnik on his descent into Orahovac, the day he witnessed the four dead horses and passed the doomed caravan of Kosovars. But Boris's slide into the war would continue, and he would descend so far that he would wonder whether it was possible ever to come back.

CHAPTER 18

"What, if she doesn't want to be found?"

December 2000–February 2001

Sofia had been attempting to communicate with me since before the October 5 revolt, but I wouldn't understand this until after our trip to the border area known as the Preševo Valley in December 2000, to visit the site of Serbia's latest insurgency.

We arrived in the fog on December 16, easing into the big town of Bujanovac, the centre of the unrest, at about 4 p.m. Bujanovac sat at the epicentre of a slip of territory hard on Serbia's southern border that was in revolt. The Preševo Valley was not only hard on the Kosovo border, it was the Kosovo war all over again. I noticed this the moment Sasha and I got into town, and spotted Serb civilians lugging deer rifles down the street, and armed *milicija* on patrol, and VJ armour at intersections.

The Preševo insurgency was easy enough to understand. This border area was home to a sizable Albanian population (Bujanovac was 50/50 Serb/Albanian, the town of Preševo itself was 95/5 Albanian/Serb) that hadn't fared much better than the downtrodden Kosovars during the Milošević years. So after NATO won virtual autonomy for Kosovo, the border region gave birth to its own Albanian army of independence, which started shooting at Serb police patrols only months after the end of the Kosovo conflict. While Milošević was still in power, the region had threatened to implode. But after the election the reformers dispatched Nebojše Čović—one of the DOS alliance's leaders—to Bujanovac. Čović set up a government in crisis and was listening to all sides. There was some hope bloodshed could be averted, but not a lot.

I had come to Bujanovac to cover the insurgency and to look for Momo. I had theorized that Momo had been a paramilitary; but I still wasn't convinced, despite finding no mention of him at the Mitrovica police HQ in Kraljevo last September, that he wasn't a *milicija,* or a member of some other branch of the security services like the PJP, JSO, or SAJ. I had heard rumours before leaving Kosovo last June that the Preševo border area was manned by former Kosovo-based security forces who were fighting their old war in their new home. Was Momo Kneznanović among them?

To find out, I wanted to talk to cops and soldiers. I also wanted to talk to Kosovo Serb refugees, of which Bujanovac reportedly had a lot, to see if any displaced citizens of northern Kosovo had recognized hometown cops among the local constabulary. Because Bujanovac was a military zone and the authorities could eject us at will, we decided to talk to the cops last. So Sasha asked around and received directions to the nearest refugee centre. When we pulled into the parking lot of the Motel Bujanovac, Sasha announced, "We're here."

The Motel Bujanovac was a former hostel that had been converted into a haven for Kosovo Serbs driven from their homes by Albanians after the war. I didn't find Momo there, or anyone who was in a position to know him. Of the 140 Serbs billeted in this facility, most were from the Gnjilane area, right across the border; a few others were from Prizren and Uroševac.

But I would learn something important from the visit and these sad, kind, and dignified people who were yearning for homes they would probably never see again. These folks had been through a lot and their troubles were far from over. They had been displaced by one Albanian insurgency and now another wave of violence threatened to drive them off again. But war seemed to have become commonplace for the residents of the Motel Bujanovac. These refugees were either amazingly self-possessed or bored. After entering the lobby, Sasha and I chatted with two refugees whom we had found smoking behind the reception desk. Minutes later three brooding men appeared. One of the men looked to be about sixty years old. His name was Ljubiša, and he was wrapped in a heavy mustard-coloured jacket. Another fellow was heavy-set, wore an army-issue camouflage vest, a grimy baseball cap, and a deep frown. His name was Bata.

After I established that none of them knew Momo or hailed from northern Kosovo, I decided to try something. "Let's say one of your sons came to you and said, 'I want to marry an Albanian.' What would you think?"

The men said nothing. The question swept across the room like a cold draft. Then Ljubiša worked up the courage to speak. "It's very possible," he said.

Bata, who had stood brooding until now, cut him off. "It often happens that Albanian girls are interested in Serb men," he said. "We're irresistible to them." He didn't smile when he said this.

Ljubiša continued. "I have a daughter-in-law who is Albanian. She lives in Belgrade with my son. They've been married for twenty-two years. But these things are rare. A pure-blood Albanian marrying a Serb—rare. It's another thing if a Catholic Albanian marries a Serb. That's what happened with my son. My daughter-in-law's father was Muslim, but her mother was Catholic. She is mixed. She was a school friend of my daughter, and since she was a little girl, my daughter brought her to our home to play. That's how she met my son."

A suggestion of a smile appeared on Ljubiša's face as he spoke and I imagined he was picturing his son, daughter-in-law, and any children their union may have produced. Otherwise he was stoic and matter-of-fact. If he felt betrayed by his former Albanian neighbours for chasing him from his home after he had accepted one of their daughters into his family, he didn't reveal it.

"How do you feel about having an Albanian as a daughter-in-law?" I asked.

"I love her like she's my own daughter," he replied. "She's a wonderful mother. She's a wonderful girl. The moment they got married, they moved to Belgrade. My son was afraid of revenge."

I was about to ask about this revenge. I was about to ask my real question: what would you think if your daughter wanted to marry an Albanian man? But a man in a soiled red track suit stopped me. "What's with you?" he said. "You're more interested in marrying Albanians than in what's going on in Kosovo."

Bata's brooding silence had made me uneasy. And I was nervous when he invited us to his room to meet his family. But he smiled kindly, so Sasha and I followed him upstairs and into the motel room that was his home. Bata's wife met us at the doorway. She was a sturdy but youthful-looking woman. She had large peasant hands and looked to be in her late thirties. Bata's home was a single room with an adjoining toilet. It was painfully clear how the life of his family had been compressed into this seventeen-square-metre room. As I glanced around, I noted two beds, an electric stove, a small refrigerator, and a TV.

"Three of us live here," Bata said as he sat us down and reached for a plastic bottle. The third resident of the unit was Bata's thirteen-year-old daughter, who scribbled in an exercise book in the corner of the room. Bata opened the bottle and poured clear fluid into glasses, then handed one glass to me. At first I thought it was water, but when I sniffed the contents of my glass I discovered it was *rakija*— probably brewed by a local farmer. It smelled as pure as jet fuel, and went down smooth only to burn three seconds later.

Bata called his daughter over and proudly introduced her. His little girl didn't alleviate his gloom. "We're dying," he said. "One old lady from our village froze to death in a barracks near here. She was healthy, but there was no heating. Two guys died in this building recently. They were my age. They just died."

"This whole thing is stupid," he said, working himself up. "It's ridiculous. My mother watched Albanians burn down her house. They kicked her out because they found an army uniform inside. I brought her here, but she died a little later."

Bata clearly had good reason to hate his former neighbours. So I asked him what he thought of Ljubiša having an Albanian daughter-in-law. Obviously no one in the Motel Bujanovac knew Sofia Kneznanović, but it occurred to me that it might be important to know what they thought of her romantic predicament.

"That story my neighbour told you doesn't happen often," Bata said. "There was only one Serb in our village who married an Albanian. But I heard of other cases in other villages of Serb girls marrying *Šiptars*. The men carried them away to Albania, and if the girls didn't like it, they locked them up."

Bata's outrage increased with every gulp of *rakija*. He was a man who had lost everything—home, livelihood, past, and future—and there was no doubt in his mind who was responsible.

"Serbs are honest and peaceful people," he said. "Albanians are a whoring nation. You can't trust them on their word . . . An Albanian can't let his wife go to his brother's home alone because he can't trust that his brother won't rape her. They're a dog nation. They piss like dogs. They're savages."

Around this time another neighbour arrived. She was a twenty-nine-year-old Bujanovac woman who operated a hairdressing salon from her home next door to the motel. When the hairdresser entered, Bata mercifully lightened up a bit, and began recalling how he and his wife met. It was a simple story of country courtship. Bata had noticed a shy local girl. He invited her for a ride in his car. She accepted, and he married her. He married, he said, because she was decent and honest and pure.

The hairdresser listened to Bata's story and laughed. "There's none of any of that any more," she said, referring to purity. "The only fun for poor people is sex. During the air strikes that was our only recreation."

But sex and love seemed to be the last things on her mind these days. She invited all of us to her house for a coffee. When we got there, an old man with a face as grey as soot shuffled into the room and exchanged a few words with the hairdresser and Bata's wife. The moment he shuffled out, the hairdresser whispered that the old man was her father or father-in-law—I wasn't sure. "He has leukemia," she said.

"We haven't told him he's dying. We don't because he's not strong. We're worried he'll just give up."

The hairdresser explained that the family was giving the old man injections of interferon. "He needs the injections every second day to live. But one shot is eighty Deutschmarks. To cure him we would need to do this for two years. This would cost ten thousand Deutschmarks, and we can't afford it." The hairdresser paused a moment. "I've heard that Albanians in Kosovo get medicine like this for free. We're a few kilometres from Kosovo, and I have to pay eighty Deutschmarks. You know, if we had a war here, I could get this medicine for free."

While the hairdresser contemplated poverty so onerous war would be a relief, Bata returned to his rant on love and sex in small-town Kosovo. "The Albanians in my village used to trust me more than their own brothers," he said in a very drunken voice. "If their women were sick, they'd ask me to take them in my tractor to the hospital in Gniljane or Priština." At this point he slowed the delivery and lowered the volume as if to make clear how much he disapproved of the conduct he was about to recount. "Sometimes these women made their intentions clear with me," he said. "One night this Albanian woman says she has something in her eye. It's painful, she says, she needs to see a doctor. I want to help, so I load her in my tractor, I drive her to the hospital. But at the hospital the doctor inspects her and says there is nothing in her eye. We start back, and then she tells me there is still something in her eye and she wants me to get it out. I understand what she wants. I tell her, 'I'm an honourable man.' I tell her I don't want what she wants, and she should take a taxi home." Bata concluded his story with a solemn gesture. I wasn't completely sure what to make of Bata's story. I found it hard to believe he had been a magnet for Albanian peasant women. But it was interesting he felt the need to tell me these stories. Whether his accounts were fact or fiction, Bata offered another example of the sexual tension that burned just beneath the surface of Serb-Albanian relations in Kosovo.

After Bata had finished his story, his wife laughed nervously, and Sasha and I announced we had to leave. It really was late. Despite his troubling appraisal of his former neighbours, Bata had been a kind host. He had virtually nothing left of his lost life but still he was willing to share with us what remained. Bata and his wife escorted us to the parking lot and kindly waved goodbye as we drove off. The Motel Bujanovac was the closest I would get to Sofia while on the border.

Sasha went off alone and spoke to one or two Serbian police manning positions around town. The cops were as upset as everyone else. They wouldn't tell Sasha much, but they did tell her they knew no one named Momo Kneznanović. And they didn't know of any Mitrovica police officers posted in the region.

"He said to me the Mitrovica guys are in Kraljevo," Sasha told me later. I shook my head. There was no point in staying.

On Sunday, December 17, we left the border area and headed for Belgrade. We edged along the road in a thick fog. Because we met few cars, the trip had a lonely dream-like quality. Every now and then a green armoured vehicle appeared from the mist and passed us with a roar.

I sat in the back seat and thought about what we had achieved, which was nothing. The cop had told Sasha to look in Kraljevo, a city where we had been four months earlier. By going to Bujanovac, we had travelled full circle.

We arrived in Belgrade late the next day and the next morning I caught the train to Budapest, where I was living. The trip was sombre and not because of the cold and barren countryside that moved past my window. The year ended and I had nothing to report to Gjorg.

*

When 2001 arrived, I didn't realize how close I was to the end. In late December I had dreaded getting another phone call from Gjorg. I couldn't bear the thought of hearing his lonely voice. Six months had passed and I had achieved nothing, except for a general certainty that Sofia was some-where in Belgrade.

In January 2001, I set to the project with renewed opti-mism. It was a new year. It was a new Serbia. Since Milošević's ouster the previous October, DOS reformers had shored up their position by winning a landslide victory in the vote for the republican parliament. But no sooner did I set foot in Belgrade than I fell frustratingly ill. It wasn't serious; I had caught a flu. It proved to be a debilitating one, how-ever, and within two days of my arrival I was languishing, bedridden, in a musty room in the Hotel Toplice. I stayed in bed for three days, hoping to sleep off the illness. After a week I felt no better but decided I had to do something. So I pulled myself out of bed for an hour or two every evening and met with Boris and Sasha, usually for a dinner of soup and tea.

Sasha had refocused on Sofia. "I have a plan," she had said soon after I arrived in Belgrade. "Zoran knows a guy in an NGO, and this NGO has a list of Serb refugees from Kosovo. They won't give names and addresses to anybody outside of the NGO. But his friend can look at the list for us. The only problem, we'll have to pay for the information."

I was dubious. I was sick of refugee centres and lists. Before getting ill, I had drafted a final plan myself. My inten-tion was to pick up Sasha and travel together to northern

Kosovo. It was time to return to where the story began seven years ago. Kosovska Mitrovica was the last place Sofia had been spotted, and the backdrop for her turbulent love affair with Gjorg. I was wasting my time in Belgrade, but I was just too ill to leave.

On February 4, after two and a half weeks in Belgrade, I felt no better. I still lacked the strength to conduct a search of northern Kosovo with Sasha, but propelled by sheer frustration I decided to do the one thing I had postponed for so long: travel to Kosovo, cross the Ibar River, and meet with Gjorg. I was far from recovered, but I was well enough to sit on a bus. On February 5, I climbed on an express bus heading south, which coughed its way into the northern Serbian enclave of Kosovska Mitrovica seven hours later.

The city was dark by the time I arrived. Very dark. Midwinter cloud cover blocked out any light from the stars, and a power outage had extinguished any white light from within the city. As I plodded from the bus stop down Mitrovica's main street to the bridge, I passed a circle of severe and bored men warming themselves around a small fire that licked out of a trash can. Other men sat at tables in cafés, huddled over candles. Glancing inside, I could just make out the ghosts of their faces from the light of the flames and the glow of their cigarettes. This was my first visit to north Mitrovica since the search began. Wading through a darkness as thick as smog, I really wondered what Sasha and I could ever hope to uncover here.

Within minutes I was at the Ibar River. I waved KFOR press credentials at a startled French peacekeeper, and he waved me across the bridge into south Mitrovica and Albanian Kosovo. Despite the late hour I caught a taxi on a muddy street beside the city's central mosque, which ferried me to Priština and the entrance of the Grand Hotel where I spent the night. I slept soundly, awoke early, and by 9 a.m. I was standing in the farmyard of Gjorg Isufi.

It was our first meeting in eight months. I marvelled at how fast the time had passed. Gjorg appeared on the porch, looking as he always did when I arrived unannounced—as if he had been expecting me all along. I was prepared for a certain moodiness from Gjorg. I was prepared for him to be hurt and disappointed that I had gone away eight months before on a mission that would define the rest of his life, and had returned with nothing. But Gjorg was as stoic as ever. He ushered me into his basement *óda*. We sat on cushions and drank tea delivered by his older brother Ibrahim. He asked me nothing about Sofia. Nor did I expect he would. The rules still applied; she would not be discussed in his home. So Gjorg filled me in on news. Some of it was happy. Gjorg had bought a car. His brother Rexhep—the UÇK war veteran—was planning to be married. A date hadn't been set yet, but Gjorg said he would call when it was.

"I'll do my best to be there," I said.

I wanted to discuss the project, so I asked Gjorg to meet me in Priština the following day. He agreed, and gave me a lift to the outskirts of the Drenica Valley so that I could catch a bus into the capital. The drive to Komorane took almost thirty minutes because Gjorg drove agonizingly slowly. On the way I asked how he was getting on in life. "Not good," he said, and predictably his gripe was political. "NATO and UNMIK must know we must have independence.[1] This is the only important thing."

"The important thing is rebuilding Kosovo and having a normal life," I said.

"They must know we will fight them if we don't have independence," Gjorg said.

"You want to go to war again," I said.

"Not real war, but political war. We must have independence."

Gjorg pulled up to a taxi stop at the junction in Komorane, and leapt from the vehicle to negotiate a reasonable fare for me with the driver of the Kombi bus that was about to leave.

The next day, I met Gjorg in a café in Priština. He had news about Momo and the murders. He said he had information that a unit called the 1st Četnik Company had been involved in the cleansing of Rezallë. Gjorg then gave me a sheet of paper. It contained a list of five Serbian names. Three appeared to be nicknames preceded by the title "Paramilitar," which obviously denoted paramilitary or volunteer fighters. The list said one fighter was from Raška, and the other two from Vojvodina. The fourth name carried the designation "Potpukovnik," which meant Lieutenant-Colonel. The fifth name, "Pukovnik," meant Colonel. The Pukovnik was a Raška man. The Potpukovnik was the only one with a first and last name, and the only one without his origins specified.

"What's this?" I asked.

"These are Serb men who did massacre in my village."

I sat up and looked hard into Gjorg's face. "How do you know all this?"

"I cannot say to you," he replied. I pressed him and Gjorg hinted that the names were provided by a witness.

Wherever the names came from, Gjorg's meaning was clear: if you find these men, you'll find Momo and perhaps Sofia. Despite Gjorg's calm demeanour I felt he was getting desperate for me to produce something. He had given me information he felt was dangerous, and he did it for the sake of finding Momo and Sofia.

I left Priština that day with a new sense of energy.

The end came soon after I returned home to Budapest. I wasn't getting any better, and decided to return home to see a doctor and convalesce. There was no point spending any more days in a cold hotel room in the middle of winter. A day or so after my return, I had a late evening coffee with two Serb friends who had left Yugoslavia a decade before. They were a man and wife named Vlada and Vesna. Like most of the members of their generation, they had left Yugoslavia because of the wars and the poverty. I had met them in the early 1990s in Budapest not long after they left home to forge a new life in Hungary. Loyal and tirelessly hospitable, they were the first Serbs I had ever known, and they were the beginning of my love affair with Yugoslavia. I trusted them implicitly, which is why their message to me that evening had such an effect. Earlier I had told the couple I was doing some research work in Yugoslavia, but I had given them no specifics. That night Vesna asked me what I was doing.

I decided to tell her the gist of the story in order to get her read on it. I told her about the Serbian girl and the Albanian boy. I told her I was looking for this girl and had almost found her. I told her about Momo, and the murders in Rezallë, and about Mrs. Lukić and the cousin, and that we had found Sofia's former apartment only two weeks after she left it.

"I think she knows someone is looking for her," I said. "But I think this girl doesn't know what it's all about, and she's spooked."

I was smiling, boasting, revelling in the drama of it all. I expected Vesna to smile back, but her face turned dark and serious. Her expression revealed that she didn't believe what I was saying was worthy of a boast or a smile. Then she asked me two questions that I have to admit I had never asked myself.

"What are you doing?" she asked.

I stopped my story, and paused. What was I doing? "I'm looking for this girl," I answered.

What she had really been asking me was: Do you know what you are doing? I acted as if I didn't. She told me she knew of inter-ethnic affairs between Muslims and Serbs and Serbs and Croats in Bosnia that had gone terribly wrong—so wrong that lives had been destroyed. She was telling me that this was not a love story, or a game, or a fine drama, or a fascinating journalistic assignment. This was real and dangerous, and lives were at risk. The risk, of course, was Sofia's father, Momo. I reminded myself that he wasn't your average stiff and conservative dad. His vice wasn't surliness, tirades, or occasional drunkenness, although he might have been guilty of all three. The best evidence so far made him out to be a stone-cold serial killer.

Then Vesna hit me with the second question, which really put it all in perspective. "What if this girl doesn't want to be found? I lived in Bosnia. I know how these things work."

I silently chewed on that question, the best one I had heard in eight months. What if she didn't want to be found? Throughout this research project I had considered myself and Gjorg, but I had considered Sofia only from our perspective. When I guessed she had instructed Mrs. Lukić and the cousin to cease communication with us, I rationalized that she was frightened because she didn't know who we were or what we were doing. I had refused to consider the less encouraging explanation: she was scared because she guessed exactly who we were and what we were doing. If Sofia had told Lukić and her cousin to lie to us, she was sending me a message. She was saying she wanted to stay lost. And if Sofia wanted to be lost, what right did I have to find her?

I also knew that Sofia had secrets. Gjorg had shared a few and hinted at others when he confided to me under duress about his clandestine relationship with Sofia in south Mitrovica. These secrets, which Gjorg had told me in front of the empty schoolyard in Gllogovc eight months before, were the real reason Vesna's words cut me so deeply.

It was over.

CHAPTER 19

Lucky

Kosovo, May–June 1999

In Orahovac, Boris had slid so deep into Kosovo and the war, he wondered whether he would ever find his way back home. Dying there wasn't his only fear. There was the possibility of losing oneself—one's mind, morality, sanity . . . soul—so completely that if a man did emerge, he came back a different person.

Boris would soon face that. His descent continued. He laboured in the hospital. During quiet periods he explored the city, which was named after the Serbian for walnut, *orah,* and had the deep roots of a tree. Orahovac had its own language, a strange cocktail of Macedonian, Serbian, and Albanian called Raovacki, which Boris struggled to learn. He stole a few hours and visited the nearby village of Velika Hoca with a few doctors. Velika Hoca was located about ten kilometres away, and it was a microcosm of the Serbian soul. It had one thousand inhabitants and about a dozen churches. It was a place where you might sniff the holy aroma of incense, candle smoke, and molten wax on the street. At Velika Hoca, Boris and the others were met by the village's highest-ranking priest, a tiny man lost in robes and a grey beard, who told them the war was revenge for the Great Schism.

"These Albanians don't respect the Orthodox religion," the priest said. "They don't respect Serbia. They don't respect Christianity. They just want to destroy. But the Pope, that devil, is the real reason for this war. Albanians didn't really want to start the war. They were turned against us."

"Holy Father, are you sure about this?" Boris asked.

"The West wants to destroy the Serbian people because the Serbs live on the crossroads between the East and West," the priest continued as his wife served the soldiers coffee. "They want the Serbs to be slaves. We want to be free, but they won't let us—especially that devil the Pope. He wants to rid the world of the Serbs because the Serbs prevented him from spreading Catholicism here."

Boris left Velika Hoca having difficulty mustering any sentiment for God. He tried to bolster his soul by leading a local choir of boys in Orahovac. He found moral and spiritual solace in the choral music, even if the choir sometimes sounded to him like the yapping of a pack of wild dogs. He loved choirs because of the energy created by the group, and he particularly loved compositions for choir composed by Tchaikovsky. For Boris, Tchaikovsky was the first Orthodox composer, who diverged from the rigours of the canon, and wrote from his soul. The only other composer of merit was the Serb Stojanović-Mokranjac. His contribution was to revolutionize the Serbian Orthodox liturgy, and give it depth, complexity, and ornamentation that was true to the spiritualism it was meant to reflect. He turned the liturgy into a religious euphony that the Orthodox churches in Russia and Romania coveted and adopted. Boris's favourite Stojanović-Mokrnjac composition was the liturgy of Sveti Jovan, or St. John, the central liturgy of Serbian orthodoxy. Sung in choir, in full force and solemn prayer, it had the power to bring tears to his eyes.

Any solace Boris received from the music diminished somewhat when one of the priests approached him. Inter-ethnic suspicion had infected even the clergy. "I know you are a Catholic," the priest told Boris. "I'll be watching you."

Boris's faith was being challenged. So was his humanity. Both were tested a few days later when the military police arrived at the Dom Zdravlje with an Albanian prisoner, a cap-tured UÇK terrorist who had been injured in the field. As soon as he heard this Boris made an excuse to go to the man's room. He had to see what a UÇK looked like. He imagined a mean-eyed fanatic, cruel and bearded.

What he found was a simple man dressed in civilian clothes, who lay quiet and still in his bed. Boris walked in just as a surgeon was changing a plaster cast on the man's left leg. The prisoner had been shot and the wound was serious. The leg was mangled and the kneecap almost gone. The wound was so fresh it still bled. It had leaked blood all night, and the surgeon was adjusting the dressing to stop the flow.

"I don't have any money," the prisoner told Boris and the surgeon. "But I wish I could give you a hundred Deutschmarks for doing this."

Boris was puzzled, perhaps a bit disappointed. The pris-oner was neither fearsome nor particularly soldierly. He looked like an unremarkable Albanian, a guy who had lived a hard life. His creased, knotted face looked ten years older than the man's recorded age of forty.

Somebody later told Boris that VJ soldiers had spotted the man in a field. They shouted for him to stop. He ran, and they shot at him just as other soldiers had shot at Gjorg Isufi when they saw him from afar. But this time the bullet found its target.

Boris decided not only did the terrorist not look fearsome, his capture was anticlimactic. When he looked at the quiet Albanian, Boris had to wonder: Is this the face of the creature I am so afraid of?

The next time Boris went to see the prisoner, he noticed that something wasn't right. The prisoner was in his bed, but the room reeked of urine. There was a glass of water just out of the man's reach and a plate of meat on the table beside him.

"What's going on?" Boris asked.

Standing beside the bed, Boris saw that the meat on the plate was bacon: pork. Then he understood. The man was being tormented. Someone had taken away the Albanian's bedpan, forcing him to foul himself. They were also denying him water, and trying to force the man—presumably a Muslim—to ease his hunger by eating forbidden pork.

"Are you hungry?" Boris asked. The man said, yes. Boris went to the kitchen and filled a plate with cheese and hard-boiled eggs.

"You had your breakfast," one of the cooks said.

"It's for the Albanian," Boris replied.

The cook chuckled: "He's got bacon. Let him eat that."

Boris left with the eggs and cheese and returned to the Albanian's room. The prisoner acted shy, and somewhat amazed, perhaps that a Serb was feeding him. He wolfed down the food. Boris handed him the glass of water and a bed pan.

"I would like to pay you for what you are doing," the Albanian said.

"You speak Serbian very well," Boris said.

The prisoner explained that he had worked in Croatia as a shipbuilder. "That's where I learned," he said.

The next day Boris entered the room and found another glass of water just out of reach. He later overhead two order-lies talking. "I'm going to visit my *Šiptar*," one said, "and see what he has to say."

Boris went to his room and asked: "Has anyone been beating you?"

The man said, "Yes."

Boris began to take heat too. That same day one of the orderlies angrily confronted Boris. "Are you our *Šiptar's* private nurse?" he asked.

"He's a patient," Boris told him. Boris went to one of the senior physicians. "Do you know they're beating that Albanian?"

The surgeon reflected. "I'll do what I can to stop it," he said. "But you have to understand, this is life." The physician was neither condoning nor apologizing for the abuse; he was simply giving a diagnosis. There was that much hatred in Kosovo.

Boris thought about it. Was he being a traitor by not mistreating the Albanian?

The next time Boris went to the Albanian's room to inspect his leg, he found an empty bed. The terrorist was gone. "Where's the Albanian?" Boris asked an orderly in the hallway.

"The cops took him," he was told. And that was that. Boris never heard what happened to the man. He never even knew the name of this timid terrorist who once built ships at Rijeka. But it didn't matter. The Albanian was now in the hands of the *milicija*. His troubles were just beginning.

All these incidents greased the slope of Boris's downward slide. But just when he believed he had slipped too far, Boris was given what he thought was a reprieve—two weeks' leave to write his medical exams in Belgrade. Lieutenant Vlada balked at letting Boris go, but a senior doctor intervened. He wanted Boris sharp and qualified.

The circuitous bus trip out of Kosovo was more terrifying than the journey in. The driver was a fat man they nicknamed Buddha, who drove like a lunatic. They had only just begun their trip, and were outside of Zrze, the first village south of Orahovac, when Boris spotted a man waving his arms as the bus barrelled along a straight stretch.

"What the fuck does this guy want?" Buddha said. The man was wearing a Serb VJ uniform. Buddha stopped the bus.

"Fucking help us," the man screamed into the window. "Fucking help us." He motioned ahead to a vehicle that was lying on the road like a dead deer.

Boris and his colleague Zvonko, who had also wrangled leave, grabbed the first aid kit and ran to the car, which was pierced with bullet holes. A man sat in the driver's seat, bleeding, trembling, staring straight ahead, clutching the steering wheel. At a glance Boris could see he was shot in both arms, perhaps with the same bullet.

The dazed guy who had stopped the bus danced around Boris and Zvonko. "Help him," he said. "Help him. If he dies, I'll fucking kill you."

Boris and Zvonko patched the man up, and a *milicija* truck that was accompanying the bus rushed him to Orahovac. Boris then had occasion to look at his hands. Blood covered them like plasma gloves. No matter where Boris went in Kosovo, he eventually found himself wearing other people's blood. Zvonko and Boris washed their hands and lit cigarettes.

"God, we're stupid," Zvonko said. "We should never have left Orahovac."

Boris went to Kraljevo and met with his parents. He went to Belgrade and had an awkward reunion with old friends he had trouble understanding, and a girlfriend—Jelena—he felt distant from. Boris prayed the war would end before his leave was up. It didn't. Boris contemplated deserting, staying at home, and not reporting for duty. He didn't. He climbed on board a bus and returned to Orahovac with fat Buddha at the wheel.

In late May a rumour began to spread that the army was launching a new offensive called Operation Typhoon. No one quite knew what Operation Typhoon was. Boris knew it was directed against the UÇK, and he knew it was starting right away. He also knew there would be casualties. The end-game of the war was apparently beginning, and survival was getting more and more difficult.

Typhoon's force was felt only a few days later. The *četa* dispatched an ambulance to the field to support VJ units engaged in Typhoon. The ambulance was driven by Aleksandar,[1] a Kosovo Serb boy who had begged his way into the unit in Kraljevo. Somewhere near the village of Mala Hoca, the ambulance ran over a tank mine. Everyone survived, but the blast blew off Aleksandar's leg and blinded him in one eye. "Look at me," young Aleksandar screamed to a comrade seconds after the blast. "I don't want to live like this. Kill me."

Aleksandar's mutilation was the *četa*'s numbing inauguration to Typhoon. It unnerved everyone in Boris's unit. Aleksandar was mutilated on or around May 27. On May 30, Lieutenant Vlada approached Boris. "OK," Vlada said. "It's your turn. You're going to the field."

Boris was overwhelmed by fear. It was his first assignment as a combat medic. He would be working with the physician Dr. Gulja. As they gathered their supplies, Gulja took Boris aside. "Look, don't do stupid things in the field," he said. "Let's look after each other. I'll look after you, you'll look after me. We'll get through this thing."

Boris, Dr. Gulja, and a driver nicknamed Rabbit left in an ambulance at 3 p.m. that day. Boris donned a helmet and held his rusty rifle. He was terrified the entire way to Mališevo. Several villages along the way were reported to be terrorist strongholds, and he braced himself for bullets that never came. The ambulance rounded a corner and Boris spotted a sign. *You are entering east Beirut,* it said. *Minimum speed: 200 km per hour. Take care, good luck.*

Nothing much happened that day. Rabbit brought them to a hill at Crni Lug—Black Woods—where they observed a UÇK position. But there was no fighting and were no wounded. Boris and Gulja and Rabbit spent the night in an abandoned house in Mališevo. The night was quiet. The stench of rotting animal carcasses started them on a conversation about death. Both Boris and Gulja knew the war would be over sooner rather than later. How ironic it would be to die so close to the end. "We have to focus, focus on surviving," Boris said.

Two days later, survival would be more than talk. They took a routine trip to Crni Lug and were having coffee when an officer ran up. "There's wounded," he said. "You have to go to Mališevska Banja and get them." Boris put on his helmet and they left.

Boris had heard that this road was littered with tank mines, and that scores of VJ vehicles had been destroyed along this route. "I'm going to have to drive fast," Rabbit said, pumping the wheel. "We're just going to have to trust in God's will."

Rabbit and Gulja sat up front, Boris in the back. He started thinking: If we hit a mine, where is the safest place to be in the car—in the front, in the back, in the middle?

Rabbit powered on at top speed, and the ambulance heaved like a motorboat on a surf. Boris bounced around. The window was covered with steam, so Boris opened it and watched the ground for signs of the enemy, but all he saw was charred villages, destruction, a mosque with a buckled minaret. Boris's mind was as empty as the villages; no thoughts, just fear and worry. "*Will we hit a tank mine? Will we be shot by a sniper?*"

Suddenly the landscape changed. Boris saw soldiers running from a field. Explosions ruptured the air. Boris actually thought he could see bullets flying. The ambulance stopped, the back doors opened, and there was Gulja. "Let's go. Come on," he said. "There's wounded."

An injured man lay on the ground. Two hundred metres away, mortar shells went off. They were incredibly loud, like thunder claps in your head. Bullets struck the ambulance. Boris could hear the hollow thumps as the rounds entered the vehicle's soft metal. "Sniper!" someone screamed, and everyone went down. Boris and Dr. Gulja embraced the dirt but rose almost immediately, as if the ground were a trampoline, because they had a casualty. While bullets flew and mortars exploded and men shouted, Boris and Gulja secured the man to a stretcher, and loaded him into the ambulance, and piled in themselves.

Rabbit gunned the engine and they charged off. Boris lay flat beside the casualty, grabbed his hand, and whispered: "Are you OK? Are you all right?"

The sounds of war rapidly faded away, and Gulja said, "We're out of trouble, go ahead and see what's wrong with this guy."

Boris took scissors and cut away clothing. The man had an injured hand and a wound on his abdomen. Boris asked: "What's your name?" The wounded man mumbled something and it sounded like the name "Abdullah."

Boris couldn't believe it. Abdullah, he thought; this guy is a Muslim.

Boris focused, and the injured man repeated his name. "Valerij," he said. "I am Russian." He was a Russian volunteer. Boris and Gulja took him to the hospital in Orahovac.

Boris got out of the truck and collapsed at the hospital entrance, burying his face in his hands. Someone—an unrecognizable face—offered Boris a cigarette and a coffee. Boris took them, and shook like a man with fever. Lieutenant Vlada walked up to Gulja and Boris, and said, "All right, you guys can stay. We're sending another team to Mališevo.

Boris nodded, went to his room, and wept. He emptied himself. He felt ashamed for crying, but he couldn't help it. About three hours later the field medics who had been sent to replace Boris, Dr. Gulja, and Rabbit came back with two wounded and one dead. The wounded were hideously mutilated. The surgeons stopped their bleeding and sent them on to a larger hospital in Prizren. Boris learned that the men had been in a vehicle that had rolled over a tank mine on the same road that Boris, Gulja, and Rabbit had just travelled.

On June 3, Boris and his friend Zvonko were ordered to the field. They arrived in Mališevo in the morning, but despite the early hour the air was already trembling with heat. A cop stationed in the town told them to stay put. Boris and Zvonko found a damaged shop that contained a chair and a cot, and they declared it the Mališevo clinic.

The next day, Boris met Lucky. The encounter happened just before dinnertime. Boris and Zvonko were scheduled to pull out that evening, but they were hungry, so Boris entered a house that the army used as a barracks. He was searching for bottled water. When he entered the kitchen, he found a man hunkered over a table, writing a letter. The man's face was bearded and handsome, and would have been as familiar as his own had it not been so drawn and troubled. But Boris recognized the man anyway. It was his friend Srečko, which means Lucky. Lucky was the father of a dear friend from Kraljevo. The two families, his and Lucky's, had become as close as kin over the years. Boris had grown to love Lucky like an uncle, and when he saw him, he was surprised and elated.

Lucky had been expecting Boris. "Hey, there you are," he said. "I've been looking for you for months."

He was a captain in the VJ and was fighting on the front lines of Operation Typhoon. Boris had known that Lucky was fighting in the region and had been looking out for him as well. He was sure their paths would cross eventually, and now they had. But seeing Lucky in uniform in a war zone was a strange experience for Boris. There are certain men whose bodies fit easily into uniforms, but Lucky wasn't one of them. Boris knew he wasn't the soldierly type. He was a lover of fun. He joked incessantly. His laugh was contagious.

Back home in Kraljevo, Lucky was one of those guys in perpetual motion. When he talked to you, he never simply relayed words; he touched your arms and shoulders as he spoke. And this was when he was calm. When Lucky was trying to perform, he bombarded listeners with puns and pokes. Anything could set the guy off. Boris remembered visiting Lucky's home one time. He was speaking with Lucky's daughter Nataša, and Nataša had exclaimed in English—for some reason—"What a pity!" Lucky had just entered the room, and when he heard "pity" he recognized the Serbian word *pita,* which means "pie"—cheese pie, meat pie, spinach pie. "Pita! Sounds delicious. I want a pita," he said. "Dad, I said 'pity,'" Nataša said. "Dragana, now," he said to his wife. "Make me a pita." That was Lucky—making a joke where there was none.

That was the old Lucky, the Lucky whom Boris knew in Kraljevo, a man in constant quest of a punchline. But this was not the man whom Boris found in the VJ barracks in Mališevo. Not only did Lucky's sagging face suggest deep worry, but his entire demeanour reflected the strain he was under. Lucky told Boris he had been fighting the UÇK in the nearby hills, and the fighting was going badly. Boris understood that Lucky, despite his gentle character, knew what he was talking about. Like many citizens of Serbia over the past decade, Lucky had been exposed to multiple wars. He had served in Croatia and narrowly escaped death there. Lucky hadn't served in Bosnia, but he was an army reservist when the Kosovo war broke out. Over fifty years of age, Lucky should have been too old to fight, but he went anyway. He went for the same reason that Boris returned from his leave when he knew he didn't have to. Lucky had told his wife and a few close friends that he felt a responsibility to the young men of Kraljevo. So many Kraljevo boys, like Boris, had been conscripted into the war. Everyone knew that the city was being punished for its support of the opposition, but the reasons for the mobilization were irrelevant. An entire generation of young men was being marched to the front, and Lucky couldn't bear the thought of abandoning them.

Boris and the doctors in Orahovac weren't the only ones who read the writing on the wall and realized the war was in its final stages. Any soldier could see that the Yugoslav military was teetering and about to collapse. Two months of NATO air strikes had smashed the army to bits. There were even hints out of Belgrade that Milošević was about to cave in. The soldiers in the field knew this better than anyone. Like Boris, each was striving to stay alive until the war ended. But Lucky was fighting a private war. His aim was to keep the boys under his command alive until the conflict came to a formal end. And his face and normally jubilant voice were downcast because keeping his men alive was proving more and more difficult with each passing day.

He told Boris he was now writing a letter out of desperation to army HQ to inform them of the real situation on the ground. Lucky read out portions of his letter to Boris. "We don't have enough weapons and munitions to protect ourselves," Lucky had written. "I'm getting orders that place my men in unnecessary danger. I'm informing you now that I will not follow orders that will result in needless casualties."

"Typhoon is the most moronic military action there ever was," Lucky told Boris.

Lucky vented the same worries in a letter to his wife, Dragana, which he was composing at the same time. It wasn't clear why he was writing both letters at once. Perhaps his frustration was so profound that he needed to know at least one of the letters would be read with sympathy. Boris could see that Lucky was subdued and overwhelmed. But he was Lucky after all, and Boris's presence seemed to bolster him. He quickly put the letters and Operation Typhoon aside, and adopted something of his old persona. He launched into a rat-a-tat staccato monologue, catching Boris up on news from home. There was so much to tell. Lucky too had just been in Kraljevo on leave. His daughter was pregnant! Boris could see that it hurt him to leave home on the brink of becoming a grandfather, but nothing could diminish his enthusiasm for the coming child. Lucky told Boris the latest about his wife. Lucky told Boris of his short, precious time with his other daughter, Nataša, Boris's close friend. Lucky talked and talked and talked. He spoke like a man who didn't have enough time to say what he had to say. For some reason he recalled the war in Croatia, when he had been in a vehicle that hit a mine. Two men in the truck died, and Lucky never quite understood how he survived. "My godfather named me Srečko, and that was right," he told Boris. "I'm lucky. I was lucky then, and I'm lucky now."

When Lucky mentioned Operation Typhoon and the fighting now going on, he didn't give details. Boris still had no idea what Typhoon was meant to achieve. Was it a bid to seize territory? Was it an effort to kill as many terrorists as possible before the war's end? Typhoon could have been both of these things, or neither. In any case, its objective was immaterial to both Kraljevo men, particularly Lucky. He was going to keep his men alive, and stay alive himself. He told Boris he had had the same general attitude in the Croatian war. "But Croatia was a different war," he said. "There things were organized." Boris could see that Lucky had been a different man back then, too; he was younger, better able to endure the hardship of fighting. Lucky complained to Boris about his health. He told Boris he had a hernia, and he was recovering from a broken hand that made it difficult for him to operate a rifle. Boris offered to arrange for medical papers that would ensure Lucky a discharge. "Come to Orahovac as soon as you can," Boris said, "and I'll arrange it for you."

Lucky smiled, and agreed. He would come after Typhoon ended. They parted without emotion. They knew they would be seeing each other again soon.

Boris left and returned to Orahovac, where the next day he rose at 7 a.m. for duty. When he went outside the hospital for air, he heard the sound of far-off sirens coming from Mališevo. Boris went into action. He put on gloves, cleared civilians from the reception area, and made sure he was outside just as the ambulance pulled up.

A doctor from another unit got out of the ambulance. "There's two in the back," he said. "One wounded, one dead."

While the doctor helped orderlies carry the injured man into the hospital, Mane, the ambulance driver and a Kraljevo boy, mounted the back of the vehicle to help lift the stretcher carrying the dead man. Mane had loaded this stretcher in Mališevo without looking at the casualty. Perhaps it unnerved him to see dead soldiers who had so recently been very much like him: ordinary decent guys from Serbia who somehow found themselves at war. Or perhaps he was growing too accustomed to loading corpses into his ambulance and didn't much care who the dead man was. But for some reason at that moment he looked into the face of the lifeless soldier and screamed.

"Oh my God," he said. It was Lucky.

CHAPTER 20

Lies and Secrets

Kosovo, June 2000

The real reason I abandoned the project had to do with something Gjorg had confided to me in Priština during those three days of interviews that marked the beginning of the search. At the start of the interview Gjorg went over some of his wartime experiences.[1] He talked about growing up in the Drenica Valley, and about his fear of the police.

When I felt he had talked enough about his past, I turned to the subject of Sofia. That was the reason for our meeting, after all. I was about to leave Kosovo, pick up a one-month visa, and enter Yugoslavia. I would have less than thirty days to find Sofia, and I needed to know as much about this girl as possible.

Gjorg started at the beginning. He spent almost two days describing the minutiae of their first eighteen days together, when Gjorg had been hospitalized in Mitrovica with Sofia's father.

When we finally left this epoch Gjorg told me how he decided to attend school in Mitrovica. Sofia resided in a community in northern Kosovo, but they were able to meet in Mitrovica. At this stage Gjorg's account became fragmented.

He spoke about spotting her on the Mitrovica bridge, and how she whispered for him to meet her in the café where they usually met.

"There will be a war in Kosovo soon," she said to him in the café. "It's too dangerous for us to meet any more." She terminated the relationship. Gjorg left her standing on a leafy street in the hills above the city.

"I did not see her after that," he said.

I remember blinking, straining to understand. "When was this?" I asked.

"Early 1998," he said.

I fumbled through my notes. I just didn't get it. "What about the four years in between?" I asked.

Gjorg's face tightened like it did in moments of stress and seriousness. He jumped up from the table, marched down the street, and climbed on a bus that would take him back to his village. I had followed him down the street, waiting for him to tell me why he was running away. He said nothing, and refused even to look at me. I watched his bus cough exhaust and disappear down the street, listing like a sinking ship, and I reeled.

I reeled and fretted for most of the afternoon. There had been something fearful and final in his departure. What had happened? What was it that he couldn't bring himself to say?

The day after Gjorg fled Priština, I too boarded a bus. My destination was Gllogovc, the small city in central Kosovo where Gjorg had found a job with an international aid agency. I knew there were things about Sofia and her father that Gjorg hadn't told me.

As I had hoped, I found Gjorg at work. He immediately asked me how I had come to Gllogovc. "Bus," I said. He asked me the fare, and nodded approvingly when I told him two Deutschmarks. (He once went berserk when I told him I had

268

paid forty Deutschemarks to get from Priština to his village. "They did steal from you!" he howled. "Why do you let them?")

I was relieved by the chiding. He treated me like a naive innocent only when he was in a good mood. Taking an early coffee break, Gjorg led me down the street. We sat on the cool concrete steps of an empty school building, and Gjorg immediately got to the point. He was now about to reveal the secret he had kept from me—and everyone—since the summer.

"I think about our talk all night," Gjorg said. "I did not tell you everything yesterday."

"Yes," I said.

"I did not tell you, because you do not need to know everything. I know I did say I would tell you everything. And I did want to. But yesterday we talk about things that I did not talk about with nobody before. We talk about things I did not think about for years, and I did not like to think about." He paused and I stayed silent. "So I decide not to tell everything, only what you must to know. That is why I jump the story."

I said nothing, afraid that if I interrupted him, he'd jump again.

"For many years I did carry this story," he went on. "And I tell no one about her. This story was like a burden on my back. I decide last night I do not want this on my back no more."

I still couldn't understand it. Why was this chapter in his life, a romance between two innocents, such a burden?

His voice emphatic, almost apologetic, Gjorg told me that much of the shame and horror he felt about Sofia had to do with her father. Gjorg had already told me that Momo was a policeman of some description. He had already told me that Sofia terminated their relationship because of dangers to them both. Now he admitted that the peril was from her father, not from the war itself. In trying to articulate the

269

danger to him, Sofia had apparently uttered these parting last words: "My father wears camouflage."

Camouflage? I thought. "What does that mean?"

"It means he is a paramilitary," Gjorg said, looking away from me.

A paramilitary was a volunteer or private soldier. These militiamen, organized in small units or *četas,* have arguably been a fixture of Balkan history since the rebel leader Karađorđe raised a militia of brigands, peasants, farmers, and patriots to fight Ottoman Turkish occupation of Serbia (including Kosovo) in the nineteenth century. In the Second World War, in which Albanians allied themselves with Germany and Italy, *Četniks* developed a reputation that made their name a by-word for brutality. But paramilitaries had gained special notoriety during Serbia's recent wars in Croatia and Bosnia-Herzegovina for the unimaginable cruelty they meted out. By 1998, when Gjorg and Sofia last saw each other, *paramilitary* was synonymous with *butcher*.

This was exactly where Gjorg was going with his story. "You know I did tell you a massacre did happen in my village?" he said. I told him I knew, and recalled the eighty-four villagers who had allegedly been shot. "There is a woman who was there when the Serbs did come with tanks," he said. "She saw the police and soldiers who did do this massacre. She told me about one man she did think was a leader. He was very big man with green eyes. He did not wear a uniform like the *milicija* or VJ. He was a paramilitary. By the way she did describe him, I did know who it was. It was Momo, the father of Sofia."

A year after learning the truth, Gjorg still had not come to terms with the possibility that the father of his fiancée was responsible for murdering most of the men in his community in one bloody volley. But then Gjorg turned his monologue to Sofia, and took up the story he so abruptly terminated the day before.

As he had explained the day before, Gjorg returned to Mitrovica after being discharged from the hospital, but he didn't succeed in finding Sofia. He then returned three months later to enrol in a Kosovar underground college. His classes were not until September, but he stayed in the city for two weeks to register, meet his professors, and, of course, look for Sofia.

He roamed and scoured the city's Serbian areas obsessively, but finally found her on one of the few days he wasn't actually searching. It was the weekend, and Gjorg had gone to the bazaar near the big mosque in south Mitrovica to buy bread, cheese, and yogurt. Mitrovica's market was a huge maze of stalls, goods, and jostling people. Somewhere at the centre of it, while considering a purchase, he looked up and stared into the smiling face of Sofia.

"Where have you been all this time?" she said.

This, he explained, was the real beginning. Over the next hour he told me about their relationship. He described the hushed and coded phone conversations, the apartment in south Mitrovica where they held their clandestine meetings, and her secrets. Gjorg told me strange and puzzling secrets that it would take me a year to understand fully. And he talked about the lies he had told her, the paramount one being his name and identity. This staggered me.

"But why?" I asked. "Why in the world did you lie to her? Why didn't you tell her your name isn't Kemal Isufi?"

"Because I did not trust her," he said. "I did love her, but I did not trust her."

But there was a bond of understanding between them. If it wasn't trust, what then was it based on? I pressed Gjorg to explain. Finally, he did. He told me the thing that linked the two of them. It wasn't sex. It was a strange secret that strained credulity, but if true it meant that Sofia was in great danger from Momo. Gjorg had told me Sofia had once confessed to him that Momo was not her real father. Her real father was Albanian and she was fascinated with the fictitious Kemal Isufi because he was of mixed blood just like her.

If she wanted to remain lost, who was I to find her?

CHAPTER 21

Last Casualties

Kosovo, May 28, 1999

Boris had come to the ambulance to help with the wounded, When he heard Mane's scream, he experienced a jolt of disbelief. "Lucky?" said Boris. "Which Lucky?" Mane the ambulance driver groaned. "Our Lucky. It's our Lucky."

"Impossible," Boris said. "I just saw Lucky last night. He was alive." Not just alive, he was—even in the sad and retrospective mood Boris had found him—a life force. Boris decided his Lucky couldn't be dead. He peered into the ambulance where the dead man was still lying on the stretcher and saw a body mostly covered by a blanket. "That's not him," Boris said, and turned immediately. He stumbled through the doors into the hospital, found Zvonko, and said: "It's not him."

Zvonko grimaced, "What are you talking about?"

"It's not him," Boris said.

Zvonko was confused, but he sensed something bad. He took Boris aside, gave him a glass of *rakija,* and said, "OK. What's going on?"

Boris drank a gulp. "Mane said Lucky is dead."

"What Lucky? You mean Lucky you saw yesterday?"

"Yes, Lucky from yesterday."

"Did you see him?"

"No."

"Well, maybe it's another Lucky."

Yes, Boris thought. It has to be another Lucky. Srečko is a common name.

"We have to go to the morgue," Zvonko said. "You have to check. But you have to be prepared for what you might see."

They went down to the basement and entered the morgue. A body lay covered on a stretcher in the centre of the room. A candle burned nearby. Boris was terrified, not of seeing the dead—he had seen enough of that—but of seeing the truth. Boris approached the body and slowly raised a corner of the blanket, unveiling the dead man's face. He looked down—and stared into the lifeless face of Lucky. His Lucky.

Boris uncovered the entire body and tried to fathom it. Later, Lucky's daughter would ask Boris questions: "What did my father look like?" Boris would say he didn't know. And she would accuse him of lying, of trying to protect her from the dreadful reality of his death. But Boris wasn't lying. Lucky looked like any dead man—plain and horrific. Seeing him was unforgettable, and infinitely forgettable. The face was recognizable as Lucky, but it wasn't the face of his friend. An unstoppable life force had defined Lucky, and without that energy this face looked like a mask.

Boris had little time to mourn. Wounded flowed into the clinic all day. Boris left the morgue and entered the emergency room, where men stood, sat, and lay trembling, coughing, and bleeding. Blood seeped from gashes and pooled on the floor. Doctors and orderlies tracked the blood out the door and onto the hospital grounds. Wounded men groaned and pleaded for help. But Boris couldn't respond to them.

At one point Boris retreated mentally. He was there in the emergency room, but he wasn't. He heard a voice. "Boris!" It grew louder. "Boris, what are you doing?"

Boris looked down. A bare-chested doctor was sitting on his own bloody shirt. The shirt was pressed against the hemorrhaging femoral artery of a dying soldier. "Help me," the doctor shouted. Boris surfaced, saw the man and the blood, and got back to work.

One by one the wounded were brought to the operating room, or were dispatched to another ward. One by one the bodies disappeared. But Boris stayed on, working. Finally the room was empty and Boris found himself alone, except for Zvonko. Boris looked down and saw that his hands and clothes were red. Boris told a gypsy orderly to mop up the blood, and said to Zvonko. "I'll stick around and work with the civilian outpatients." Zvonko said: "Are you sure?" Boris nodded, and Zvonko said he would stay and help him.

There was still blood on the floor when an Albanian man in his mid-thirties, and an older woman, who might have been his mother, walked into the room. The old woman walked up to Boris. "Doctor," she said, "My blood pressure is high."

Boris blinked. "What?"

"Doctor, my blood pressure is high."

Boris couldn't believe it. Lucky had died fighting Albanians, Serb blood dirtied the floor—and this woman complained of hypertension. This was callous, Boris decided. This was disrespect. There was blood on the floor!

Boris exploded. Without really knowing how it came to pass, he found himself being restrained by Zvonko. He clawed and shouted. "Get out of here, you fucking Albanians. Murderers! Get out." The Albanian man and the old lady cowered, and retreated from the room. Boris followed them, and the Albanians continued to cower. Some of the others in the unit said, "What's wrong with you?" and Boris told them to fuck off and shut up. Some of the orderlies complimented Boris. The Albanian-lover, the man who had fed terrorists, had come to his senses! Boris told them to fuck off too. Boris went to his room and brooded. It was June 4, and he knew he would always remember this day as Lucky's death day.

Later, a surgeon approached Boris. The surgeon said he had heard what happened. He said he understood that Boris's friend had died. "Don't ever do that again," he told Boris. "Don't ever turn away patients."

"Yes," Boris said. "It will never happen again." After his outburst, he had grieved about his conduct as much as he had mourned Lucky. He understood what he was, and that was a doctor. And he understood what he had done, and that was to refuse medical aid to a person in need.

Boris later met with some men from Lucky's company, and asked how he had died. The men were sombre and confused, and said they didn't really know. It was the strangest thing. They found Lucky's body in a tree.

NATO fighters had attacked their company in the hills near Mališevo the night Boris and Lucky had met in the VJ barracks. Lucky ordered his men to withdraw and they pulled out in a such a frantic hurry there was some confusion whether everyone had come back safely. Not every man had been accounted for. So Lucky went back to the strike area, fearing that someone had been left behind. He didn't come back. The next day a patrol returned to the area to look for him. There was no sign of him. Then one of the men looked up and saw a bearded officer being supported in the air by the limb of a tree. It was their captain, Lucky. The only thing the men could figure was that a NATO missile had detonated near him and the concussion of it had instantly swept the life from him, lifted his dead body high into the air, and set it down on the limbs of that tree where his men found him the next morning.

Other men from home died in those final days, too. Boris's cousin had a husband named Slavko. Before the war Slavko had been a garrulous small-time criminal, business-man, and bullshitter, a modern-day *hajduk,* the old Serbian term for an outlaw, although not as successful in his smug-gling and fencing endeavours as many. Boris's family wasn't crazy about Slavko. He drank, and committed crimes, and occasionally raised his hand against his wife. But she loved him anyway, and for her sake Boris's family accepted him. When war broke out, Slavko was conscripted into the VJ and posted near Orahovac. Boris met with this cousin-in-law from time to time, and as the war progressed, Boris noticed how Slavko grew more and more despondent. For Boris, Slavko's slow discouragement was the first sign of Serbia's defeat. Slavko was not a man of wit and emotion like Lucky. He was a tough guy. He had spent his life straddling the fence between the criminal and legitimate worlds, but he was clearly more comfortable on the lawless side. And even his comfort with violence and his moral flex-ibility couldn't help him make sense of what was going on around him.

On April 30, Slavko had come to the hospital to talk to Boris. "I can't take it any more," he told Boris. "I just don't understand. I don't understand any of this." Slavko said he wanted to change his life and his ways. He wanted to get a job, be a father, be a good husband, stop getting angry, stop beating his wife. Slavko had slid as far as Boris had into a dim world of fear and hate, and in that darkness he was seeing things with utter clarity. He was a bad man and he wanted to change, and maybe this was the deal he was trying to strike with the God of Kosovo and the Serbs. Save me, and lift me from this place, and I'll be good.

The next day Slavko got drunk, grabbed a gun, and declared: "I'm going to kill all of them." He climbed on a farm tractor like the ones Kosovar refugees used, and rumbled off towards the nearest village. He was never seen again.

*

Berishë was a high mountain village, and the air at night was brisk and cold. But Gjorg slept better there than anywhere else in Kosovo since March 24. For the first time in months he felt he could sleep in safety. For the first time in months sleep was something he could savour.

Thousands of others had also come to the conclusion that the mountains near Berishë were Kosovo's last best sanctuary. Gjorg figured there were one hundred refugee families in Berishë itself but tens of thousands of others in makeshift tents on the mountainside within walking distance of the little village. Gjorg had found peace in Berishë. He had decided he was invincible to Serb bullets—not immortal, but simply and wonderfully impervious. He understood that no Serb soldier or bullet could end his life; that privilege belonged to the entity that had given him this life to begin with. This inner peace made the hardships they still faced in the mountains easier to bear. There was no room in the village of Berishë itself, so Gjorg, Kadri, and Ibrahim ventured into the high country. This territory looked like a wilderness, but it didn't feel like one. The summit had become a refugee city. There were lean-to tents everywhere you looked, and each was a home around which children played, women worked, and men brooded. The three wandered through the community, and Kadri spotted a family he knew.

The family comprised a man by the name of Sylejman, his wife, and their daughters—six-year-old Jetmira and nine-year-old Mirjeta. They invited the Isufi brothers to stay in their shelter. Right away, everyone pooled their money. Gjorg and Kadri took the collection and hiked to the village of Krojmir, the only community in the area with food supplies. Berishë sometimes had food. But Krojmir was close to Lipjan and received steady supplies. Krojmir had become a black market paradise. With so many hungry people in the vicinity, a sly businessman could set whatever price he wanted for staples like flour. The boys bought a bag for fifty Deutschmarks, and hiked the precious powder back to the camp. That night the women of the shelter baked *búka* in a makeshift *saç,* or oven, and everyone feasted on the hot bread. Feeling almost secure, with a few mouthfuls of fresh food in his shrunken stomach, sleeping under a shelter, and surrounded by kind friends, Gjorg felt happy.

The flour eventually ran out, and food proved hard to come by. But it always came somehow. The UÇK had a kitchen nearby where they prepared potatoes, macaroni, and corn. (There was rarely any meat available.) But the UÇK needed more than a single kitchen to feed the multitude hiding there. The fighters took to distributing any foodstuffs they could find. It was strange to see these hard and bearded men so accustomed to violence and fighting delivering bags of wheat. But at that moment it was the best thing they could do to protect their people. People mixed the wheat with water to create a mush called *mullin,* which was far from appetitizing but it kept people alive.

The isolation of the mountains might have compensated for the hunger if the security had been complete. But it wasn't. NATO fighters screeched overhead some days and most nights. Because of the high altitude the jets seemed closer, and the children squealed and screamed every time a plane appeared. Every now and then Yugoslav forces lobbed artillery into the area. In addition to all the refugees UÇK fighters were concentrated on the mountain, and lower down they periodically traded mortar fire with Serb forces. Gjorg heard that there had been close bitter battles where UÇK lobbed rocks down the mountain to keep the Serbs away.

But there were more good things about Berishë than bad. A river ran nearby and streams wound through the trees like arteries. There was a pipeline that delivered mountain water to villages below, and the refugees had tapped into it, so there was no shortage of fresh water for drinking, and even washing. What a comfort it was to wash your hands and face. Gjorg made a mattress out of an old blanket filled with wheat chaff. He went into the trees and searched for food. He found great bushes of red *dredhëza* and black *manaferra* berries, and brought them home.

Gjorg developed a daily routine. He rose early, usually at 6 a.m. He kept water for himself in a plastic cola bottle, and he would heat the water in a pan to wash his hands and eyes. He would then fetch water for everyone else. He would scrounge for food during the day. But there was not enough food to occupy a day of foraging, so when it was hot and there was no food to be found, Gjorg sat on a wooden bench in the shade of a tree with his brothers. He gossiped with other men. Later, he would say that he spent a lot of time wondering: Will I ever get home? And he thought about his girlfriend.

Gjorg grew attached to Mirjeta and Jetmira, the young girls in his shelter. He wrote them poems and told them stories. Gjorg marvelled at how bright Mirjeta was. He would ask the nine-year-old for a poem and she would recite one. Then he would tell her a poem, and she would memorize it and recite it back to him word for word. Gjorg's poems were always about the UÇK, and a free Kosovo, and home.

The mountain became the wanderers' whole world, not just a temporary haven. There were weddings. They were brief. One homeless family would leave their shelter and walk to the tent of the family of the prospective bride. There would be introductions, and a short celebration, and then the husband would accompany the women to his shelter, his home. Almost always the couple had met as refugees.

Babies were born. Whenever there was a new baby, people donated food to the mother so that she could produce milk.

People died. Every day there were whispers. "So and so, son of so and so, from Komorane or Gllogovc or Skenderaj, has died." The dead were usually very young or very old. They usually succumbed to hunger and hopelessness. The dead were buried in a special field. But it seemed to Gjorg that no matter where you looked, you saw mounds of earth that contained the bodies of Kosovars who would never be going home.

There were radios on the mountain, and the mountain people listened to the BBC. Often they could pick up an Albanian-language service. The news always seemed the same. NATO continued its attack against Yugoslavia, the fighters flew night after night, but the war did not look any closer to ending. At one point the radio said the West was considering an invasion of Kosovo. This was something to be noted, but the radio also said that an invasion would have to take place by September at the latest. Basically, the news was bad.

Then one afternoon, the fading voice of the BBC said that a Western delegation consisting of the Finnish diplomat Ahtisaari and the Russian politician Chernomyrdin had travelled to Belgrade and was meeting with Milošević. Peace was being discussed, but for the mountain people these negotiations were drowned out by the artillery the Serbs tossed into the hills.

CHAPTER 22

Lost Letters

February–June, 2001

I had given up on Gjorg's project, and I was happy
that I had. It didn't please me that I was letting Gjorg down.
But, he didn't know I had given up on him. I should have gone
and told him right away, but I didn't have the nerve.

I wondered about Sofia a lot. I asked myself if she was
hiding from me. What could she be thinking?

I watched a movie called *Before the Rain* that chronicled
a love story between an Albanian and a Slav in the former
Yugoslav republic of Macedonia. The story was one of terrible
violence with an unhappy ending. I ordered the video over
Amazon.com in late February, and watched it again and again
for no other reason than a desire to learn how a Yugoslav film-
maker—in this case the Macedonian Milcho Manchevski—
interpreted an Albanian-Slav love story.

The movie proved to be a primer. A few weeks later I was
assigned to cover the crisis in Macedonia, which began brewing on January 27 when a Macedonian police station in the
village of Tearce came under grenade attack by Albanian
rebels. By the time I arrived in Skopje on March 15, 2001,

Macedonia was the site of yet another Albanian war in southern Europe. It was a sad, bloody rerun of Kosovo and the Preševo Valley. I told myself I was glad to be free of Gjorg, and Sofia, and Momo.

But immediately after my return from Macedonia on March 22, 2001, things began to happen that would draw me back into Gjorg's drama.

The first event didn't have to do with Gjorg directly, but it had an impact on all of us. A week after I got home, I answered my phone. It was Sasha, and she was excited. "They've just arrested Slobo," she said.

Sasha was almost right. Late on Friday, March 30, when she called me, the Belgrade media was reporting that Milošević had been taken into custody to stand trial for unspecified crimes, or to be delivered to The Hague, where he faced a war crimes indictment. The reports were wrong. Two hours later Milošević appeared briefly before a crowd of supporters who had gathered outside his villa, which had once been one of Tito's official residences. At midnight a squad of police stormed it, but they were repelled by Milošević's bodyguards. Milošević's mansion in affluent Dedinje had been under guard and surveillance by security forces for months. Inside his bunker Milošević was surrounded by family and a loyal volunteer guard who were determined to fight to the end.

Milošević's life had changed little after the street revolt that toppled him on October 5, 2000. Before the revolt he had been living in seclusion, surrounded by family, guards, and sycophants. After being toppled, he lived in seclusion, surrounded by family, guards, and sycophants. He no longer lived with the satisfaction that he was the most powerful presence in Yugoslavia, but in the end maybe it didn't matter so much.

After the failed arrest, negotiators tried to talk the former president out. For the longest time Milošević refused to budge. He threatened to kill himself. He threatened to kill his wife, Mira, and his thirty-five-year-old daughter, Marija. Finally, on Sunday, April 1, Milošević relented. He surrendered himself, his twenty bodyguards, and an armoury that included two armoured vehicles, three machine guns, thirty automatic rifles, thirty grenade launchers, twenty-three pistols, and two cases of hand grenades. The Milošević regime, dead for six months, had now been interred. The October 5 revolution seemed irreversible.

A few days after that, Gjorg called. He had been calling from time to time to give me news on his brother's wedding. The ceremony was constantly being postponed. Rexhep had applied to be a member of Kosovo's new indigenous police force, and he did not want to set a wedding date until he knew when he would have to go to the academy. So Gjorg kept calling with the various potential dates. "We want you to come for this," he said. "You are like family." These conversations were torture to me. He was pushing me to get on with it and come up with something, and faced with such expressions of loyalty I couldn't summon the nerve to tell him I had given up. But Gjorg continued sending out messages to me, and some of his communications were ingenious and haunting.

Soon after he called, I started going through old Kosovo files for 1998 and 1999, the period immediately before and after the air strikes. One file was filled with paperwork that I had obviously transferred directly from a suitcase into the folder without checking the contents. The folder contained old press releases, photocopied maps of Kosovo and Serbia, literature from the World Food Programme, and a few business cards. As I thumbed through the file, I noticed a sealed envelope that had been buried among the morass of papers. The envelope was yellow, and my name was typed on it. I turned it over. A return address had been typed on the back. It was Gjorg's village.

I had no recollection of the letter until I opened it and read the contents.

> Dear my friend John
>
> This is my first letter after the war
> First I like to thank you for everything
> I feel much better this week, but sometimes
> I feel like I am in bondag for something in
> my past.
> Im trying to make my future but it is so hard
> for
> me.
> I dont know why I writ you but I feel
> I have to.
> I believe that you are generous. gentle.
> Come back please. We must finish the story.
> All the story not just half.
> COME PLEASE
> Im happy to have friend like you
> it is my pleasure
> THANK YOU
>
> GJORG
> ISUFI

I remembered now where it came from. It was the letter he had given me in the summer of 1999. In our previous meeting, on his farm in Rezallë, he had informed me that he had given up on Sofia and never wanted me to mention her name again. When I didn't return, he thought I'd left Kosovo and he wrote me this letter, which he handed me when I called on him some time later. I had stuffed it into my bag, never to see it again until now.

I studied the letter. Gjorg's words amazed me. Pain and obsession radiated from the warped paper. I noted his strange reference to feeling "bondage for something in my past." He had written this almost two years before, but I was getting the echo now, and it was like he was asking me all over again to help.

"Come back please. We must finish the story." I couldn't help but feel he had written the note *then* so I would read it *now*.

The phone calls, the lost letter recently discovered, and the conversations I found recorded in the notebooks made me think there must be a way to continue the search without endangering Sofia. But I felt obliged to respect the possibility that she didn't want to be found.

In June I returned to Macedonia to continue coverage of the crisis there. Since I left, rebels had seized the village of Aracinovo, just outside Skopje, and once again the war threatened to spread into the capital. Negotiations between Albanian politicians and the Macedonian government collapsed in mid-June, but a fragile ceasefire had been hammered out, thanks to the intervention of foreign negotiators.

Skopje wasn't the only Balkan capital where things were happening. While I was in Macedonia, Milošević re-entered the news. In an effort to secure US$1.28 billion in aid and reintegrate into the international community, Belgrade's new masters surrendered Milošević to U.S. forces in Bosnia for delivery to The Hague to stand trial. The irony of the date of the surrender—June 28—was lost on no one, including Milošević. Just before being carried away from Belgrade by helicopter, Milošević wished one of his police escorts happy Vidovdan, or St. Vitus Day. On that day 612 years before, the Serbs met the Turks on the field of Kosovo Polje. On that day eighty-seven years before, the Austro-Hungarian Archduke

Ferdinand ignored his aides' advice that a parade on St. Vitus Day would provoke Serb nationalists, and was assassinated in the street in Sarajevo by Gavrilo Princip. World War I followed soon after. On that day twelve years before, Milošević appeared at a rally at the Kosovo Polje battlefield and officially launched an era of war and equally ruinous nationalism. Now, on St. Vitus Day 2001, he was leaving Serbia to face judgment.

Sasha and I spoke on the phone about her thoughts on the Milošević extradition. It was either in this phone conversation or another one around this time that Sasha gave me the news that brought me back to Gjorg's quest. It started when I asked Sasha if she was happy that Slobo was in The Hague.

"I hate Milošević," she said. "But it's blackmail. We're giving him away for money."

"Hey," I said, "you're getting a billion dollars for your lousy leader. We have lousy leaders in my country we couldn't get ten bucks for. Just take the money."

Sasha said, "Maybe." And then she dropped the bomb. Like Gjorg's question to me on that bend of the road in Drenica in June 1999, like my friend Vesna's caveat months before, Sasha's words altered the landscape.

"I have information on Momo," she said. "I found out from my friends." She didn't have to explain who her friends were; the tone of her voice suggested she had pushed her police contacts hard, called in debts, and perhaps incurred a few. "There was a Momčilo Neznanović in the DB," she said, and she spelled his name. "He was born in Mitrovica in 1949. He joined state security in '87. He was activated in 1998. He was in Glogovac[1] during the war."

I could hardly believe it. Finally we had Momo, the information was from a documented source, and it fit Gjorg's account. "Do they know where he is now?" I asked.

"He died in June 1999," she said.

So, Sofia's father didn't live through the war, dying only days before peace between NATO and Yugoslavia had been sealed. Gjorg no longer had anything to fear. More importantly, neither did Sofia. I thought about that bond that linked them, the secret about her past that he so reluctantly told me. Only Momo could have used that against her, and now that he was dead, she in a sense was free.

I could almost hear Gjorg's voice. *We must finish the story. All the story, not just half.*

CHAPTER 23

Going Home

Kosovo, June 12, 1999

Slavko was the first family member Boris had lost
in the war. Lucky was the second and this loss was far more
traumatic to him. But his last casualty in Kosovo, the one that
touched him the deepest, was a stranger.

It happened on June 12, the day NATO crossed the border
into Kosovo. That evening, a party broke out in town. Boris,
Zvonko, and friends drank wine and *rakija,* and ate the flesh
of a roasted pig. Most of the doctors and soldiers were rejoic-
ing in their defeat. You could hear gunfire as soldiers here and
there across the city celebrated the war's end by shooting into
the air. Yes, Yugoslavia had lost the war, but they had won
their lives. Others thought differently. A few at Boris's party
stood on the periphery of the dancing and drinking, and
brooded over Kosovo. But the party came together when
those who cared about Kosovo and those who didn't broke
into song. One song was an old Serbian tune about Kosovo
and Metohija. It was called "Lastavice."

Preleteše ptice lastavice
preleteše žalosti moj dilber
al nigde ne padoše.
al nigde ne padoše.

It was an old Serbian song that used a form of the language so archaic Boris had difficulty translating the lyrics word for word. But he, like all Serbs, knew what it meant. The song was about change and irrecoverable loss. A *lastavice*, a swallow, leaves for the winter. Seasons are changing and time is passing but the swallow does not return. When the war started you could sing that song believing that the swallow, missing now for centuries, might still appear. But the night that Boris and the other weary soldiers sang they knew the swallow was gone forever. Kosovo as they knew it was gone forever.

Not that everyone thought this was a bad thing. Loss sometimes brought new life. In this case Boris and the others consoled themselves that the loss of the war had brought peace and the assurance that those still living would not die in Kosovo. Listening to the voices, both sad and joyful at the same time, and drinking in the wine and the mood, Boris might have thought the nightmare was over. But he would witness one last tragedy.

After the party, Zvonko and Boris were standing in front of the hospital. They were chatting quietly and breathing in the cool summer air when an Albanian ran up to them carrying his sixteen-year-old daughter in his arms. The man was frantic. The girl was bleeding from the head. The father explained that his daughter had been sitting on the balcony of their flat when a bullet struck her in the skull. It had come from the gun of a drunken soldier who had been shooting volleys into the air to celebrate the war's end. A lone bullet had ricocheted from something and careened into the back of the girl's head.

Gjorg and Zvonko rushed her into the emergency room and placed her on a table. Boris marvelled. She looked unhurt. She looked angelic. She was beautiful—long black hair and a lovely slender face. You might have believed she was only sleeping if it wasn't for her flickering eyes and senseless mumbling, which grew softer and softer with each utterance.

Boris took scissors and cut away the girl's thick hair so that Zvonko could inspect the wound. Surgeons arrived and said the damage to the brain was too severe for the girl to survive.

Boris and a few others sat in chairs around the girl. It was sad and fascinating, watching this beautiful child slip away. They stayed because they didn't want to give up on her. But Boris and the others could do nothing but watch transfixed as her breath grew weaker with each exhalation. Zvonko had lost interest in the girl, so Boris sat with Miško, an anaesthesiologist. "Look at this," Miško said. "Life is a *kučka.*" It's a bitch.

The parents knew their child was dying. They stood beside the table and wept. The father pleaded with Boris and the doctors. "I always liked the Yugoslav army," he said. "I once worked for the police and the army." It was hard to figure what he was after. Was he trying to encourage the army doctors to work harder? Or did he really believe the Serb military—masters of Kosovo for so long—were the final arbiters of everything, including life and death?

A half-hour later the girl opened her eyes. To Boris it looked like she had been awakened from a sleep and was about to say something. Then she fell back into coma and breathed on in violent little gasps. Then her chest stopped heaving. Finally she gave out a long exhalation that echoed like a farewell, and her chest stopped moving. It was as if life had left the child in one shudder.

That night Boris went to another party. He guzzled white wine and did everything in his power to forget about the dead girl. But he never would. She was his last casualty of the Kosovo war.

On June 14, German NATO troops deployed in Orahovac gave word to the local army command that the hospital staff could redeploy at 2 p.m. that day. The medical unit could go home. Boris was elated. He and Zvonko decided to travel together in a first aid vehicle, the same one Boris had entered Kosovo in.

When their convoy pulled out, it consisted of about five vehicles. The day was oppressively hot. The convoy went first to Mališevo and then to Kijevo, where it stopped for the night. Kijevo was a Serb village, but there were no Serbs there any more, just soldiers. In addition to the medical convoy, other army personnel were bivouacking in town. Boris saw no civilians. The only inhabitants were chickens, confused dogs, and pigs that roamed the streets and squealed. Where were the villagers? It never occurred to Boris that they had fled for Serbia already and were spearheading a mass migration of historic proportions that would virtually empty the Serbian Holy Land of Kosovo of its Serbian population. But if Boris fretted about the fate of Kijevo's villagers he didn't for long.

Another party was breaking out, and it enveloped him and everyone else. Drunken soldiers waved flags and shouted, "Kosovo je Srbija!" ("Kosovo is Serbia"). The army had turned into a circus. One APC in the village used a toilet seat as a hood ornament. That night the men killed orphaned pigs and feasted. Lieutenant Vlada got "drunk like a Russian," which in Serbian means highy intoxicated. "You know, Boris," Vlada said, "I like people. All people. Polish people, Jewish people, German people. Any people who are honest people."

That night Boris slept in a house where about forty soldiers were bunking. Before turning in, he looked to the hills. He saw the flashes of firefights and exploding grenades. The war was supposed to be over, but clearly it wasn't. The day before, a Jeep had pulled up to Orahovac and an officer approached a couple of partying soldiers. "OK boys, we need twenty volunteers," the officer said. "You, you, you, and you. We've got to fight the UÇK." The men looked at the officer like he was a clown. They laughed and continued to pour brandy down their throats. The officer drove off empty-handed. But obviously he had found volunteers somewhere, because Boris had witnessed how the typhoon against the UÇK was raging on in the hills.

The next day, the military convoy that had camped in Kijevo summoned itself early and prepared to leave. Just then, another convoy drove up. Boris recognized some faces in the windows. The people were Serb civilians from Orahovac. Yesterday they had decided to stay put and take their chances with NATO. After the convoy stopped, Boris overheard a conversation. A woman said that the UÇK was already hunting down Serbs and torching Serb homes, and NATO soldiers were doing nothing to stop it. So all the Serbs decided to leave. "This is what had happened to the Serbs of this village," Boris thought. They had fled NATO and the UÇK. They had fled so quickly that there was no time to pack. They left dogs and pigs, and sped north towards Serbia, their last refuge.

Seconds after the medical convoy left Kijevo Boris turned and watched as UÇK soldiers entered from the other end of town, and raised a red and black Albanian flag on top of a school. He watched UÇK terrorists shooting into the air. It was nightmarish. An Albanian flag was already waving above the most Serbian of villages. What did this mean? Was Kosovo already being absorbed into a foreign nation, and had the old Serbian village of Kijevo become a place name on the map of Greater Albania? This was the nightmare of Serbs, Macedonians, and Montenegrins alike, all of whom had Albanian citizens in their border regions. As a Kraljevo boy

Boris knew well of the Albanians in Bujanovac in southern Serbia. During summers in his childhood his family had vacationed in a village on the Montenegrin coast where the Albanians were numerous. For generations Slavs in all these territories warned that Albanians were planning someday to rise up and forge a great Albania with Kosovo at its centre. Was this the beginning of it?

When the convoy reached the Slatina airport, Boris saw a NATO soldier for the first time. He was British and impressively trim. His camouflage uniform, an explosive design of green, black, and brown foliage, was clean and complete. The APCs and the tanks were modern and monstrous and very lethal-looking. Boris couldn't remember the last time he had seen a soldier so well equipped. And in two wars he had never seen armour like this. As the ragtag convoy passed, one of the guys in his unit jumped up and shouted at the Brit, "We'll be back. Kosovo is Serbia."

The convoy passed through Priština. Boris glimpsed the medical faculty where he had studied years before. The convoy rolled on all day long, and exited Kosovo at the village of Merdare. As the trucks crossed the border into Serbia, men brandished guns and shot into the air. Everyone felt relief. For Boris it was the first time in three months he felt free and safe and in possession of a future. Zvonko and Boris sat in the back of the ambulance in chairs, and stared out the open back doors at Kosovo as it drifted further and further away.

Boris vowed he would never go back. Two years later he would break that promise to himself for the sake of a woman named Sofia, whom he had never met.

*

On June 3, radios told the mountain people that the Serb leader Milošević had agreed to peace terms delivered by

Ahtisaari and Chernomyrdin. A final deal over the Serb with-drawal was scheduled to be struck in Macedonia. Serb forces now controlled the route to Krojmir, which cut off the food supply to the mountains. Gjorg and the others had to rely on berries, but there were not enough to keep everyone alive.

Rockets now fell on the Albanian encampment in the mountains. UÇK fighters told the refugees at Berishë that the rockets were shot from the back of a truck. The rocket launcher was designed to be a mobile anti-aircraft weapon, but in this case it was perfect for attacking Kosovars high up the mountain. Whenever a truck was spotted down below, the UÇK spread word to expect an attack.

Gjorg knew it was impossible to escape a rocket if God willed that it should hit you. One afternoon in early June, Gjorg and a friend named Bashkim decided to go and fetch water. On their way, rockets started to come down. One exploded very close. Gjorg and Bashkim were unhurt, but shrapnel from the explosion tore and mangled the hand of a young girl. It was hard to see the mutilation of this innocent. Gjorg always feared mutilation more than death. He had come to terms with death, but he was afraid of an injury that might render him an invalid and force him to be a burden to his brothers. He decided he would rather die than be injured.

Around this time Gjorg noticed a solitary man living beneath a tarp near his shelter. He had arrived in the flood of homeless, but he kept silent, kept his own company. No one paid attention to him. Gjorg wondered why until someone told him that this man could neither hear nor speak.

Gjorg became fascinated with this man's situation. He was in danger, the same danger as everyone else, but he didn't know fear because he couldn't perceive the threat. He couldn't hear the rockets. He couldn't hear the warplanes ripping the sky overhead. He would never know death until the instant it took him. Gjorg thought about this man, and sometimes he envied him. Gjorg wished he too could hide in this world. For almost eighty days Gjorg had been seeking sanctuary, and this man enjoyed the best hiding place of all, within himself.

And so it went. Words of peace shot from the radio. Rockets and artillery fell from the sky. And because of the lack of food and the spread of disease, more and more mountain people died. Gjorg himself developed a cough that seemed to rule his body. If this peace continued, Gjorg knew he would end up in the cemetery field under a mound of earth and stones.

Then, one morning, Gjorg awoke under his shelter to the sound of excited chatter. The night before, a helicopter had arrived carrying two NATO soldiers, people said. The soldiers said that a peace deal had been signed in a Macedonian city called Kumanovo. According to the deal, the Serb police and army would leave Kosovo. NATO soldiers would come in their place. The mountain people could return to their homes.

It was unbelievable. Everything was the same in the mountains—the filth, the sick people, the crying children. Graves and plastic tents. Everything was the same except for the world itself. If the news was to be believed, Kosovo would soon be without war and Serbs.

Later that day, two American soldiers appeared in the camp. One of the men had black skin. Gjorg had never seen a man with skin so black. He asked the black soldier when he could go home, and the soldier said, "You should wait three or four days." He explained it would take that much time for Serb forces to leave the area. "But don't be afraid," he said. "They won't shell you any more up here."

Despite the soldier's warning, people started down the mountain on their way home that very day. Some fired up tractors, and piled belongings and family in the wagons. Some families started off on foot. Lonesome souls long separated from friends and family headed down alone.

On June 14, Gjorg and his brothers decided to set out for home. Nearly everyone on the mountain had left already. The three Isufis had found an Albanian flag and carried it triumphantly. At Berishë, the Isufis leapt into the wagon of a tractor. Their tractor was part of an endless line headed for Gllogovc. Gjorg's tractor was the lead one, and as they made their way down the mountain to homes they hadn't seen for months, Gjorg waved his flag.

The tractor left the Isufi brothers at Komorane, on the outskirts of Drenica, because the tractor driver and his family were from that town. The boys gave the driver their flag as a gift, and then they walked to Gllogovc. There, Gjorg and his brothers went to the home of a friend, where they ate their first full meal since the beginning of the war. It was *fli,* a layered flour pancake that had always been one of Gjorg's favourite dishes. Gjorg's stomach was small, but he forced all of the steaming food into himself.

During the war, Gjorg always ate sparingly. He made sure he did not consume too much so that extra food could be shared with his brothers or given to children. But now that the war was over, Gjorg gorged himself. He drank from a bottle of mineral water that the NATO soldiers had left at Berishë. There had been fresh water in Berishë, but before Berishë he had to drink brown water from puddles. This water was clear as air, and it sparkled magically. It was an elixir. Gjorg had never felt happier. He would soon be home.

Kadri and Ibrahim decided to linger in Gllogovc a few more hours. Gjorg said he would return to their village immediately to check on things. The prospect of going home excited him until he encountered a neighbour in Gllogovc who told Gjorg of the killings that had reportedly taken place. There were fresh burial mounds, and a corpse already unearthed.

Gjorg climbed aboard a tractor heading into Drenica. The ride was slow and sad. He was going home, but the rumours and stories of "massive graves" and dead neighbours frightened him. He worried. He knew nothing of his family other than Kadri and Ibrahim. What of Shota, and Rexhep, and his mother?

Just before his village, the tractor was overtaken by a strangely modern car. Gjorg could see that it contained foreigners, but they didn't look like NATO soldiers. The car stopped. A voice called out in English. Gjorg jumped from the wagon, sauntered up to the car, and looked inside. Then he saw my face in the back seat. And he recognized me immediately from Qirez. Gjorg thought of a name and address he carried in his wallet, the same wallet he had carried with him for the duration of the war.

PART IV

Finding Sofia

CHAPTER 24

City of Kings

August 2001

My train rumbled into Belgrade on a typically sweltering August day. Two days later, Boris and I climbed into Sasha's new car, and headed south. We were going to Kraljevo. The search was back on.

The decision to resume Gjorg's project came easily and instantaneously. Sasha's news meant that all the good reasons for abandoning Sofia no longer existed. Momo was dead and could no longer hurt Gjorg, Sofia, or us. And there was no need to assume that Sofia wished to remain lost. Ms. Kneznanović of Belgrade, the former tenant of Mrs. Lukić who had given us ample reason to believe that she did not want to be bothered, was not Gjorg's Sofia after all. The girl we were pursuing carried the family name Neznanović. Sasha's police contacts had provided documentation of this. According to their records, shortly before the end of the air war in 1999, one Momčilo Neznanović, a native of the Mitrovica area and a reactivated member of the SDB, had died in Kosovo after being stationed in the Gllogovc area.

Of course, it was not absolutely conclusive that this man

was Sofia's father. But this Momo fit perfectly the description given by Gjorg. The name, age, birthplace, and state-security affiliation were consistent with Gjorg's story. Moreover, Sasha's sources placed this Momo in the Gllogovc area of the Drenica Valley during the war, which put him in the vicinity of Rezallë at the time of the killings in April 1999. Yes, this had to be our man. This had to be Sofia's father.

Now we were rumbling south along a familiar road to prove this, and to answer the question: where exactly had Momo been before he died, and where was his daughter Sofia now? I was also curious about the circumstances of Momo's sudden death so near the end of the conflict. Did this have anything to do with the story?

I had hatched a plan before leaving for Belgrade. It was a straightforward scheme that required the participation of both Sasha and Boris. I had called Sasha from home and pleaded for her help. "I need you and Boris for one last push to find this girl and end this thing," I told her. "Will you do it?"

Sasha agreed immediately. She spoke to Boris, and sent word that he was on board as well. We arranged to rendezvous in Belgrade when both Boris and Sasha could take time from their lives to go on the road.

I arrived by train on August 16. The republic I entered was surreally different from the Serbia I had visited before. Exactly a year ago I had made the same trip in an empty and lonely train car to cover the presidential elections and begin Gjorg's search. Serbia then was a paranoid fortress on the verge of combustion. Its frontier was patrolled by brooding border police, and its citizens discussed war like others would the likelihood of rain. But on this trip my train was crowded with American backpackers who complained about the fifteen-minute delay while waiting for genial border cops to issue tourist visas at the Subotica crossing. Fortress Yugoslavia of the Milošević era seemed as ancient as the Iron

Curtain, and as I stood beside the nasal-voiced college kid from Boston with baggy knee-length shorts and a Peter Frampton hairstyle, I couldn't help missing the good old police state just a little.

Time was passing. The most telling reminder came when I met Sasha at the train station. She was dressed in her customary jeans and T-shirt, but she no longer looked like a tomboy. There was something womanly and settled about her, and she gave me the reason. "I'm getting married," she said.

I stared, wide-eyed and silent. Sasha had broken up with a boyfriend last autumn. When I last saw her in February she wasn't yet seeing anyone. Now she was engaged. As we walked off the platform, Sasha told me she had met a local fellow shortly after my previous visit. They had been together only months when he proposed to her in the candlelight of a Belgrade power outage. Sasha accepted, but a date for the wedding had not been set.

"I didn't tell you, because I didn't want to do it over the phone," she said, levelling those dark, beautiful eyes at me. "I wanted to tell you in person."

I understood Sasha's sentiment. I had tried as best I could to keep our relationship strictly professional. I think Sasha felt the same way. But we had experienced a lot together: an election and revolt that had changed her life and this strange search for Gjorg's fiancée that I'm sure had altered mine, although I still wasn't certain how. Sasha had joined this project and this had created a bond between us. I understood why she wanted to give me the news in person.

I smiled when she said it and I was happy for her. But I also felt a little panic. Sasha's graduation into the adult world of marriage revealed how time was passing. In the face of it I felt as inert and lost as a perpetual grad student. Everything was changing. Everyone was moving forward in life. Only

Gjorg stayed in one spot—frantically pedalling a stationary bike, exerting energy but getting nowhere—while he waited for Sofia. Only Gjorg and I.

When Boris bounded up to me the next day for a meeting in our old haunt, the café in Dom omladine, I learned that he too had firm but as yet unscheduled plans for matrimony. "I am happy man," he said quietly. After the trip I had planned for the south, I hoped Gjorg might be saying the same thing in a year's time. Huddled around a table in the café, we discussed the next step.

"I want to finish this thing," I said. This was my plan. We would go to Kraljevo and use Boris's intimacy with the city's dense population of war veterans to find somebody, anybody, who had fought in Drenica. A large force had rolled into Rezallë that terrible morning in April 1999, and I was convinced there were men in Kraljevo who had been there. I needed an eyewitness to tell me what had happened there and to confirm whether or not Momo had been there and participated. (I also wanted Boris to check into the paramilitaries whose names Gjorg had given me during my last visit to Kosovo.) More than anything, I needed Boris to find someone like him, someone who would explain that day with the same intelligence and openness with which he spoke of his war. If we were lucky, whatever we found on Momo might shed light on the identity and whereabouts of his daughter. If not, Sasha and I would continue on to Mitrovica—Sofia's last known abode—to find out as much as we could about her past, and her present. She had to have left some footprint that would lead us to her now.

Boris wouldn't be joining us in Kosovo, because he didn't know about Momo or Sofia or the details of the shootings in Rezallë. As far as he was concerned, I was writing about the ethnic cleansing of one particular village where a lot of bloody fighting had occurred, and I wanted Serbian eyewitnesses to corroborate the stories told to me on the Albanian side. I was keeping Boris in the dark not because I didn't trust him—there was no one in Serbia apart from Sasha whom I trusted more. But as much as I had an emotional intimacy with Sasha I suppose I had also established one with this missing girl Sofia. Although it pained me not to be completely candid with Boris I felt that every time I shared her story with someone I was somehow betraying her. I was still determined to disseminate information only if I had to. And there was another reason I wasn't forthright with Boris. I was aware our research might lead us inadvertently into areas I imagined might be either compromising or at least embarrassing for Boris. By not telling everything I half hoped to protect him. If he was ever accused by someone who had divined my true purpose of helping me, he could truthfully plead ignorance and say that I had deceived him. I was trying to give him every politician's dream weapon: plausible deniability.

Boris, Sasha, and I left Kraljevo in Sasha's car at 11 a.m. on August 18. We made good time. Sasha may have peered over the steering wheel like a girl, but she drove like a demon. Before I knew it, we were passing Kragujevac, and forty-five minutes later we powered down into Kraljevo. As trees became power poles, and concrete housing projects and the City of Kings took shape on either side of us, everyone was in high spirits. Sasha had always been a happy camper on our Sofia excursions. She seemed to love the hunt. I was optimistic we would get somewhere. Boris had already lined up contacts in Kraljevo. "I ask my friend about this," Boris had told me yesterday. "He was VJ in Kosovo, but not in Drenica. He give me two names of cops who were in Drenica in the war." Two names! I was happy because of this. And of course Boris was happy to be home.

When we arrived at Boris's parents' flat, Boris took his mother in his arms and squeezed so hard that a girlish giggle came out. That was Boris's mom. Boris's dad wasn't around. It was *rakija* season, and the old man was in the countryside picking plums that would soon be crushed and distilled into liquid fire. A table was waiting for us. We sat down, Boris's mom fed us a feast of boiled sausage, *kajmak,* fresh brown bread, and fried paprika, and afterwards Boris bolted from the apartment to find that friend who knew the two cops who had served in Drenica.

Boris appeared minutes later with the friend. The friend had a slight build. The skin of his face sagged but as with many Serb men it was the fleshy face of a boy, and I read something else in his face—curiosity, concern, something— when we shook hands.

"This is my friend," Boris said, slightly out of breath. "He is a neighbour, he lives just here. He knows a guy, a cop who was in Drenica. He said me he will give the guy's number if I want it."

Boris, Sasha, and the neighbour spoke for a few moments, and then the neighbour was gone. "What's going on?" I asked.

"He said he thinks it's better if he talk to his cop friend first," Boris said. "He will talk to the cop and make a meeting for tonight. He will help us, he will help us."

An hour in Kraljevo and we had the help of a VJ vet and a tentative meeting with a fighting *milicija* from Drenica. Things were progressing faster than I had dared hope.

Boris was to check with the neighbour to see about that night's meeting with the cop. In the meantime we went to another café to meet another man I hoped would help us. He was Goran, and he was rumoured to be a member of an exclusive fraternity: he was said to have been one of Arkan's Tigers. Goran wasn't anywhere in sight when we approached the white tables of the café, clustered like toadstools on a side street just off the Square of Warriors. But Goran's young wife Jelica was working at the café as a waitress, which meant that Goran wasn't far away. "Goran he is little jealous," Boris said. With short blond hair and full lips, Jelica was a woman to be jealous for. Jelica smiled at us with eyes that looked tired and disappointed. Her discouragement may have been attributable to her husband, who—sure enough—sauntered up ten minutes later. Goran was a welterweight of a man. He had a fierce wiry body, a face as long as a bayonet, and, due to a few missing teeth, the gummy, jagged smile of a ten-year-old. When Goran saw Boris, he cried, "Borko," and they embraced almost violently. I felt excited and scared. Here was Goran the Tiger.

I had heard Boris speak about Goran before, and he was exactly the type of guy I wanted to meet for the search. He was a local gangster. When Jelica and Goran had married, Goran was an up-and-coming warlord. "He was very handsome," Boris had said to me earlier. "He was popular. He had many many thousands of Deutschmarks he got somehow in Switzerland." But the money disappeared. These days Goran scraped together some cash through various blackmarket enterprises, and then gambled most of it away.

Goran sat down in a chair at our table, and Boris asked what he was up to. "I lost three hundred Deutschmarks this afternoon on football," Goran said, shrugging. I wanted to talk to Goran to see if he recognized any of the names of alleged ethnic cleansers that Gjorg had given me in February, particularly the "paramilitar" from Raška. After a bit of gossip Boris asked Goran about the nickname of the fighter Gjorg's list identified. Goran raised an eyebrow.

"I know of this guy," he told Boris. "He's bad guy. He's not going to talk to you. And if *he* tries talking to him," he added, pointing at me, "this guy will just shoot him. He won't say a word. Just shoot."

Just then a tall young guy walked up and sat himself down at an adjoining table, and the conversation turned to him like a weather-vane. I could see Boris getting excited, but I didn't pay much attention. Goran's description of my potential interview with the Raška paramilitary had shut me up. Sasha and I drank coffee in silence. Then Boris—after ten minutes of chatting—leaned over and whispered: "This guy was VJ. He was in Drenica."

I sat up, and Boris asked the new arrival if he had ever fought in Likovac. I wanted to ease my way into Rezallë and the killings. "I never fought on the Likovac side of the road," he said, referring to the Glogovac–Srbica highway.[1] I asked about paramilitaries, and the 1ˢᵗ Četnik Company that Gjorg had mentioned. He had never heard of this company, but he talked about the cleansing operations. "The point is, the volunteers"—the men Gjorg described as *paramilitars*—"and the tanks always went in first and did the work," he said.

The VJ guy said the war had pissed him off. "I mean, what were we fighting for?" he said. "Once, our column was on a main road. Two bitches pull up in a shiny new car. They're girls from Kosovo. They pass us and roll down the window. They ask, 'Are you rusty lizards?'" *Rusty* means horny, and a *lizard* is an infantryman, a grunt. "We had to stop some of the guys from killing them. It was war, and these bitches are driving around in cars."

"Those volunteers were bad fuckers. They used to make jewellery from fingers and ears. They showed me."

Everyone stayed silent except for Goran the Tiger. "A Tiger wouldn't do that," he said. "They'd never make jewellery from fingers. They'd go straight for the eyeballs." Then he laughed.

We left to find Boris's friend who was arranging the interview with the Drenica cop, the man I hoped would have first-hand knowledge of Rezallë. Before I left, I leaned over to

Goran and asked him about his time with the Tigers. He had trained at the infamous base at Erdut, and had fought in Croatia. He shook his head. "It was a bitch war."

Boris's friend arranged the meeting for the next night. The cop said he wanted to talk. I could almost see Momo's squat, bearded form in the weak early light of Rezallë. We—Boris, Sasha, and I—met the friend at Boris's flat on Sunday night, and drove in Sasha's car to a dark parking lot about five minutes away. The parking lot was like a ravine; apartment blocks towered on all sides. After we parked, the friend led us out of the ravine somehow, and onto the terrace of a small coffee shop. The cop, a predictably monstrous character with big head and big hands, was there waiting.

He sat at a plastic table, and we joined him. I was introduced by the friend. The cop shook my hand but spoke only to the friend and a little to Boris. Boris squirmed, and Sasha stayed silent. I waited for the friend to disappear. The moment he excused himself I planned to ask Sasha to leave us as well. I wanted to talk to the cop with only Boris present. I didn't think he would be candid with a woman or a local friend there. But the friend stayed and smoked. The cop smoked. Neither said much. It was the kind of non-conversation I saw a lot in Serbian cafés. But I felt I had to let the interview progress at its own speed.

Finally, after fifteen minutes of lazing, the cop and the neighbour rose, ushered us inside the café, and motioned us to a long, dirty picnic table. The cop sat in the centre, the friend to his left, Boris to his right. Sasha and I sat across from them. It was clear that the friend had no intention of leaving. His face radiated the same expression I saw yesterday, of concern and curiosity. I decided to begin.

"I'm interested in a battle that happened in a village in Drenica, in early April 1999," I said through Sasha. Then I named Rezallë. "I spoke to Kosovars who lived there. They gave me their story. But I want to talk to Serbs who were there. It's important to me to get the Serb point of view." I flashed a harmless smile.

The cop shifted in his seat. "That village," he said. "I can just imagine what those *Šiptars* told you about that place. Those *Šiptars,* they talk soft and friendly."

Electricity shot up my spine. He had been there. I decided to back off a bit, to take a detour to Rezallë. I wanted to take my time getting to Gjorg's hometown. "Yes, they do," I said. "So tell me, what was the war like? It must have been a terrible time."

The cop sighed, as if to say, You'd never believe it. "It wasn't just Serbs fighting," he said. "There were *psi rata,* dogs of war, mercenaries there too." He mentioned a Serb girl from the city of Jagodina. She was a volunteer. "She had five notches on her rifle," the cop said. "The Belgians paid her to come and fight. She'd been in the Belgium army." The cop said there were a lot of Russian volunteers in Kosovo, and I paid attention to this because of the Russians who were alleged to have been in Rezallë. "The Russians drank more than they fought. We didn't want to grease their guns because they were shooting each other." He said the Russian contingent consisted of about twenty men.

"Look," he said, lowering his voice to a soft and friendly tone, "it was war, and there were many situations—extreme situations. But I assure you my guys didn't kill anyone."

I hadn't asked if his guys had killed anyone but I didn't get a chance to say this. The cop's mood turned like the weather, and he began to rant. "I'm not interested if a *Šiptar* left his wife in a house," he said. "It was war, and if someone is fighting from a house, we will destroy that house. War is a dirty thing."

"We went to Kosovo because we were patriots—not to kill and rob. It's never been a problem for Serbs to be warriors."

"Is that why you became a cop?" I said, trying to placate him. "Because Serbs are warriors?"

"I hate junkies, criminals, and faggots," he replied. "That's why I became a cop." He told me a Kraljevo cop story, and I let him digress because telling it seemed to calm him down. "A couple of years ago I was in a park downtown. It was night-time, and I found these two guys fucking. *Pičku materinu!* One had the other pressed against the wall, screwing him from behind. I walked behind them and I hit the guy doing the fucking in the back of the head. I hit him so hard the face of the fag in front smashed against the wall. I pulled off the guy in back, and then I fucked his mother. I beat him a bloody mess. Then I grabbed the other faggot, who was on the ground. But when I looked into his face, I recognized him. *Pičku materinu!* He was my neighbour, a big-shot manager in a factory. I had gone out once with this guy's daughter. What was I supposed to do? I just threw him back down on the ground and took off." He shrugged a shrug that said, *Pičku materinu!* What are you going to do? "I wanted to be a cop," he continued. "I didn't want to go to war . . . But being a war-rior is in our brains."

"We are a nation with a soul," the neighbour said. "We are proud of our country, and we have the best-looking women in the world."

"We are a proud people," the cop said. "And we won't accept anyone telling us what to do if we don't want to do it. You people in the West don't understand this. The Kosovo battle was the most important in Serbian history." He had now shifted back 612 years to the first Kosovar war. "In that battle we were conquered by the Turks. And so many Serbs died— 75 percent of the Serb population died then. They died to save Europe from the Turkish invasion. All of our history is about capture. We are a funny people, because we celebrate our defeats. I go to church at Vidovdan and light candles for those men who died six centuries ago. But that's not the reason I went to war. I'm not for Slobo. I fought in Kosovo because my father was born in Kosovska Mitrovica, and he's buried in Kosovo. When I decided to go to Kosovo to fight, I thought about my family. I thought about some *Šiptar* sitting on my father's grave. That's why I went to war. But I was afraid."

"It's normal to be afraid," said the neighbour.

"Only a crazy man is not afraid," said the cop.

I closed my notebook, put it away, and put both hands on the table. "On April 5, 1999, a force made up of VJ, police, and volunteers conducted an operation in Rezallë," I said. "I'm interested in what happened that day. Were you involved in that operation? Were you in Rezallë on April 5?"

The cop stared at me. The neighbour stared at me. "I was at Likovac for ten or fifteen days," the cop said. He mumbled on a bit, and then grew animated. "This is what happened in Likovac. A soldier went to the creek for water. A civilian shot at him and hit his canteen. It was a civilian! He was UÇK. That was the point—we were fighting civilians. It was like Vietnam."

"Did you fight in that village and that part of Drenica?"

"*Šiptari su pičke.*" The *Šiptars* were pussies, he said. "They'd hit us, and when we fought back, they threw down their uniforms and put on track suits and sneakers. Every civilian was a UÇK! In 1998, during the day, we'd politely ask them for their ID. At night they would attack us!"

"Were you in that village on April 5?"

He stopped his rant. "No," he said.

You're lying, I thought. I know you're lying. "You're saying you've never been there?"

"I passed through it," he said. He shrugged, and sat, and stared at me. The friend sat, and stared. The interview was over.

Something was taking shape, but it took three more days for me to understand. I wasn't overly disappointed by the cop's refusal to talk. Sasha, Boris, and I discussed the interview. They agreed the guy was holding back, and they suggested he might come clean or at least tell us more if we talked to him again.

While another interview with the cop was being arranged, Boris hunted for veterans. He came up with a great idea. Why not contact a war invalid association, one that offered support to disabled soldiers? Who better to speak critically and candidly about a war than a man who has been scarred by it?

On Monday, Boris went to the office of the invalid association, situated in the basement of an old Turkish-style building near the Ibar, which cuts through Kraljevo as well as Mitrovica. He met the association secretary, who was an invalid himself. He had all his limbs, but he confided to Boris that he had lost his testicles.

Boris didn't say much, because what do you say to a man who has lost his testicles? Boris told the secretary he was looking for veterans who had fought in Drenica. He told the secretary about me. The secretary said, "Come back tomorrow at 10 a.m. I'll have something then." Then he added: "By the way, we're selling exercise books and pencils to raise money for invalids." The message: buy pencils and you'll get some names.

The next morning Boris returned to the office with me in tow. Boris would retrieve the names from the secretary. I came along to ask a few questions. I figured that association members would have an idea of the composition of the fighting force that had been mobilized in Kosovo during the war. I guessed the association's secretary wouldn't mind discussing this issue. The war was over; the revolution was over. For Serbia it was a new day.

When Boris and I descended into the office at 10 a.m., we found a massive water boiler of a man who sat at a desk and growled into a phone. His voice, an octave lower than Boris's, sounded like someone rubbing the strings of a stand-up bass.

There was a conference table in the centre of the room, and a few men sat and smoked at various spots around it. One was the association secretary that Boris had met with the day before. Another was a balding man somewhere in his late twenties whom Boris had treated during the war. He had been a lieutenant and on the verge of death. Boris seemed amazed to find him alive. I was shown a seat and sat down beside an old man. He had a face as brown and furrowed as a ploughed field, and a grey moustache. Boris told the old man I was a journalist, and that I was interested in Kosovo. "Everyone is interested in the boys who died in Kosovo," the old man said. "No one remembers the boys who died in Croatia and Bosnia." He told us his son had died in Bosnia. "My second son went to Kosovo," he said. He crossed himself. "Thank God, he survived."

On the wall I noticed the association seal. It said *Udruženje Ratnih Vojnih Invalida Opštine Kraljevo* (Association of War Invalids from the Community of Kraljevo.) Also hanging on the wall was an icon of a Serbian saint, as well as several portraits of generals.

Once his phone call was concluded, the man at the desk stood up and limped over to us. "He is the association president," Boris said.

We shook hands, and the president told his own story. "I lost my lower left leg in Croatia," he said, explaining his limp. He had been an officer in the old Yugoslav People's Army (JNA) and had stepped on a land mine. He announced this because of his delight over the new French-made prosthesis he was walking on. The French branch of CARE International had provided the association with eighteen artificial limbs, and he had taken one for himself. I listened to the president give a spiel on the association—about the 122 disabled veterans and 108 children of disabled or dead veterans whom the association supported. He told me the association supported every branch of the services —army, police, and volunteers. He told me it was now canvassing for cash to provide wood and oil for families under its care, and Christmas presents for kids. Remembering the deal sealed yesterday, I asked if I could make a donation. The president nodded, and I gave the secretary fifty Deutschmarks.

Sticking to our plan, I asked the president about the war in Kosovo. I said I was interested in the force that fought in Drenica. Did he have any information? "There aren't too many men from here who fought in Drenica," he said. "That unit was the Raška Brigade." I already knew that the brigade that had fought in Drenica was centred out of Raška, a city due south of Kraljevo. "You should talk to people in Raška."

I asked the president if he could tell me roughly how many army units and personnel were mobilized in Kosovo. He levelled that look of concern I was now getting accustomed to in Kraljevo. "I don't know," he said. "I wasn't in Kosovo."

"You must have some records of the units that were mobilized there," I said.

He shrugged and said, "No."

Boris asked, "Is there any local veteran registered with you that we can speak to about Kosovo?"

"Go to Raška," the president said. Then he got on the phone to the war invalid association in Raška. Just before he ushered Boris and me out of the office, he said: "I fixed things. They're waiting for you in Raška."

"I do not understand," Boris said on the street outside the building. "Yesterday, my friend the secretary say we will get names."

I didn't understand either—until later that evening. At 5:10 p.m., I was in the local Internet café, checking the news.

Macedonia had stepped back from full-blown civil war by forging a shaky peace deal. A political crisis was flaring in Belgrade because of a rift between Yugoslav president Kostunica and Serbian prime minister Đinđic. I was reading about this, and contemplating writing an article on Đinđic, when Boris ran in the door of the café, panting. "Come, come," he said. "You have five minutes."

We climbed into Sasha's car and Boris explained. He had arranged an interview with Dragoljub, who was related to Boris's brother-in-law and had fought in Kosovo in the VJ. We drove to Dragoljub's farmhouse just outside the city and met him in his garden. Dragoljub looked to be about forty-five years old. He wore a white muscle shirt, and he sat us down underneath a canopy of grapevines on the edge of a large lawn. I knew that this interview would be as farcical as the others when Dragoljub's wife and children sat down with us. What man would discuss the shooting of eighty people with his wife and children at hand?

Seconds later we were told that Dragoljub wasn't in fact a veteran. His brother Marko, who lived next door, was the veteran. Marko hurried over five minutes later. He sat in a lawn chair beside me.

Marko was forty-eight years old. He was mobilized on March 25, 1999, into the VJ's Raška Brigade. He operated a mortar. He said his unit was stationed in Srbica on April 1, and later went to Likovac. "We were a civilized army," he said, perhaps defensively. "We didn't burn any houses." He said he had passed through Rezallë but had never fought there. He said he had heard no stories of loss of life in Rezallë.

Boris put it best as we sped away in Sasha's car. "We got nothing," he said. "We got nothing."

At that point I understood what was happening. Boris would understand it too a few days later, when his neighbour told Boris's parents that I was asking about Kosovo, and that no one should know what had happened there, and that Serbia must be protected, and that Boris should break all ties with me. For Boris this revelation was reinforced when he next met Dragoljub. "I didn't know what that reporter wanted to find out," he told Boris about our meeting. "But I was happy when he left because I could see from his face that he didn't get it."

In the end, Goran the Tiger did nothing to find volunteers for us to talk to. And the invalid association president spread the word around Kraljevo and Raška that I—a journalist and spy—was asking questions, and that no one should co-operate.

After the Marko interview, Boris, Sasha, and I went to dinner and discussed what had happened. Boris was so agitated that even a heaping plate of grilled meat couldn't soothe him.

"I'm angry," he said. He knew that Marko held secrets. "Once, when you were talking to Dragoljub, Marko leaned to me and said something. He said that during the war they found some Albanian men dressed like women in a refugee column. 'They push their women ahead of them just to save their stupid lives,' he said to me. He actually said this, 'their stupid lives.'"

"I don't understand. Why they do this? Why can't they say what happened?"

Of course, I knew why Marko and the cop avoided Rezallë like a leper colony. Terrible things had happened there. I knew it and they knew it, and it was time for Boris to know it.

"Boris, I never told you why I was interested in that village in Drenica," I said. "This wasn't just a battle." Then I told him the entire story as it was told to me by the villagers. Boris listened without a word. He stopped eating and stared down at the red tablecloth. His face was clenched, and he shook his head.

"You know, I believe this, and I don't believe it," Boris said after a long period of silence. He was wrestling with himself. "It can be that they didn't shoot them for no reason. It can be they were UÇK."

"Maybe," I said. "That's why I want to find someone on the Serb side who will talk to us."

I asked Boris to keep looking. While he searched for a witness, Sasha and I would go to Mitrovica and focus on Sofia's past and present. It was time to go to the place where the story had started.

"This will be difficult," Boris said quietly, reassessing our task in a new light that exposed eighty dead Kosovar men. "I told you everything what happened to me. But you must know I wouldn't say anything if I had done killing. If I killed, I wouldn't tell you."

CHAPTER 25

The Hospital

September 2001

Kosovska Mitrovica is where I had started the search for Sofia sixteen months before. It was not Gjorg's home. Neither was it Sofia's home, but it was the common ground where they had met seven years before. It was my next stop after Kraljevo. But just as Sasha and I prepared to take the bus south to Kosovo, I was commissioned by my newspaper chain to rush to Skopje, Macedonia. On August 22, NATO officially authorized the deployment of 3,500 alliance troops to collect and destroy the arms of Albanian rebels. On August 23, I caught a bus for Skopje. I asked Boris to keep looking for an eyewitness among Kraljevo's veterans, and I told Sasha to be ready to go to Mitrovica when I returned from Macedonia.

On September 9, I returned to Belgrade. I was determined to leave for Mitrovica immediately, but the next day I met with Boris first to see if he had come up with anything after I had gone to Macedonia. Boris had worked hard. He had gone to Raška, the headquarters of the army brigade that had fought in Drenica. His plan was to find army doctors or nurses who might have invaded Rezallë in the wake of the troops. Boris had conversations with a couple of doctors. One was young, a cousin of a guy with whom Boris had gone to med school. "I was in Rezallë, Likovac, all over," he had told Boris. "Ask me where I wasn't. It was horrible." Boris asked about Rezallë, but the young doctor didn't react. "I understand why you want to know about Drenica," he said. "The resistance from the terrorists was terrible there."

Boris cornered a forty-six-year-old military doctor who was attached to the brigade. "This is interesting for you. Why?" the doctor asked.

"People have to know," Boris replied.

"These things people don't have to know," the doctor said. He didn't say much more, but he did say: "I didn't agree with the clearing of villages, and I didn't agree with what was done to prisoners." Boris spent considerable time trying to find one particular doctor, a musician and young father, who he believed might have the sensitivity to speak honestly about the war. But the doctor always appeared to be out when he came calling, and Boris eventually decided he had been warned away.

That night I went with Boris to the opera house and sat in on a choir practice. The next day Sasha and I would be catching a bus to Kosovska Mitrovica, and just before the practice got underway, Boris apologized for not coming along. "When I left Kosovo after war, I tell myself I will never go back to that place," he said.

I told him not to worry, that I understood completely. Boris gathered with the singers at the front of the room and I sat off to the side. The conductor gesticulated and voices filled the room like a dense mist. The air quivered. "Oh Lord, I need you, I need your soul," they sang. "I haven't enough power to see you, hear you. Please help me. . ."

Please help me. The next morning at 10 a.m., Sasha and I climbed aboard a southbound bus. It was raining in Belgrade when we left, but sunny when we crossed the Kosovo border seven hours later. But no one noticed the weather. During the last leg of the trip the driver broadcast news in Serbian over the bus's speakers. After one report there was a muffled cheer. Sasha sat upright in her seat. "There was an airplane crash in New York," she said. "A plane, no, two planes, hit a tower."

"You mean the control tower of an airport?" I asked.

Sasha didn't know, and I couldn't imagine. But not long after we arrived at the Serbian enclave of north Mitrovica, all became clear. I should have suspected something from the commotion we witnessed after crossing the Kosovo border. NATO peacekeepers were out in force. Armour was on the move. The scream of tank and APC treads on asphalt ripped the air.

In Mitrovica, Sasha and I took two rooms at the Hotel Bešavac, and sat in the lobby in front of a TV set with a satellite link. The day was September 11, and Sasha and I, and a lobby full of Mitrovica locals—who sat at tables, smoking, drinking coffee, and staring at the screen—watched the towers of the World Trade Center collapse again and again and again. The men in the room were hard cases. Some were bearded. They drank brandy and held cigarettes in dirty bear paws. No one in the room was likely to be a supporter of NATO or the West or the U.S. However, most looked moved and saddened by the images. But the reaction had been different on the bus. There, a cheer had rung out, and I asked Sasha why. "They cheered because of the air strikes," she said. "They cheered because they think now America knows what it's like to be bombed."

I tried my best to put the whole thing out of my mind and focus on the task at hand. I wanted to find an official record of Sofia's life. I wanted to be able to draw a direct link between the Momčilo Neznanović who died in Kosovo in June 1999 and Sofia, who I hoped still lived either in Kosovo or somewhere in Yugoslavia. To get documentation on these lives we needed a local contact. We found a friend in Niki, a twenty-seven-year-old music enthusiast. Niki was Sasha's friend, and he had been at the bus stop to meet us shortly after we arrived. Niki had booked us into the Bešavac, and he met us later that night, which descended suddenly and completely due to a power outage. Mitrovica was as black as a city about to be blitzed, but Niki said it was still possible to get something to eat, and led us to a restaurant just off of Kralj Petar, the main street leading up from the Ibar river, where they grilled pork, chicken, and hamburger over hot coals.

I told Niki I was a foreign journalist and that I had come to Mitrovica to profile the city. Niki barely gave it a thought. There had been so many foreign hacks in Mitrovica over the past two years that he had stopped paying attention. Niki talked about Mitrovica, and basically confirmed things we had been hearing for the past year—that only about 20 percent of the population were original Mitrovica inhabitants. "The most of peoples are refugees from other places in Kosovo," he said. "Mitrovica people are in Kraljevo and Belgrade. Mitrovica is a difficult city now. These people are not clean. They're primitive."

While we ate, Niki told us about his life, and what a story that was. Niki was a testament to the invincibility of youth. On the surface his life was sadly simple. His father had left shortly after he was born. He was raised by his mother, and still lived with her. Niki went to school but left early to work in the nearby Trepča mine. He was injured, and partially disabled, and then turned to his real love—music. Niki reinvented himself as a disc jockey, and played at clubs and parties in postwar Mitrovica. The town was poor, and radicalized, and occupied. For all these reasons it had become a party town. Idle unemployed residents, especially the city's youth, had nothing better to do than rave, party, and hang out at one of many bars, restaurants, and nightclubs that made their real coin catering to NATO soldiers, UN cops, and western NGO workers. Niki parlayed the party environment into an avocation. But Niki would go only so far into the local scene.

"I like techno music, he said. "But techno—*dadang, dadang, dadang*—it's not good to listen to too long. There was a rave in Zvečan last weekend. You know, Zvečan is the next town. It's older than Mitrovica. A lot of kids did go to this rave, but techno is impossible to listen to without drugs. I don't like drugs. My friends do. Not me. It kills your health, and it takes your money."

Niki would know. Situated on the brink of Asia and along major trafficking routes, Mitrovica was an outlaw town that was lousy with narcotics, particularly soft drugs like hash and marijuana. Niki had just said no to drugs, but he had other pleasures. Square-faced, handsome, and as dark as a Spaniard, Niki the DJ had earned a certain amount of celebrity. "Every girl comes up to me at parties and says, 'Can I be with you, Niki? I want you, Niki,'" he said, shaking his head, marvelling at the beauty of it. He had women, he had music—but he had no money, and few prospects for getting some. "The eighty Deutschmarks in my pocket are my life savings," he said.

After dinner, Niki suggested a drink. We walked down the street and entered a bar on the ground floor of a concrete tenement. By this time the power had returned, and the bar radiated with blue light. "This is Sale's place," said Niki. Sale's place looked almost normal, like a tiny two-room bar you might find just about anywhere in Canada or the U.S. Blues music played over the sound system. We sat at an empty table and ordered drinks. The one thing that made this spot unique: the majority of the customers were men. All of them wore black leather, and most could have passed as extras on *The Sopranos*. One of the few women in the room was in her early twenties. She had curly black hair and carried herself like someone accustomed to life's extremes—be they political, temperamental, or sexual. Niki nodded at her.

"Her father, he is an escaped prisoner," Niki said. (Several Kosovar Serbs charged with war crimes had overpowered guards and escaped from a UN jail the previous year.) "He's in Kraljevo these days. And she acts like she's higher than everyone else—'My father is an escaped prisoner.' But she is a whore."

I excused myself and went to the washroom. While I was gone, Sasha casually asked Niki a question. "Have you ever heard of my cousin Sofia Neznanović? She's twenty-five years old. Went to school here. Her dad died in the war." Later, at the hotel, Sasha gave me the answer. "He said he doesn't know Sofia."

Niki was twenty-seven and grew up in Mitrovica. Sofia was two years younger and lived here. It seemed likely he would know her. "But he said the name is familiar," Sasha said. "He thinks it rings a bell."

I was strangely glad he didn't know Sofia. Still paranoid about security, I didn't want him remembering Sasha's question. The point of this visit was to get documented, irrefutable proof of Sofia's life. To do this, Sasha and I decided to explore the one place where Sofia most certainly existed: Mitrovica's school. If we were lucky, the local school would have her name, her records, and maybe even a photo of her. Sasha planned to hit the school tomorrow.

We retreated to our respective rooms. The electricity had gone off again, so I lit a candle on the nightstand, lay down in bed, and contemplated catastrophe. A dark community swollen with displaced, disillusioned people—explosions, implosions, and ruptured lives—unthinkable violence.

Tomorrow Sasha would check at the school. She would find something there for sure.

Sasha and I got up early and went for a walk. Sasha was scheduled to go with Niki to the school, but for now there was another place I had to see again; the Mitrovica hospital. This was the only place I considered common ground between Gjorg's memory and the real world. In most of Gjorg's stories about Sofia, the backdrops were as conceptual as the memories themselves. The apartment where he and Sofia had met, the café where she had worked, and the specific spot in the market were places I could never find to visit. But the hospital was another matter. I could visit it and in a sense share in their joint past. For no other reason than a pilgrimage, I wanted to visit the hospital, the shrine of their relationship.

Sasha and I walked west from the hotel, crossed Kralj Petar, passed a French APC at a corner, and wandered into a leafy residential area. At the next corner we turned and hiked up a steep incline towards Partizansko Brdo, or Partisan Hill, which towered over the city and was festooned at its summit with the Spomenik, a monument that looked like a big cement trough. This monument was meant to be an ore bucket commemorating the sacrifice of local miners in World War II. About two streets up we turned west again, and minutes later found ourselves at the gate of the Mitrovica hospital.

The facility had changed since my first visit here over a year before. Sixteen months ago, it looked like a derelict factory surrounded by a field of weeds. Then, the dark windows of the complex made it difficult to imagine this place as a hospital. The jungle that pretended to be a garden at the centre of the compound reinforced the sense of decay. Now the grass of the garden was manicured, and the hospital buildings, particularly the north one, had been renovated somehow. The building was like a woman fresh from a beauty salon. It looked different, but it was difficult to tell what exactly had changed. Maybe the building had been painted. Maybe the roof was different. Perhaps it was just the atmosphere. Patients sat on benches in the pleasant garden, taking in air or smoking cigarettes. Cars and white ambulances sat in the driveway. Medical staff in white marched in and out of the buildings.

The day was overcast but not cold, so Sasha and I took seats on a garden bench. I went over Gjorg's story. He had been a patient here for eighteen days in May 1994. This was where he had met Sofia and Momo. This was where it all began.

I knew the details by heart. Gjorg had told me the story in Priština in June 2000. The tale was simple, romantic, and bizarre. On May 1, he was placed in a room with three other men. One was an elderly gent named Milan who needed help to get to the toilet. The other was a crazy man who mumbled all day. On May 3, nurses moved the crazy man out and a stocky bearded patient in. The nurses called this patient Momo.

There was something about Momo that frightened Gjorg. Maybe it was his piercing green eyes. Maybe it was his Chetnik-style beard. Maybe it was Momo's authoritarian manner. Or maybe it was the incident that occurred two nights later.

Momo suffered from some sort of delirium. He would lose consciousness and begin moaning and thrashing. When Momo became delirious on his first night in the hospital, nurses rushed to his bed and gave him an injection, which calmed him down. On the next night he became delirious again. But no nurses came, and Momo thrashed so violently that he yanked an IV drip from his arm and papers spilled from his pyjamas. So Gjorg rose from his bed, shouted for the nurses, and collected the papers. In the dim light, Gjorg noticed that one document was some sort of police/military identification. The words were Serbian, but he could read it. The ID said Momo's family name was Neznanović. The ID said he belonged to Serbian state security, something Gjorg knew as UDB.

Gjorg now knew he had good reason to fear Momo Neznanović. Soon he would have even more reason to be afraid. On May 3, Gjorg was sitting at a table in the room. He looked up—and there she was. A young Serb girl. She had dark hair and a round face, and she wore a red sweater and black pants. Gjorg thought, This girl is wearing the Albanian flag. Gjorg saw she had a thin scar above her left eye. He decided she was beautiful.

This had been the beginning. The next day Gjorg placed himself in the hallway so he could speak to her. It didn't work. He had waited for hours but she arrived after he had given up and returned to his bed. But then inexplicably a chance came from Momo himself. He asked Gjorg to lead his daughter to the administration office to pick up some paperwork. Gjorg climbed from bed and led the Serb girl to the office, which was across the garden in another building. As luck would have it the administrator was absent. So the two sat in the waiting area and talked.

"What is your name?" she asked.

"Kemal," Gjorg lied, using the bogus name he had given the hospital in the belief that he wold be given better medical attention if the doctors thought he was a Kosovar Turk, rather than merely an Albanian. He had continued in the charade, and it appeared to have worked. Now the girl seemed intrigued by his mixed bloodlines.

"My name is Sofia," she said.

She spoke enough Albanian and he enough Serbian that they could make themselves understood. Gjorg was amazed at this Serbian girl's sense of humour and openness. She was different from the timid and skittish girls he grew up with in his village. This girl asked questions and made jokes and discussed movies played on RTS (Radio Televizija Srbije) and was not afraid to engage your eye.

They chatted for only an hour before the administrator finally arrived. But it was enough. Something had begun. After that he placed himself at the window in the hospital lobby every afternoon and waited for her visits. He loved being able to watch her cross the garden on her final approach to the hospital door. He would be able to stare and drink her down with his eyes without anyone knowing what he was doing. Often she would see him at the window and she would smile at him. As enjoyable as they were, these long gazes were not enough. Gjorg needed to be with her and speak with her alone. So one day he waited for her in the garden. When she arrived they crept away together into a leaf-protected corner where they spoke in private.

They talked about their lives. Sofia asked many questions. Gjorg was forced to lie to her, caught as he was in his earlier deception. But Gjorg was able to share real parts of his life without contradicting his lie. He talked about life at home. He said he was a writer. He said he wrote a love story called "Mixed Blood" and Sofia said she wanted to read it. He didn't have it with him of course. But he wrote it out again in school exercise books she brought him the next day. She took the story away with her to read.

The story was about young Albanian lovers in Drenica who wanted to marry but couldn't because the girl's father had promised at her birth that she would marry into another family. The Albanian word for promise is *besa*. A *besa* can never be broken. In this case it succeeded in forcing the young girl into a loveless union. Sofia returned visibly moved by Gjorg's story. "I saw myself in that girl," she told Gjorg. They continued meeting. One afternoon they crept from the hospital and sipped coffee in the back of a café.

Then Momo got better. He left the hospital, and Sofia never returned.

Standing in the garden between the two main hospital buildings on the north and south ends of the compound, I tried to imagine these visits. At a glance it appeared that the southern building, which looked older, was used mainly for administration. The northern complex seemed to be for patients, and I assumed this was where Gjorg had stayed. In fact, it had to have been. He spoke of standing at the window, watching for her and waiting, and only the north building offered a vantage point. I looked, and tried to picture Gjorg's face at the foyer window, his eyes trained on the gate of the yard. It was fun to do this, and perhaps even necessary. But there had been enough daydreaming in this project; what we needed was proof.

When recounting his time here, Gjorg had shared more than love stories. He had told me the floor and number of the hospital room where he and Momo convalesced together. He had even sketched a diagram of the room. I wondered how lost Gjorg was in the bureaucracy of this building. Did the room still exist as it had then? Was there any record, receipt, or file here that bore the name Kemal Isufi? I flirted with the idea of marching into the hospital and simply asking, but as a stranger I didn't think they would help me. Why would they let a foreigner from a NATO country snoop through their hospital records for reasons I wasn't prepared to tell them? For now, the school was the first and best place to make an inquiry.

It was stirring to be here. It was also troubling. There were still things that didn't make sense after a year and a half of investigation. I thought about the languages Gjorg and Sofia and Momo had spoken together, and the subject matter of Gjorg's story "Mixed Blood"—which he once dictated to me in all its three thousand words—and Momo's UDB identification, and a lot of minor details that just didn't seem to fit.

331

"Do you think it was possible in Kosovo in 1994 for an Albanian to register in a hospital under an assumed name?" I asked Sasha. But Sasha didn't answer. She just gave me a puzzled look. I knew what she was thinking. Yugoslavia was a bureaucratic and officious socialist state where you carried internal passports with you everywhere and needed identification for virtually every transaction with a government body. I knew she was thinking this because the expression on her face seemed to say: What are you talking about?

Around 1:30 p.m. we met Niki, as ebullient now as he had been the night before. The clanking metallic roar of tanks patrolling the city streets, which had seemed to go on all night, had apparently not disturbed his sleep as it had mine. Niki took us on a tour of the city, and I marvelled at how the place had changed. Apart from passing through in February during a late evening power outage, I hadn't been here since June 1999, when the project began.

Before, Mitrovica had always seemed so dreary and isolated. Now it hummed. People loitered on the streets, lugged straw baskets weighed down with groceries, and relaxed on the terraces of cafés. French peacekeepers, rifles in hand, wove through the crowds, and no one seemed to notice or care. There were old people on the streets. There were middle-aged men lazing about. There were a lot of women with babies. For the first time Mitrovica looked like a place where a person might live a normal life. Except for a bunker-like apartment building on the west side of town that was bordered by razor wire and guarded by French soldiers, there were no Albanians in the enclave to speak of, and the Serb exclusivity of north Mitrovica necessarily came at a price of merciless vigilance.

The logic was clear enough. North Mitrovica had become the Serbian Alamo. It was surrounded and outnumbered and now that the *milicija* and VJ were gone, the enclave considered itself defenceless. To preserve it north Mitrovica's leaders had implemented a zero-tolerance policy towards incursions. They would allow not a single Albanian to enter. It didn't matter if it was a bearded, gun-toting UÇK monster or an old lady with a cane. If an Albanian was seen crossing one of the bridges the Bridge Guards (or Watchers) monitoring the enclave would whip up a mob to drive them back. Niki told us the entire enclave was on alert. He spoke as if the war was still going on.

"I was a Bridge Guard," Niki said, "I had a Motorola. If there was trouble, they would call me and I would spread the word. We could have all of Mitrovica on the streets in minutes if there was trouble." Niki said he wasn't a Bridge Guard any more, but he was ready to take to the streets if called on. "We have to protect our home," he said.

Niki brought us to the sandbagged border of the Bosnian Quarter—home to north Mitrovica's surviving Muslim Slav population. The quarter was on the north side of the Ibar but razor wire, NATO armour, and stern-looking French peace-keepers prevented access from the Serbian enclave. Tensions over the past year had become so acute there had been attacks against Muslims living in the quarter, forcing KFOR to seal the area off from the north. You couldn't go inside but you could look inside and in the distance we could see inhabitants of the quarter crossing the bridge into south Mitrovica. Niki led us to the gypsy ghetto on the outskirts of town. We retraced our tracks, headed south along Kralj Petar avenue, and stood at the mouth of the main bridge. We then headed west up the long hill towards Brđani. During our walk we passed the vacant lot that had been the Ministry of Interior police building, and a large building that was an economic-technical college before the war. Now it was the enclave's school. Sasha nodded at me.

I excused myself, saying I had a meeting with someone from the UN. Sasha knew this wasn't true. This was her cue to go to the school's record office and request the transcripts of Sofia Neznanović. We of course told Niki nothing about Sofia or our real purpose in Mitrovica. For the sake of security I wanted no part in Sasha's query at the school. I didn't want Niki or anyone in the enclave making a connection between me and Sofia. I didn't want Niki or anyone even to know that I knew her name. This was to be a bit of personal business Sasha was completing on the side. Her story was that she was looking for the school transcripts of a distant relative who was unable to come to the city herself. After leaving them I trudged back up the hill to the Mitrovica hospital, stood on the grounds, and again imagined how it was seven years ago. Gjorg at a window, Sofia sauntering in the gate. I was still imagining when Sasha called. She had been at it only about twenty minutes. "Where are you?" she asked. I told her, and we arranged to meet at the hotel.

She was alone at a table in the lobby smoking a cigarette when I arrived. The BBC was on TV. Colin Powell was telling the world, "This is war." I sat down and searched her slender face for a sign. "Did you find her?" I asked.

"No," she said. "There was no Sofia Neznanović."

Sasha told me that she and Niki went into the school and found an administrator on duty. The administrator was an old woman, and friendly enough. Sasha recited her story. Her cousin, formerly of Mitrovica, now lived in Belgrade. She had asked Sasha to obtain a copy of her transcript. Sasha specified the girl's name and age. The old lady checked records and class lists. They found no mention of Sofia Neznanović or any name even similar. Just in case the age was wrong, they checked the records of earlier years, and found nothing. The administrator admitted that the records were not complete. Before the war the community's school had actually been in south Mitrovica

—the Albanian side of the river—and it had been hurriedly transferred to the north in the frantic days after the war.

"Maybe the girl's records are still there," I said.

"She said to me she has worked at the school for years," Sasha replied. "And she doesn't remember this girl."

How could this be? I thought. How could Sofia have attended school here without leaving records behind? Why did both Niki and the administrator have no knowledge or memory of her? Was this girl an illusion?

After I got over the initial disappointment at our failure, I realized I had to discipline myself, and focus on and explore only those things I knew for certain. Sofia's school life was conjecture on my part. Gjorg had mentioned she went to school in Mitrovica, but he gave me no details. The only thing I knew for certain—that is, if Gjorg's story constituted certainty—was that Sofia had visited her father in the Mitrovica hospital.

Sasha and I left Mitrovica on a late afternoon bus on September 15. As we raced north towards the border, I was already planning my return. I would come back as soon as possible with someone—the only person I knew—who might be able to get access to the medical community. I would return with the former army medic Boris Postovnik.

CHAPTER 26

Burying the Dead

Kosovo, June 1999

Not even the terrible sight of dead neighbours was powerful enough to erase the euphoria Gjorg felt at being home. Of course, these deaths hurt him profoundly. But the dead almost made his homecoming—and life itself—more precious. Gjorg had decided in the mountains at Berishë that he would not fear the Serbs. They could not kill him; only God could take his life. The dead were a reminder that his survival had been fated. Before March 24, they had shared many or all of Gjorg's feelings. They felt fear and uncertainty, and hunger and thirst and hope. But for some reason God had decided that they wouldn't survive; and for some reason God had decided that Gjorg would. It's not that God had prevented him from dying—He had given him a life. Living was a gift, and so was returning home. And that's why it felt so good to stand hungry and weak amid the stench and destruction of Rezallë.

Nevertheless, Gjorg couldn't avoid the grief for long. After I left Rezallë that first time, Gjorg visited the home of his sister Shota and her husband Hakif. He wanted to see who from

Hakif's family was back, and if there was any news of family. As Gjorg left the road, set foot on Hakif's farm, and walked the twenty-five paces to the family house, he sensed the news would be bad. Signs of devastation were everywhere. The cattle house that stood at the edge of the farm had been reduced to a mound of scorched wood, broken tile, and earth. The family house almost shared the same fate. The *milicija* had set fire to it during the war, but it had not been completely destroyed. Moments later Gjorg found Shota, Hakif, and their youngest children living among the ruins.

Shota wept and embraced Gjorg when she saw him. Maybe she wept from relief. Most probably she wept for her missing son, Agim.

Gjorg was relieved to see Shota and the children safe, and surprised to see Hakif. During the last days of the war Hakif had made his way to the mountains near Berishë. He had left for home around the same time as Gjorg, Kadri, and Ibrahim, but had taken a different route and arrived earlier.

But there was no sign of Agim.

"The police still have not released him," Shota said. "Now the war is all over, they will release him any time. He will be home soon."

Gjorg spoke gently to Shota, and agreed that Agim would be home soon. Gjorg spoke out of kindness, not conviction. After seeing the bodies in the graveyard and the trench, he doubted he would ever see Agim again. But there was nothing to do but wait, for Agim and all the others. Agim wasn't the only neighbour and relative who was missing. When Gjorg walked back to his home village from his sister's farm, he found it empty of people. Would any of them return? he wondered. Of course, he knew that many would return just as he had.

Every day he watched them trickle back to Rezallë. They returned from sanctuaries in the mountains or in towns like

Gllogovc or Qikatovë or Skenderaj or even Priština. They returned from exile in Macedonia and Albania. They arrived limping on foot or, like Gjorg, huddled in a tractor wagon. The women arrived with children, sisters, and grandparents. Men came back with brothers, sons, and fathers. Sometimes men trundled home alone, suddenly appearing in the village after months of wandering and flight. Such men were greeted with tears and cries when they appeared at the threshold of their home.

Gjorg was there to greet every member of his family. First there was Kadri and Ibrahim, who returned from Gllogovc to take stock of the damage. (Because the family house had been torched and levelled, both brothers decided to live elsewhere until a new house could be constructed.) Then Rexhep appeared, scarred but alive, from the hills above Likovc where he had been hiding and fighting since the air strikes had commenced. Then Gjorg's mother returned, and his aunt. Gjorg secured a tent from a local aid agency and erected it on the grass beside the rubble of his father's house, and this became home to Gjorg, his mother, and his mother's sister.

Of course, some did not return. Thirteen people from Gjorg's tiny corner of the village had gone missing during the invasion in early April. This was not including the eighty-four who had allegedly been killed on April 5. According to witnesses, all thirteen had been shot in a separate round of killings on the north edge of town three days earlier. The thirteen included thirty-seven-year-old Xhavit, who was completely deaf, and his crippled ninety-one-year-old mother Hajrije. Twelve of the executed were men, most elderly. Three were visitors.

Their deaths appeared real enough. Witnesses told Gjorg they were shot in front of a cattle house, and when Gjorg went to that cattle house he found bullets lodged in the wall and clothes littering the ground. But there were no other signs of them. There were various stories. Some said that the victims had been buried—and later disinterred—with the eighty-four who were killed three days later on the other side of the village. But this was not the case.

Eventually, the dead trickled home just like the living. Minutes after his arrival in Rezallë, Gjorg had gone to the cemetery and seen the swollen body in the open grave. At first no one had any idea who this person was, but he was soon identified as Rizah, seventy-six, one of the thirteen. Seven of the missing later rose from the fresh mounds beside the open grave. Eight of the dead were now home. And then villagers found shallow graves on the edge of town. The contained twenty-three-year-old Ajet and forty-five-year-old Nezir.

In the summer of 2000 a farmer ploughing a field came across a shallow grave that held sixty-three-year-old Hamit Rukolli. A year after the war the father of Ismet Rukolli, the young survivor of the Rezallë massacre, came home.

They were the last returnees. The bodies of old Hajrije and her ninety-one-year-old husband, Kamer, victims of the April 2 cattle-house massacre, were never discovered. And except for a few bones the remains of the eighty-four men and boys who died on April 5 on the south side of Rezallë were never found. There were still more. From Gjorg's quarter of the village alone five entire families did not return. Five houses remained eerily empty. A three-storey house, which stood empty on the eastern approach of the village, awaited one of the missing families. Russian peacekeepers, mobilized in the area, wanted to use the empty building as a base. But the village refused. They would not give up on their neighbours. They would not help the Russians kill their memory. They would wait for their return, even if everyone knew they would never be coming back. For appearances, Gjorg and his neighbours told themselves that the missing might have been transported to havens in western Europe or as far away as

Australia. It might take months or even years for them to return. This is what they told themselves, but everyone knew it was a lie.

Eventually, Gjorg and his family came to realize this about Agim. Gjorg believed from the beginning that it was unlikely that Agim had survived, but Shota never gave up. She waited; she refused to give up on him. She said there were many Kosovars still in prison in Serbia, and that Agim and the others were among them. The others were the seven other men who had been rounded up that day—March 31, 1999— as Shota and the women and children were marched away. These men too were unaccounted for. Shota's neighbours knew better and combed the area for graves, but no evidence of an execution or gravesite was found. So Shota clung like only a mother would to a son's memory.

"Agim will come home," she said. "We will hear from him."

And Shota was right. She did hear from him. One night she had a dream. Agim came to her and said: "Mother, I am home. We are home. You have been looking for my body everywhere in the village but where we are." Then Agim told his mother exactly where he was. "We are here. Look for us here and you will find us."

The next morning Shota told her eighteen-year-old daughter, Naxha, that Agim had spoken to her in a dream. "He told me where he is," Shota whispered. Then Shota told Naxha where this was, but throughout the day Shota did not go there. The location Agim had described was so near, Shota had only to walk to the edge of their farm to see it. But she refused to budge.

Later that day Naxha announced that she was going to fetch firewood. She left the house and walked to the mound of wood and debris that had once been her father's cattle house. It had been destroyed after the *milicija* came to their village on March 31. Nothing remained of it but charred shards of wood. Naxha climbed into the foundation and began collecting boards. After moving a plank lodged deep in the debris, she glimpsed sodden and rotting clothing, and knew she had found what she had really come for. She dropped the wood, approached her father, and told him she had found Agim. As honest in death as in life, Agim was exactly where he told his mother he would be.

When the men of the village excavated the cattle house, they found the remains of all eight missing men. Five of them had been from the village. Three were from out of town. The oldest was sixty years old. The youngest was sixteen-year-old Agim.

The eight were buried. Families grieved. Closure came to everyone in Agim's family except Naxha. Almost immediately, ghosts from the cattle house began appearing to Naxha. They visited her daily and spoke openly and kindly to her. Naxha did not rant or rave. She attended to her household work, obeyed her mother and father, and helped her younger siblings as much as she ever had. But she was visited daily by dead men who spoke to her as nonchalantly as any living neighbour or member of her family. And not just at night or in private moments. Once, in the middle of the day Naxha, surrounded by family, attending to some household chore, broke out in laughter.

Shota asked, "What's so funny?"

"Did you hear what he said?" Naxha said. "He told a joke."

"Who told a joke?" Shota asked.

"Nazim," she said. Nazim was a man from her father's cattle house.

Another day Naxha approached Shota. "Where are the playing cards?" she asked. "I want to play cards with Nazim and Isa."

"These men can't play cards with you," Shota replied. "They're dead."

"But Mother, they're right here," Naxha said. "Why can't you see them?"

*

When the convoy returned to Kraljevo, Boris went home. He embraced his mother, and he embraced his father with special passion. He was home from war. It was his second war. Yugoslavia under Milošević might have even more wars, but he knew that this one would be his last.

Boris was determined to live well. He returned to Belgrade. He moved back into his room in the student residences. He continued his medical studies. He pursued singing.

Boris put the war behind him, but others he knew and loved could not. One was Dragana, the wife of his friend Lucky. Kosovo was Lucky's second war as well. When he was drafted into the Kosovo war, Lucky reflected on the explosion during the war in Croatia that had killed two men sitting only inches away from him and spared him. He decided that the event held a different meaning than he had previously thought. It wasn't just that he was Lucky, like his name. "It was a warning," he told his wife.

Lucky had a dream just after he received his draft papers in late April and left for service in Kosovo. (A broken arm and a hernia operation had prevented him from being mobilized in March.) A dead comrade-in-arms from Croatia appeared to him. "You survived Croatia," the dead soldier said. "Let's see what happens in Kosovo."

While Lucky was away, Dragana worried constantly. His daily letters were both solace and a source of concern. They were loving but filled with desperation. "I don't know what we are doing here," he wrote from Mališevo. "This is not our land." Lucky wrote about the men in his unit, and about the hopelessness of the situation. He had gone to Kosovo because of the local boys—"his sons"—who were obliged to fight. He had gone to try to help and protect them. But he couldn't, and his letters were charged with frustration over this.

The sadness in the letters revealed a part of Lucky that Dragana rarely saw. Her Lucky was fun-loving. They rarely quarrelled, and when they did, Lucky always turned the spat into a joke. But his mood darkened when the war started. In early 1999, Lucky had broken his arm. He was convalescing at home when the air strikes began, and watched helplessly as his son-in-law was drafted into the army and sent to Kosovo. He fretted as so many other young men from Kraljevo were sent to war. He raged when scenes of the war appeared on television. When his arm healed and he received a call to arms in April, he reported for duty—even though he could have parlayed his injuries into a permanent reprieve.

Faced with the prospect of his second war, and visited by dead comrades in his dreams, Lucky tried to remain upbeat. During his last day in Kraljevo, he and Dragana went out into the city and said goodbye to friends and neighbours. "Don't worry," he told everyone. "I'll be all right. We'll beat those aliens . . . Anyway, it's got to be better in Kosovo than here."

During May, Lucky's letters arrived daily with the regularity of air strikes. Dragana was terrified that she might lose him, but there was hope. By mid-May there were signs that the war was reaching an end. Then Lucky returned home on leave on May 28. For a moment it was as if he had never been gone. He was the old Lucky, happy and hopeful. He told Dragana the war would not drag on much longer. In fact, they both believed it might end before he was required to return on May 31.

This didn't happen. May 31 arrived and Lucky boarded a bus back for Mališevo. Although Lucky was sad to return, both he and Dragana seemed to believe the end was near. In this they were right.

On the afternoon of June 5, a neighbour phoned. "What are you doing?" the neighbour, a woman, asked. "Can I come over to visit?" Dragana said, "Yes, of course, why not?" There was something in this woman's voice that Dragana understood only when the bell rang and Dragana opened her apartment door. Standing at the threshold were her neighbour, an army doctor, a colonel, and an official she could not identify.

The men looked grim and uncomfortable. There was momentary confusion, but Dragana suddenly understood, and then she tried to intercept and ward off the inevitable. She looked at these taut-faced men and spat at them. "What are you doing in my home?" she said. "Get out."

When she couldn't chase away what was about to happen, Dragana tried fleeing. There was no other door to the flat, so she ran out onto the balcony. She had not closed the apartment door, though, and the visitors entered her flat and followed her to the balcony, which overlooked a green and treed square. They gave her the news they were commissioned to give.

"Be brave," one of the men told her. "You have to be brave."

At first Dragana simply couldn't believe it. Standing on the balcony, looking out at the Kraljevo horizon, the world was exactly as it had been seconds before—the familiar rooftops, the unchanging skyline. But it was a world in which her husband Lucky no longer existed, and it would never be the same again. It was a mystery. How could everything look so familiar and be so utterly, unalterably different? How could there be a living world when her Lucky was dead?

In an instant Dragana's confusion turned to anger. She started to seethe. She stared into the pained faces of the army officers. "Do you really think," she asked, "we give birth to sons to be killed in wars?"

If the officers answered this question, Dragana did not hear them. But she did hear one of the officers ask: "Is there anything you need?"

Do you need anything? Dragana pondered this question. What did she need? Her partner, the father of her two daughters, was gone. What did she need?

"Cigarettes and coffee," Dragana said.

The officers left. They promised that Lucky's body would be transported home the next day. It was. And the army was true to its word on another matter. A short time later ten cartons of cigarettes arrived at Dragana's door. She was grateful for them more than the officers would know. During the air strikes cigarettes had become a scarce and expensive commodity in Yugoslavia. Tobacco had been her only solace during Lucky's absence, but black market prices made smoking an unaffordable luxury. Now at least she had cigarettes.

Dragana received little else from the army. She did get some food, which she considered inedible. And she received a government pension. The sum included Lucky's pension, for a grand total of 1,500 dinars a month, approximately US$45.

Two days after Lucky's death his last letter arrived from Kosovo written on the last day of his life, brooding over the insanity and futility of war.

Sadly, much of Lucky's last letter read like a military report. It was matter-of-fact and declarative. He wrote: "I will tell you how little human life is valued here." He wrote: "I refuse to lead these kids to their death." But the letter did contain one thought that made Dragana realize that Lucky sensed how close he was to his own end. He had closed the letter with the instruction, "Spend as much time as you can with the children."

On June 6, the army held an official funeral for Lucky. A red, blue, and white Serbian flag was draped over the coffin.

An officer approached Dragana. "Are you satisfied with the decorations?" he asked.

"The decorations are great," Dragana said.

Lucky's real funeral took place on June 26. Sixty-three soldiers attended. Most of the men had known and served with him. Lucky's gravestone was crafted by a young man. He offered to do the job without charging a fee, but he insisted he was not doing it for free. He told Dragana he was repaying a debt. "Lucky was the only officer who checked his men every day," the stone-maker said. "No matter if there were snipers, no matter what."

After Lucky's death, the war ended. Their daughter gave birth to a beautiful little girl. Daily life ground on. But with the exception of her granddaughter, Dragana accepted that there was no joy in life without her husband. She decided she would go on living, and smoking; she would do her best for her daughters and her granddaughter. But her life had become a lousy copy of the one she had once had with Lucky.

Dragana last saw Lucky on May 28, 1999. But months after his death, Dragana was able to speak to him one more time. Lucky came to her in a dream. He teased and joked as he had in life, but there was a timbre of seriousness in his voice. Dragana pleaded with him. "Why did you leave me?" she said. "Why don't you ever visit me?"

"Don't be silly, woman," Lucky said. "Now, tell me how old are you. You're sixty-three, yes?

"Srečko, you're my husband," Dragana said. "You know I'm fifty-three years old."

"But I am sure you are sixty-three."

"Srečko, I'm only fifty-three.

"All right," said Lucky. "I believe you. I'll be back for you in ten years."

CHAPTER 27

"I need you" To end this

October 2001

I arrived back in Belgrade on October 3, met up with Boris, and made plans to head south, to Kosovo. I knew this would be a difficult journey for Boris. It would be his first time back in the province since the war. I had been so nervous about asking him to do this, I had Sasha approach him while I was at home. Then I called him to get an answer.

"Boris, I need you," I said. "I need you to come with me there."

I was braced for rejection, but he readily agreed. "OK, guy, I go with you," he said. "I know I say I will not go back to there, but maybe it is time. Maybe it is good for me to go back." I worried that I was taking advantage of Boris. He was upbeat because he was that type of guy. He was upbeat because he was in love and hoping to get married. But I knew it would be a difficult trip. I knew Kosovo remained nightmarish terrain for him.

The plan we devised was to go to Kraljevo first. We would check once more for veterans who might have been at Rezallë. Then we would continue south, cross the border into Kosovo, and head for Mitrovica. Boris still didn't know what I was up to. He didn't know about Sofia or the truth about Momo. I told him that one of the fighters who had been at Rezallë had been hospitalized in Mitrovica, and I thought his medical knowledge and connections might help. I should have felt bad about keeping things from him, but I had grown accustomed to the lies and secrecy of this affair. Boris seemed to have accepted them as well. He didn't query me about anything.

We arrived at Boris's home in Kraljevo on October 5, revolution day. When we appeared at the door, Boris's mom stood at the stove making jam. The anniversary was not lost on me. Exactly a year ago protestors in Belgrade had seized the government, turned away the police, humbled the army, and paved the way for Milošević's resignation.

"Are you going to celebrate the revolution?" I asked Boris's mom.

She frowned. "Last year they set our parliament buildings on fire. Hitler didn't manage to burn that building, but the Serbs did." There would be no celebrations in her home—just jam.

Boris and I went out for dinner that night to discuss strategy. Because time was passing, I had decided this trip south would be *the* trip, the last leg of the search for Sofia and Momo. I was prepared to push things so that this time we achieved results.

The next day, October 6, we boarded another bus heading south. It climbed into the mountains on the way to Raška, and the entire time Boris chatted happily about his fiancée, his imminent marriage, and future plans. But he grew silent after we passed Raška. He knew the next stop was Kosovo, and he began to brood as we approached the frontier. He had taken this same route to Kosovo during the war. Perhaps he was reliving past fears; perhaps he was feeling new terror. Kosovo was a place that held horrible memories for him—a place where he had lost friends and narrowly escaped with his life, and to which he'd vowed never to return. And Kosovo was still at war, at least with the Serbs. Attacks against Kosovo's dwindling Serb population by Albanian extremists were still going on. Going back was to be surrounded by Albanians.

First we passed a Serbian police checkpoint. Border cops checked the luggage compartment of the bus and peeked on board. The bus powered off and seconds later arrived at another border station. Razor wire marked the frontier. Sandbags protected the station building. NATO armour stood vigil. Soldiers in crisp fatigues glanced in the door of the bus and then waved the driver on.

"What? This is NATO?" Boris asked.

"Yes," I said.

"Welcome to democracy," he replied. And then added, "I am back here. In Kosovo."

From this point on, Boris alternated between long spells of brooding and frantic recollections of the war. He showed me the spot where NATO fighters had attacked a Yugoslav position in a valley. He had watched the raid from a crag in the Kopaonik mountains high above. It had happened on the final leg of his journey home, when he had been on leave.

He talked about his friend Lucky and cousin-in-law Slavko. Boris told me that he assumed Slavko had been killed by the UÇK that day he disappeared in a drunken rage. His body was never recovered. Boris said his cousin Svetlana hoped Slavko had been captured by the UÇK and was still a prisoner. Slavko was prominent in Boris's mind, and somehow—I couldn't imagine how—he hoped he might learn something about his fate.

The next morning, October 7, Boris and I hunkered over a breakfast of oily scrambled eggs, goat cheese, and white bread, and I told him what we needed to find on this trip. "I think a man, Momčilo 'Momo' Neznanović, was admitted into the Mitrovica hospital on May 2 or 3, 1994," I said. "I need to find out if this is true. I may have the dates slightly wrong. But I need to know if this guy was in the hospital." I didn't mention Sofia, because I didn't want to conjecture any more. All I knew for sure, if I could know anything for sure, was that Momo had been in that hospital for two weeks in May 1994. The job now was to find paperwork that went back to the beginning of the story and established it as reality. There would be no record of Sofia's flirtations with Gjorg and their clandestine meetings. But if Momo had been ill and treated, there would be a record of it. We had to find that record.

I wrote Momo's name on a piece of paper and handed it to Boris. Boris inspected the note in silence as he listened to my instructions. Again he didn't ask me how I knew of Momo or why it was important to find him. He knew it had something to do with Rezallë. Boris was now as deeply enmeshed in this thing as I was.

Boris and I left the hotel and made our way towards Partisan Hill and the hospital. Crossing the city, I noticed that Mitrovica was as busy as ever. People were bustling to shops and the market. NATO armour sat at intersections. Farmers from neighbouring villages stood on the sidewalk of Kralj Petar avenue over bags of vegetables and bottles of *rakija* they hoped to sell. The air was clear. It was both sunny and cool. It was autumn. The year was dying.

Boris and I climbed the hill, entered that leafy suburb, and wandered onto the grounds of the hospital. "This hospital is larger than I thought," Boris said, standing in the middle of the garden and taking in the entire complex. Boris suggested he take a look inside the north building. I watched him march up to the building, mount the stairs, and disappear inside. I didn't go with him because I was a foreigner, and I figured we would be stopped at the entrance and our IDs checked. I knew that many hospitals in this part of the world operated that way; you couldn't simply wander into them.

Boris came back minutes later and confirmed what I had surmised three weeks ago. The southern building had been the first hospital building, but it was now used for administration and records storage. The north building contained beds and patients. That was where Momo and Gjorg had convalesced.

We left the grounds, and I walked Boris around Mitrovica. Returning offered a revelation for him, a chance after the end of his war to view both sides of the violence. Climbing the hill to Mitrovica's Brđani suburb, we passed the charred, skeletal remains of a row of torched houses. Boris asked about them. I told him they had been Albanian houses burned by Serbs, probably during the war. High on the hill, we could look through the ruins of one house, stare south across the Ibar River valley, and take in the burned-out remains of the Roma gypsy quarter in south Mitrovica. I told Boris I had been over there the day that Roma enclave was burned to the ground and the gypsies were chased across the river to the north. Boris just shook his head at the destruction, on both this and the other side of the river—the violence done to Albanians and the violence done by them.

Boris had figured out that north Mitrovica was safe enough for him, but it was still Kosovo, and he did have one scare that afternoon. We passed a group of youngsters and he overheard them speaking. "This sounds like they speak Albanian," he said, and from the look on his face it was as if he had wandered into a crowd of UÇK rebels. One of them, a lanky kid wearing a baseball cap, suddenly bolted from the group, sprinted towards us, and shouted something in Serbian. Boris's eyes widened. The boy then recognized me as a foreigner and began speaking English. "Please, I am hungry, can you give Deutschmark," he said. I pulled a one-hundred-dinar note from my pocket and gave it to him. The kid took the money and marched off. Boris deflated like a big balloon. "They are speaking in Serb, but it sounds Albanian," Boris said. "It is strange to me."

For the rest of the day we discussed what to do to find Momo, and the secrets in that hospital. At dinner, over a bottle of Vranac in one of Mitrovica's best restaurants, Boris told me he had an idea. He went over the plan in detail. It entailed yet more lying. It had a good chance of failing. Incredibly, it involved his own determination to find some news of Slavko, his cousin's husband. But this plan was the safest strategy I could think of to get information on a citizen of Kosovo who had obtained medical treatment in 1994. Boris, it appeared, had a firmer connection to Mitrovica than I had ever imagined. He had his own sources.

Boris held up a glass of dark wine and said, "Tomorrow is D-Day. I will find out something tomorrow."

The next morning, October 8, I awoke early. I couldn't sleep. We shared a tiny room, and Boris's bed was only a few feet away. I listened to him snore and wondered if he could actually pull this thing off. Everything was converging, moving to a conclusion, and I almost didn't want to continue. I knew that today we might learn that Sofia and Momo were lost forever.

At breakfast I saddled Boris with facts and details. I gave him the dates. "It's 1994," I said. "My sources tell me it was 1994, but you never know. So maybe it was 1995. So if you can check both years . . . I'm pretty sure of the month. I'm almost positive it was May."

Boris was nervous too. "I have to make sure my story is right," he said.

"You are looking for a name like Momčilo Neznanović," I said. "But it might be different. Close but different. Look for something that is close."

"I cannot make a mistake, because if I do, they will know," he said. "I have to be very specific."

"Charm them," I said. I meant the people whom Boris would be seeing—the officials, the contacts. "Make them love you, and trust you."

We parted at about 10 a.m. "I need you to do this," I said, shaking his hand. "I need you to end this."

I stayed in the lobby of our hotel, drank a coffee, and wrote notes. If all went well, Boris would be back in two hours. I suspected trouble when I looked up twenty minutes later to find him sitting across from me.

"I went to talk to this lady," he said. The lady was his local contact, the official who could help. "She was friendly, and she want to help. But she could not help."

Oh shit, I thought.

"But it still maybe will work," he said. Boris had been directed to someone else, another friend, another office. He had an appointment to go there tomorrow. There would be one more day of waiting.

The next morning Boris and I ate in silence. There was no use going over it all again; he knew what he was looking for. A satellite-fed TV blinked in the lobby. On it were images of the war then raging in Afghanistan. After breakfast Boris left to meet his contact. He winked at me. "It will be OK," he said.

This time I decided not to sit and wait. I wandered around Mitrovica. I went to a local Internet café and tried in vain to get a connection. I had another coffee, and then I returned to the hotel. There was no Boris. I exhaled a long breath of relief. If he wasn't here, he was out there finding . . . something. I sat down, ordered a *rakija,* and watched the TV. The news had been switched off. A few men watched a grainy black-and-white drama on Serbian state television.

An hour later, Boris arrived. I could see from his anxious expression that he had had some success—but something was wrong.

"OK," he said. "I found medical records. I said I am doctor from Belgrade and I ask for records. And they are there. 1994. It's big book. It lists names, but the names are listed by patients when they are admitted to hospital. There is one column for name, one for date of birth, and one for diagnosis. But I don't find this Neznanović."

"Is there a name like it?" I asked.

"There is no one like him," he said. "I look at the birthdates. Most of the people are very old. You say he was forty-five years old. There was no man less than sixty years in that time."

"Did you check the next year—the year before or the year after?" I asked.

"No. I could not do this. I had to be specific. I couldn't say I am looking for a man in one year and then say, 'No, I am wrong, it is the next year.'"

I was stumped. In my stomach was that butterfly sensation of disappointment. I wondered if this was ever going to work. "Come on," I said.

We left the hotel and went to the hospital together for a second time. The day before, I had let Boris inspect the hospital alone. This time I decided to go in with him. I had to see for myself. That north building was the only place where I could compare Gjorg's memories with the physical world.

I bought some groceries at the kiosk on the grounds and walked with Boris to the entrance of the hospital. I was shaking. I was nervous about being detected by a nurse, doctor, or orderly. I was a foreigner and had no right to be there. But I was more nervous about what I might not find.

We sauntered into the main lobby without being stopped. We passed an inattentive orderly, two patients in robes, and a pretty brunette nurse who had her mind on other things. No one noticed us. It was visiting hours, and everyone assumed we were bringing food to a loved one. I went over in my head what Gjorg had told me about his time here—the floor number, the number of the room where he stayed, and its general location. I tried to remember how he described the room and the bed.

We found the main staircase and climbed to the floor where Gjorg had told me he resided. The interior was clean and appropriately antiseptic. Sure enough, the stairwell led to a lobby area, and big windows faced the garden. I stood at the window, and looked out at a panoramic view of the compound. You could see all of the garden, and yes, you could see the path that led from the gate. If a girl had entered the grounds, you could watch her travel almost all the way to the entrance. Was this the very spot where Gjorg had stood, waiting, watching?

We passed through double doors and walked down a hallway. Doors lined the hall, but they weren't numbered in the sequence that Gjorg had described. If the doors had once been numbered in another sequence, the digits had been painted over. I stuck my head into a room, pretending to be looking for someone. The room was large—much larger than Gjorg had described—yet it could have been the room. It was simply much larger than I had imagined from Gjorg's memories.

We passed nurses. An old woman worked a mop. No one noticed our presence, and I started to calm down. I was satisfied. The window in the foyer confirmed Gjorg's story about the view, and one of these rooms could conceivably have been where he and Momo convalesced seven years before. But why wasn't Momo's name listed in the records?

That evening, again over dinner, I told Boris he had to go back. "You have to look in the other years," I said.

Boris nodded. "OK," he said. "I can try."

"This time I want you to look for something else." I wrote the name *Kemal Isufi* on a page from my notebook and gave it to him. "This guy is an Albanian. He was admitted to the hospital a couple of days before Neznanović."

I then came clean with Boris. I told him the whole story—about meeting Gjorg, about learning of Sofia, about the executions in Rezallë, and the boy's belief that the girl's father was complicit in this crime. I told him what I was really doing. For the second time in our friendship I was admitting that I had kept things from him. I had lied to him in order to encourage him to work, risk, and lie. Boris again put down his knife and fork and let it all sink in. He didn't chide me for having kept this from him. He asked no additional questions. I gave him some excuse for keeping the real story from him, but I can't remember how long I rationalized. I don't know if he listened, or cared. He simply took the sheet of paper and put it in his pocket.

"Tomorrow, when you go back, try to find this name," I said.

Thirty minutes later, as we finished our wine, we broke into a bitter argument. It wasn't about Momo or Sofia; it was about the war. There were uniformed French soldiers munching on pizza and sipping beer in the restaurant. The local waitresses flirted with one strapping soldier, and Boris said, "You know, that's how they treated us. It was the same. They were that way with us, and now they are that way with them." Then Boris brooded about their presence, and raged against what he called the hypocrisy of the occupation. Instead of respecting his point of view, I shouted all the predictable answers back: that the Serbs lost Kosovo, that they murdered and torched, that they didn't deserve this land. That night we both went to bed seething.

The next morning we were uncomfortable with each other over breakfast. But the argument was finished. I sensed we were both trying to put it behind us. Boris left to go back to the hospital one last time. I didn't think he would find Kemal. But I had to try everything.

That is why, when Boris left the hotel to meet his contact, I headed south to the river. I crossed the French checkpoints at the main bridge using NATO accreditation from Macedonia. I took a Kombi van to Skenderaj and a bus to Gllogovc. I walked down that familiar street to the office of that NGO, and I found Gjorg at work. He was inside the office when a colleague told him I had arrived. He came outside and smiled casually. It had been months since I last saw him. He wasn't expecting me, but once again he did not seem surprised to see me.

"Wait," Gjorg said. "I will take my break now."

Minutes later we were in a cellar café. I sipped a coffee and Gjorg held a glass of orange juice. I wanted to tell him everything that was happening, but I started with news that I knew he would want to hear. It was news that would change everything—if I could find Sofia.

"I found out about Momo," I said. Gjorg's eyes widened and focused on me, but he said nothing. "I found records of him. His name was Momčilo Neznanović, just like you said. He was in the DB. He was reactivated just before the war. He was in Gllogovc, so that means he fought in Drenica. So he was in your village.

"He's dead, Gjorg. He died just before the end of the war."

Gjorg blinked, but his expression gave nothing away. I imagined the news was shocking and sobering. Hearing of Momo's death had been moving for me, and I was just a tourist on this journey. This was Gjorg's life. The man he had feared and dreaded throughout the search had been dead all along.

"How he did die?" Gjorg asked.

"I don't know," I said. "He died in a place called Luzanë. Have you ever heard of it? Maybe there was UÇK there. Maybe he was killed by an air strike."

Gjorg said he knew of no Luzanë in Drenica.

Then I hit him with the other news. "Gjorg, I think we may be very close to finding something about Sofia. I've got a friend checking on Momo right now. If we find Momo, then we'll have everything—the address, the proper name spelling. I'll know in a couple of hours."

I was excited, but Gjorg was expressionless. I could see that all this news, although not conclusive, was too much for him. He then gave me a poem that he had written for Sofia in 1998. He had been meaning to give it to me for months. He had committed it to memory, and he recited it for me now. I scribbled it down in my notebook. I noted the first lines in particular:

> Perhaps we will meet again
> It will be a surprise for you
> Perhaps this meeting will connect us . . .

I left Gjorg and ran back to the bus station. This time I took a bus to Prishtina, and phoned Shaban, my old friend the actor who almost two years before had filled me in on the sexual politics of Albanians and Serbs. We met within the hour at the café of the national theatre, Shaban's unofficial office. After spending twenty minutes catching up on news in his life—since I had last seen him he had had another child—I told him what I was doing. I told him about Momo. I told him it had been officially confirmed that Momo was a state-security operative. I told him where he had fought. I told him where he had died and asked if he knew anything about the village.

"Man, do you remember at the end of the air strikes?" he said. "There was a NATO missile that blew up a bridge just as a bus filled with Serbs was crossing it. That was Luzanë. And that was the same date."

That was it, I thought. I remembered the incident. I had been in Macedonia at the time, but the story was all over the news. NATO sources said the attack was a mistake. The fighter had fired on the bridge over the Lab River just before the bus crossed onto it. Forty-seven of seventy passengers were killed in what those responsible dismissed as fate rather than malice. (Fate must have been in a bitter mood that day, as NATO jets returned twenty-five minutes later and destroyed the ambulance that had arrived to minister to the survivors.)[1]

I arrived back in north Mitrovica about 4 p.m., but there was no Boris when I got to the hotel. I started to worry. When finished, he most certainly would have come back and waited for me. I sat down and smoked, and waited.

Thirty minutes later, big Boris appeared at the door. "Where were you, guy?" he said. "I have looked for you all day." Then he smiled triumphantly. "I have it. I have it."

He pulled a notebook from his pocket and opened it. As I had instructed, he had charmed his way back to the medical office. He turned to the records of May 1993, and found nothing. "Then I look in 1995," he said. There was no Momo Neznanović, or Momčilo Neznanović, or M.N. anything. But then I find your boy. I found this name, Kemal Isufi." Just as Gjorg had described, the record listed his home as Srbica. And almost like Gjorg remembered, it stated that Kemal Isufi had been a patient between May 5 and May 23, 1995.

It was a strange thing staring at Boris's notes. It was like I was seeing into the past. It was like I was looking into Gjorg's skull. "But no Momo," I said.

"Look here," Boris replied. "There was a number beside every name. Yesterday I thought that this was some registration number, but today I realize it is room number. So I went down list and I found everyone who was in the same room as this Kemal during the same time. There was only one name. This was it." Boris pointed at the entry. The name read: Momir N———. The last name, the family name, was not Neznanović.

The room fogged up. It wasn't right. I knew who Momčilo Neznanović was. He was state security, he was from Mitrovica, and he died at Luzanë. This man Momir N——— was different. The family name was similar to Neznanović. It began with an *N,* but it was decidedly different.

"I ask about this guy," Boris said. "One of the ladies in office say she knows him from his village." Boris named the village. It was one of several I had suspected as being Momo's residence. "She describe him," Boris went on. "She say when she knew him he had a big beard. She also say he has a daughter."

"He used to be a cop?" I asked.

"No," he said. "The lady say he was a worker all his life." Boris named the trade. It was one not even remotely connected with the military. "He was no cop," Boris said, "and he was not in the war. She say she knows that for sure. He has been very ill for years, from since before the war."

I hadn't had Momo after all. The state-security reservist who fought near Gllogovc and died at Luzanë was just another sad casualty of war. I had had the wrong name. I never took the time to consider why Gjorg's name for Sofia's father did not even remotely resemble the name we found in the hospital. I was just too elated. We had Momo's real identity and it was confirmed and documented by medical records we could cross-reference with Gjorg's records.[2]

Through Boris's inquiries I also had the name of the village in northern Kosovo where Momo now lived and where Sofia was raised. More importantly, from what Boris had learned from the office lady, Momo had neither been a combatant in the war nor had he participated in the Rezallë massacre. The "paramilitary" in question had been another bearded green-eyed man, not Sofia's father. This was the best possible news for the simple reason that there was now no reason to fear Momo and every reason for Gjorg and Momo's daughter to be together. All I had to do was make contact with Sofia and deliver Gjorg's message and poem.

After giving me the information Boris looked on quietly. He had done his job. After months of searching he had found Momo. I wasn't sure why he had done it, except for his unique determination that nothing from the war should be hidden, that all the dead should be found, identified, and buried. I was so pleased I wanted to reward Boris, to give him something in return. I thought of Slavko, Boris's cousin, last seen on a drunken tractor charge outside Orahovac days before the war's end. "My friend the Albanian has a brother who was in the UÇK," I told Boris. "I could ask him to find out about Slavko. Someone's got to remember. Would you like me to do this?"

Boris looked down, thought for a moment, then shook his head. "No," he said after a long pause for reflection. "It's better that we don't know what happened."

"OK," I said. Slavko and so many like him would have to remain lost. But I had Sofia. She was found and very close to being reunited with Gjorg.

EPILOGUE:

The Wedding

October 27, 2001

The wedding took place in the fall a short time after I learned of Sofia's whereabouts.

In many ways it was a traditional Serb affair, but as Serbian weddings go, it was relatively small, and it was held in the big city of Belgrade, far away from the Ibar River, where my thoughts lingered. Like most Serbian weddings, this one was on a Saturday. Like most Serbian weddings, the ceremony took place early and the party began immediately.

Unlike most Serbian weddings, the marriage was sealed with a civil ceremony only; there was no religious component. When I arrived at noon to witness the nuptials at the government house, located, ironically, down the street from the military prison, I must admit I was disappointed that there would be no church service. I loved the incense and mystique of Orthodox churches, and the wail of the liturgy. But you had to respect the decision of the bride and groom, and once the civil ceremony got underway, it was clear that this venue possessed enough pageantry to compensate—at least partially—for God's absence that day.

The room had the high ceilings you would find only in a palace. The justice of the peace, a middle-aged woman, conducted the service with dignity and speed. And the bride—like all brides—was beautiful. You couldn't keep your eyes off her. More elegant than pretty, more proud than graceful, but graceful nevertheless, this bride commanded the room in an understated way. Her dress was straight and simple, but the fabric's ivory-white colour gave the dress and the woman real distinction. I guess I marvelled at the bride because she was both a stranger and a friend to me. I knew of her long before I got to know her. I knew her almost entirely through the groom, and that bastard was another matter. You couldn't accuse him of being graceful. He squirmed in his grey tuxedo, like a teenager fidgeting in his first suit at the high school prom. His boyish demeanour fit him better than the tux. He was a man, the best of men, but he had the innocence and boisterousness of youth. Now he was getting married, and I couldn't believe it.

He smiled broadly when it was my turn to shake his hand in the receiving line. "Thank you," he told me.

"Congratulations, man," I said. I should have said something more. For the couple it was a new beginning, but for me it was the end to a strange endeavour—the search for Sofia and Momo. It was only at this moment that I started to understand everything: Gjorg, the war, and Yugoslavia. After years in the Balkans observing wars and revolutions (from close up and afar), it took a Serbian wedding to push home the point and bring it all together—which should not have surprised me. There is no celebration in the world quite like a Serbian wedding.

After the marriage ceremony the guests piled into taxis and sped to the Dva Jelena restaurant in Belgrade's old town for the reception. I was seated at a long table with about eight young people, all of whom I didn't know. Sasha was supposed to be there, but for some reason she hadn't arrived yet. At first I felt awkward surrounded by strangers. But Serbia is nothing if not hospitable, and a swarthy guy across the table, a medical student living in Belgrade, took pains to strike up a conversation. "What do you think?" the student asked. "The wedding or Belgrade?" I said. "All of it," he said. "I love Serbia," I said.

Over the past three years I had been asked that question a lot, by Serbs and Kosovar Albanians. I always said the same thing, depending which side of the Ibar I was standing on. On the north bank I said, "I want to be a Serb." On the south bank, "I want to be an Albanian." In almost every case my questioners were delighted by my answer. In every case, I was sincere. I found both Serbian and Albanian culture enticing, and addictive, and noble, and maddening. That was Kosovo. That was Serbia. And like the law of human attraction and the mystery of the Holy Trinity, I found both places utterly inexplicable. Which—ironically—was the theme of my conversation as the lunch was served.

"It's difficult for someone like you to understand everything that has happened," another guest said.

"An outsider can't ever understand," the student said. "I mean, you can, but it's not easy . . . Do you understand?"

"You mean the wars?" I asked.

"Yes the wars," he said.

I asked him to tell me. The reason for the collapse of Yugoslavia, the bloodshed, the denial, was a question I had asked myself the entire year I tried to reunite the Albanian boy Gjorg reunite with the Serb girl Sofia. I wondered every step of the search. Yugoslavia was a prosperous, respected, and stable power when Slovenia and Croatia seceded in 1991 and the carnage began. Made up of seven official nationalities (the six national republics plus the Albanians of Kosovo) and scores of small ethnic groups (Roma gypsies, Vlachs, Hungarians, ethnic Germans, to name a few), post–World War II Yugoslavia had been a model of ethnic harmony. Until, that is, Yugoslavia became a model for something else: genocide, atrocities, and missed opportunities.

"You had all these nations," said the student, "and each thought they were right. And then there was the hate."

"Why was there the hate?" I asked. This was the fundamental question.

"Each nation is passionate about its hate," he replied. "Maybe Serbia more than others, maybe Serbia and Macedonia, just because of their passion." He said this with uncertainty, like he was not sure he believed it. "I myself am genetically incapable of hating. My father is Serb and my mother is Croat."

As the student spoke, I listened to the music. A folk band had been waiting in the restaurant when the wedding party arrived and began to play immediately. At first they sang mournful, mellow songs, strange songs that seemed to drone on in repetitive oriental stanzas. But despite the graceful simplicity of the music, the words expressed volumes of emotion, or at least that's what the student told me.

> *My eyes are searching*
> *for you,*
> *While my wine sleeps*
> *in my glass . . .*

The student suggested that the music offered an answer when I asked him about the lyrics. But I wouldn't learn anything by having him translate a few words. "It's not just about one song," he said. "The words have more than one meaning. It's about all songs. You have to know about the people and all the songs to understand it."

Almost on cue, a middle-aged Serbian woman, still beautiful although you could only imagine how stunning she had

368

been twenty years ago, stood up and began to dance and sing "Vranjanka," ("The Girl from Vranje").

> *There was a girl from Vranje who loved me,*
> *She was the most beautiful of girls,*
> *named Jelena . . .*

She didn't just sing and dance to the music; she exuded it. After "Vranjanka" the band eased into a popular *kolo*. A *kolo* is a folk line dance. The dancers form a circle and, hand in hand, shuffle forward and step backwards, and repeat the steps. The *kolo* began as a small circle led by the bride and groom and the best man, the *kum,* who danced with extra bravado because that is how a *kum* must act. The *kum* is the firing mechanism of a wedding. He must drink more, sing louder, and dance with more élan than anyone else. The beautiful middle-aged woman shouted, "Bravo, *kum,"* and the *kum* had to be pleased. The *kolo* started small, but people left their seats and the circle grew until half the guests were on their feet, pounding circles with their arms, and articulating steps that looked simple but, like the music and the lyrics, amounted to much more.

When the band played "Vidovdan," the student and I were still seated. He translated:

> *Wherever I go,*
> *I come back to you again,*
> *No one can take*
> *Kosovo from my soul.*

"For Serbs, Kosovo is the beginning and the end," he said. I know it was for me. The search for Sofia began when I met Gjorg in Kosovo and learned of the mysterious Serbian girl he obsessed over and pursued. It ended in Kosovo when I told him I had found her, or more precisely, identified her. The identification happened on October 9, 2001, when Boris discovered her real identity, her true name. That day wasn't quite the end of the search, however.

When Boris found me in the lobby of the hotel, he had learned who Sofia and Momo were. The revelation was both disappointing and exhilarating. It was disappointing because the end was much more banal than I had imagined. Gjorg believed that Momo was a cop and a killer. Gjorg had believed this from the moment he first met him in that hospital room in Mitrovica in May 1995. For a Kosovar Albanian boy like Gjorg, the worst monster the world could manufacture was a card-carrying holder of the UDB.

Momo may well have possessed secrets. He may well have been capable of violence. But as near as I can figure, Gjorg had imagined this dark side of Momo. In 1995 the UDB no longer existed. The mid-1990s incarnation of the secret police went by other names, and I had found no evidence that Momo belonged to their ranks. Momo, in many ways, was like Gjorg had remembered him. He was bearded; he was powerful; he was, according to one account, troubled. But Momo was not a cop. Nor, as far as I knew, had he ever been a cop. He had spent a lifetime working honestly, with his hands. His power may have come from a fierce temper, but it also came from years of honest labour.

Neither was there any evidence that Momo had fought in Kosovo as a paramilitary. Perhaps I'm wrong. Perhaps the veil of denial that masked so many secrets in Serbia suppressed this fact as well. But I don't think so. A brief investigation revealed that Momo had the best of alibis. So by the time of the wedding, I did not believe that Momo had been in Rezallë, gun in hand, shooting the men of the village or standing passively by as others did the killing.

This is not to say that the massacre did not happen, even

though there were no human remains when I visited Rezallë in the summer of 1999. Villagers had alleged that the corpses of the Rezallë victims were trucked away before the end of the war. Officially, these men were missing. They were neither dead nor alive; they were rumours. Then, beginning in June 2001, Serbia's new reform government, led by the DOS coalition that had toppled the Milošević regime nine months before, reported that police had uncovered mass graves in Serbia. One, on a grassy hill at Petrovo Selo, contained seventy-six bodies from the Kosovo war. By the end of July 2001 investigators had found four gravesites in Serbia containing up to eight hundred Albanian victims of the war. Although investigations are still underway I think it is perfectly possible that these grave sites—or ones like them uncovered in the future—contain the remains of the men of Rezallë.

These men were not killed by Momo. But even Gjorg, in the summer of 1999 when we first pondered Momo's alleged crimes, admitted to me that it didn't matter. "Even if Momo did not kill there, somebody did kill," he said. Looking back, he was admitting it was unlikely that Sofia's father killed these men, but somebody's fathers (or sons) did. What mattered was that they had been murdered.

After Boris discovered Momo's identity, we left Kosovo immediately. The next step was to find Sofia for the purpose of making contact. To do this I turned to the only person in Yugoslavia besides Boris whom I could trust: Sasha.

She was now a newlywed, ensconced with her husband in a warmly furnished apartment in a monolithic housing block in Novi Beograd. Sasha had retired from the Sofia search and found a life. I called her from Budapest and told her of our breakthrough. "We found Momo," I said. I went over how we found him and what we knew—that he wasn't *milicija*, and that it appeared he didn't fight in the war.

Sasha listened. Her utter silence betrayed her fascination. She consumed every word, and questioned me only at the end. "What about Sofia?" she asked.

I told her this was why I was calling. "I need you to do one last thing," I said. Based on what we knew about Momo and Sofia's real surname, I asked Sasha to use her contacts—both official and otherworldly—to locate Sofia, once and for all. I knew that Sofia could be anywhere—Kosovo, Belgrade, Montenegro, or Australia for that matter.

Sasha promised to be discreet, and laid out a general plan. I was satisfied with the security. "Go ahead," I said. "Just find her, and let's finish this thing."

A week went by. I brooded like a father-to-be in a hospital waiting room, desperate for news, praying for a girl. I sent Sasha an e-mail requesting an update, and then I phoned. "Nothing," she said. "We're still looking."

Another week. And yet another. Then one afternoon, as I sat at my desk, my phone rang. "It's Sasha," a voice said. We had a bad line and Sasha's words cracked and broke, but one phrase emerged from the ether with clarity. "I found Sofia." I pumped her for a few facts, and braced myself for her answer to the most important question. "No, she is not married," Sasha said. Not married—was she waiting for Gjorg?

I met Sasha in a café near the Belgrade train station. The morning weather had been temperamental—bursts of rain followed by summerlike sunshine out of sync with the season. After arriving on the night train, I had spent the morning walking the streets of Belgrade, killing time until my rendezvous with Sasha. I marvelled at the change. Belgrade had moved on. Gone was the atmosphere of isolation and excess that depressed and scintillated me in the past. Shop windows looked fuller. People marched to work straighter and taller. Expressions appeared lighter. The city gave off a new-found whiff of normalcy.

I marvelled at Sasha as well. She seemed her old self, but I sensed something was up and pressed her until she confessed. "I'm pregnant," she said. *Pregnant*. I could hardly believe it. In the course of our pursuit of Sofia Sasha had made an incredible transformation: from coltish tomboy to a woman in full bloom.

Sasha and I boarded a bus and headed in the direction of the village where Sofia now resided. We would not find her in Mitrovica. Sasha had located Sofia in a village that I had visited months before, not realizing how close I was to her. I might have brushed past her on the street. Sasha and I sat next to each other on stained seats, and she went over what she knew about Sofia, which was skeletal, but fascinating since I had known so little.

"She is not married," Sasha said. "But she has a job.' The position was clerical, with a solid local firm. "I think she was lucky to get this job." Sasha spoke about the family, giving me background on one of Sofia's siblings and details on Momo's past. Sasha confirmed Boris's account. Momo had no affiliation that anyone knew of with the Yugoslav security forces. He had been sick for years. He had been bedridden during the Kosovo war and was now crippled and dying.

Sasha identified the village where Momo and the sibling were living, but this community was not where we would be seeking Sofia. She was in a community to the north.

It was not raining when our bus powered around a bend and cruised into Sofia's village, but it had stormed shortly before. The sky was overcast, and the air smelled wet and fresh. As we got off the bus, I told Sasha, "Tomorrow we finish this. Tomorrow we meet her after two years."

We spent the rest of the day settling in, hatching a plan. We decided that Sasha would make the initial contact with Sofia and invite her to meet with me. In my wallet I carried two photos: a portrait of Gjorg, looking square-jawed and healthy, and a shot of Gjorg and his mother in the backyard of the farm. When Sasha brought Sofia to a quiet table in a near-by café, I thought I'd give her the photos. I wanted to gauge her reaction at seeing Gjorg after all these years. And I thought it might intrigue her to see his mother.

The next day we found the building where Sofia worked. We walked by the concrete structure together and gave it a once-over. The building was two storeys tall and sadly institutional-looking. Its demeanour was brightened by secretaries and clerks, middle-aged and attractive local women, raven-haired and full-bodied, who breezed in and out of the main entrance. Sasha and I retreated a safe distance and went over the plan once again. I wished her good luck, and she marched off.

She returned alone ten minutes later. She had a whimsical half-frown on her face that suggested something had gone wrong. "Well, she was in there," Sasha said. "I talked with her."

"And?" I said.

"She doesn't want to meet. She said no."

I was stunned. *She doesn't want to meet?* I got Sasha to describe the encounter. Her account was true to the plan. She spoke to Sofia alone. She asked if she could meet Sofia for a coffee. There was no reason why Sofia wouldn't have met Sasha, a harmless young Serb woman much like herself.

"What do you think happened?" I asked.

Sasha thought a moment. "I told her I heard she comes from an old Kosovo family," Sasha said. "She got very worried when I mentioned her father."

I felt helpless and angry. I was actually angry at this young girl! We had come all this way—hundreds (if not thousands) of kilometres over two years. We had her. She was sitting a hundred metres away, in a cubicle in a decaying building I could see from where I stood. She was right there, but I couldn't reach her. Why the hell did she not want to meet?

This was Sofia—impervious to bigotry and hatred, open and optimistic. The possibility that she would not talk had simply never occurred to me.

Sasha and I paced around the village as I tried to figure out, what now? Sasha told me that Sofia seemed afraid. "Afraid of what?" I asked. Sasha shrugged. She didn't know. I couldn't force this girl to converse with me. I couldn't stalk her. We rejected descending on her home, hammering on her door, demanding a meeting. For want of a better idea we positioned ourselves where we would see her leave the building after work. I would not be able to talk to her this day, I might not be able to speak to her ever—but I needed to see her. As much as I was frustrated, I also ached with envy that Sasha had spoken with her face to face, and I hadn't.

We lurked like muggers—waiting silently, eyes trained in the direction Sofia would be coming . . . if she came. Time passed. People passed. Suddenly, Sasha became alert. "That's her," she said, calmly, matter-of-factly. "That's Sofia."

I saw a young woman. She was dressed stylishly—black slacks and a white pullover covered by a bulky leather jacket. She sprang slightly with each step, like a girl. Had Gjorg been similarly charmed by Sofia's girlish spring as he watched her from the window of the hospital all those years before? Even at a distance one feature—her eyes—shone out. Warm, brown, bottomless, her eyes wrested your attention and threw the rest of her out of focus. At a distance I couldn't tell whether they were eyes that emoted more than they took in. They were eyes you didn't forget.

In a moment my understanding of the project had changed. I had to doubt myself and my motives. Did I want to meet her for the wrong reason? I had become obsessively curious about her. I wanted her side of the story. About her. About Gjorg. About their strange courtship.

But in fact I didn't really need to interview this girl. This had never been my responsibility. Two years before, Gjorg had asked me to find Sofia for him and report back. I had found her just as he had asked. Now I had only one recourse: to go straight to Kosovo and report all of this to Gjorg, and learn what he wanted to do about it. I was here not to satisfy my curiosity but to do some good I still found difficult to understand.

That evening over dinner I told Sasha my plan. I would go to Albanian Kosovo, to Gjorg's home, and inform him of the breakthrough—that we had found her, that I had seen her with my own eyes.

"What do you think the boy will do when you tell him?" Sasha asked, sipping a glass of Vranac wine.

"I don't know," I said. "I'll offer to deliver a letter to her from him."

I left the next morning. I asked Sasha to stay put and lie low until I returned. "I'll only be gone a couple of days," I said.

I phoned Gjorg from Priština and told him I was coming to see him. I didn't reveal the purpose of my visit. He assumed it was a social call, and when I appeared at the door of his home, or rather Kadri's home—the post-war dwelling Gjorg called "the house of my brother"—it was early evening, and Gjorg ushered me into the basement *óda*.

The expansive wood-panelled room, bordered on three walls by a horseshoe-shaped sofa of foam mattresses, appeared the same as it had during my last visit, a year before—although the decor had hardened perceptibly. An Albanian flag, the black double-headed eagle on a blood-red backdrop, adorned the centre of the wall directly across from the room's entrance, making the nationalist symbol the first thing your eyes met when entering the room. Beside the flag was a calendar featuring a portrait of the great Albanian hero Skenderbeg, who fought the Turks centuries ago. And beside

the likeness of Skenderbeg was a copy of a famous photograph of the fallen UÇK commander Adem Jashari—bearded,
bearish, and defiantly sporting khaki and ammunition belts,
gazing out at a vista that would prove to be brief, bloody, and
more successful than the martyred guerrilla leader could have
imagined. Jashari was probably only months or weeks or even
days from mutilation and death when that photo was taken;
but now, three years after his death, Kosovo was on the verge
of becoming an almost exclusively Albanian territory.

"Do not go to Priština," Gjorg said. "You will stay here this
night. Then we will have time to speak about things."

Speak about things. Did he want to speak about the same
thing I did? I accepted Gjorg's invitation. That evening I
feasted with Gjorg, Kadri, and Ibrahim sitting cross-legged on
the floor of the *óda*. The dinner began with the customary
washing. Lean and long-faced Ibrahim approached me on the
low sofa carrying a carafe and a pail as I sat. I held out my
hands, and he poured water over them and into the pail
below. I wiped my hands on a towel draped over his shoulder.
Ibrahim offered this same service to Kadri and Gjorg, and
then Gjorg left the *óda* and returned with a large circular tray
that he placed on the floor and we huddled around. The tray
held dishes containing roasted chicken legs, rice, scrambled
eggs, and fried green peppers. Everyone tore pieces from a
round loaf of fresh *búka* that Kadri proudly announced was
baked by his wife. We drank water from a common glass, and
after the meal tray was removed. Gjorg and I reclined on the
sofa, sipped sweet tea that Ibrahim boiled on a hot plate in
the corner of the *óda*, and talked.

The horizon framed in the window faded to grey and then
blackened. Night descended with a fury. Heavy rain pelted
the house and pounded the hard soil of his farm. And Gjorg
relived the journey that had just ended when I met him at
that bend in the road in Drenica, days after the end of the air

strikes. Gjorg remounted the clearing where he feigned death to confuse police snipers and was given up for dead by his cousins. He wandered down dark stretches of road, eluded *milicija* checkpoints, endured hunger, and rejoiced as NATO fighters roared overhead. He returned to villages like Tushilë, Qikatovë, Bajicë, Qirez, and Obri e Úlët—swollen with lost and roving souls just like himself. He marched into the mountains near Berishë and foraged for food and water. He lost hope and gained the peaceful fatalism that all of his travails had been ordained by God and God alone.

At one point the power went out—a habitual occurrence in post-war Kosovo—and Gjorg spoke by candlelight. Hours after beginning, Gjorg had relived and recounted the entire war. He resurrected many of the people with whom he had survived the ordeal: Kadri, Hakif, and Ibrahim. He talked about the girl Floria whom he met at Qirez and rediscovered in Qikatovë.

He did not mention Sofia, which—for me and perhaps Gjorg as well—made her present as a memory, desire, or final destination at every juncture. I wasn't surprised by Sofia's absence from his account. His brothers lingered in the *óda*, and Gjorg had said that Sofia was a chapter in his life he would not discuss in his family home.

So I waited until the next morning to tell Gjorg the news about Sofia. He was about to drive me to Gllogovc. He was loading bags of grain into the trunk of the family's car to take to a local mill, where it would be ground into flour.

"Gjorg, we need to talk in private," I said. "Do you have time to speak in Gllogovc?"

He eyed me with curiosity and led me in the direction of the cornfield. "We can speak here," he said.

This was the approximate spot where he had confessed so much about Sofia that summer after the war. But this backyard bore little resemblance to the one I remembered. The green tent that was home to him, his mother, and his aunt after the NATO occupation was still there, but now it sheltered coal and firewood. He had torn up the grass just in front of the cornfield and built a greenhouse from clear plastic and rough timber he had harvested from the woods. Inside the greenhouse, young pepper and tomato plants thrived—because the farm now had water. Gjorg had used thousands of the Deutschmarks he had earned from his job at the Gllogovc NGO to have a well dug, a gas-operated pump installed, and a pipeline laid that would feed his father's once arid farm and his brother's house with water.

"Gjorg," I said after we had mounted the empty cornfield and marched away from the house, "I . . . I found her." I was nervous and excited. Almost four years after I learned of Gjorg's quest for the girl Sofia, the search was over. Almost over. As requested by him and promised by me, I had finally located her. There was now nothing for it but a reunion.

"Found who?" Gjorg said.

I stopped. I couldn't fathom the question. Who? I thought. *Her!* The her I had been thinking incessantly about for months. "Sofia," I said. "I know where she is, and I saw her." I smiled broadly and awaited a smile, or a shout, or some expression of thrill and anticipation from Gjorg.

Instead, Gjorg tightened his face, looked down into the furrowed ground, and then glanced back at me. "You did see her? You did see Sofia?"

"Yes, yes," I said. "She's alive. She's not married, and I know where she is. Gjorg, the name was different. That was why it was so hard to find her."

I raised the issue of her family name to get some explanation for it. Despite the fear and half-truths that coiled around their relationship, I was still not sure how he could get her name wrong. But Gjorg simply nodded when I told him her real name, and I rambled on. I told him what I knew about her current circumstances. I described her job, the village she now lived in, and what little I had culled about her family. Then I summoned Momo.

"I also found out about her father Momo. He wasn't a cop, and as far as I know, he wasn't state security." I told Gjorg his job. "And it was impossible he fought in Drenica during the war. Momo didn't kill your family or your neighbours. Whoever did, it wasn't Momo."

I figured I had re-erected a bridge between them. Everything was set for a meeting. Sofia was alive. She was conspicuously alone and—for all I knew—awaiting Gjorg. And the one obstacle—Momo, the tyrant, the suspected mass murderer—no longer separated them. Gjorg could consider Sofia without the agony of believing her own father had brought murder and mutilation to his family and home. He no longer had to fear him.

"We found her two days ago," I said. "That's why I came. I wanted to tell you right away. I wanted to ask you what you want me to do. If you want, I can deliver a message to her."

A message seemed the best course of action. Since Gjorg could not cross into Serbia to visit her himself, I could facilitate the first communication, and perhaps a future meeting.

Gjorg resumed walking. "I want you to do nothing," he said.

I shook myself. "Nothing?"

"Yes," he said.

"Why? I know where she is. I've seen her. Why not communicate with her? Write her a note, and I'll make sure she gets it." I was feeling weighed down by the same sense of frustration that had hit me two days before, when Sofia had refused to meet with Sasha. The story was ending but not how I imagined it would. And it was driving me crazy. "I don't understand why you don't want to write her," I said, exasperated.

"This is the reason," Gjorg said. "It is over between us."

I acted shocked, but I wasn't. Midway through the search Gjorg had lost his interest in Sofia. He had even started a relationship with a young Albanian girl: Floria, the brave young girl who foraged for food with him in Qikatovë. When I went to Gllogovc on October 9 and told Gjorg that I had found Momo and was close to finding Sofia, he had passed on a poem. I thought the poem was for Sofia. The first lines were: "Perhaps we will meet again / It will be a surprise for you / Perhaps this meeting will connect us . . ." But when I reread the entire poem afterwards, I realized it was a message for me. The verse was a valedictory. The next lines read: ". . . Perhaps this meeting will connect us / But I cannot believe it / Fly away, fly away my love / To somewhere / A safe place / Go somewhere far away."

Gjorg had been trying to tell me that his interest in reconciling with Sofia had waned. But at the time I didn't try to decipher his message. In truth, I didn't want to. Months before, even in early 2001 when I had briefly discontinued the search, I was moving forward under my own steam. I wanted to find this girl for my own reasons. Some of the reasons were crass and professional: by this stage the search had become a journalistic project that I wanted to see through to its conclusion. But also, I personally wanted to know. I wanted to know if Sofia existed or had ever existed. I wanted to know long after Gjorg had stopped caring.

When I look back, Gjorg's indifference was probably the message contained in all the brief and lonesome phone calls I received at home and in Serbia while I searched. At the time, I told myself that he was urging me on. And maybe he was at times. Maybe his moods and desires fluctuated. Gjorg is a complicated man, and I still don't understand him. But now I think he was asking me to stop. But the real reason is as transparent as waters of the Ibar that separates Serbian and

Albanian Kosovo. Before the 1999 war there was a belief that Kosovo could continue as a home to both Serbs and Albanians. This notion burned like a torch even in the disillusionment of NATO's occupation of Kosovo, when Gjorg returned to his village and asked me to try to find Sofia. He believed—and I believe he was sincere—that a relationship between a Serb and an Albanian in post-war Kosovo was possible. But this idealistic flame died out with every Serb villager who was chased from Kosovo after NATO's arrival. Within months Kosovo was cleansed of over 90 percent of its Serbs. More importantly, the psychological landscape of this patch of the Balkans had been altered. The NATO-monitored peace did not bring Serbs and Albanians back together. With peace, hatred in Kosovo not only continued, it intensified. By October 2001, Serbs and Albanians were too far removed for Gjorg and Sofia to come back together.

We walked the length of the cornfield and back. As we approached the farmhouse, where Kadri was loading the car, I was still pressing Gjorg, "Why? After all this time, why won't you communicate with her now that we have her?"

Stopping just out of Kadri's earshot, Gjorg turned to me and delivered his last words. "Before, I didn't know who I wanted to be with. I'm with Albanian people now. I found myself.

"It's over," he said with a tone of finality. "We'll never speak of this again."

I nodded. "We'll never speak of this again," I said.

It took Gjorg only thirty minutes to break his own vow. Standing with me in the parking lot at Gllogovc, as I waited for the bus to leave, Gjorg said, his face clenched and pained, "You told me about her. I did forget about her, and now I'll think about her for the next six months."

"I'm sorry, Gjorg," I said as I climbed on my bus. "I thought you would want to know."

382

I was sorry if I had rekindled the obsession that had tormented him for years, especially if it was an obsession he could not easily sate or solve. I was sorry because I knew the feeling well. Sofia had become a bit of an obsession for me as well—which is why I couldn't do as he had asked. Gjorg had told me it was over and to drop the matter of Sofia, but this was impossible. I had spent two years looking for this woman, and now that I had located her, I could not simply walk away without contacting her.

I returned to Sofia's community by bus as quickly as I could. I found Sasha in the café of our small hotel, and I told her about my meeting with Gjorg. She was as surprised as I had pretended to be. "So that is all?" she said. "We won't try to see Sofia again?"

"No," I said. Then I told her what I wanted—no, needed—to do.

The next morning we found Sofia, followed her, and ambushed her in a discreet corner of the village. As Sasha tried to soothe her—"Hello! What a coincidence it is to meet up again"—I stood back and watched.

At this stage I knew I no longer had any right to mention Gjorg to her or to ask questions about their past. There was so much I wanted to know, but I had no right to any of it. But I decided I did deserve contact—basic face-to-face contact. There was just one thing I had every right to know. So just before we descended on the poor girl, I drank her in from close up. I was searching for a quality—elegance, grace, sensitivity . . . *something*—that might explain Gjorg's obsession. What allure could any woman possess that would compel a man to wander a war zone for years in search of her?

I stepped forward and extended my hand. She turned to me, tentatively took my hand, and focused those eyes on me. Lord, those eyes were wet and deep. They were the type of eyes you could swim in. They were like caves you could stumble into, and get lost in, and find yourself at the mythical earth's centre. Or were they? Perhaps the depth was a mirage? Perhaps they were shiny gems that mirrored images just distorted enough to make them appear real?

For a moment I think I understood Gjorg. I think I understood how Gjorg's embellished memory of Sofia—his own personal myth—sustained him for so long. Shaban told it to me straight way back in June 2000. He said that, for an Albanian boy, to love a Serb meant that you were as good as a Serb. For Gjorg, loving Sofia created a possibility that might eradicate the ugliness of the reality he lived in. If Kosovo were a place where he could be with a Serb, then perhaps the arid poverty of the Drenica Valley need not be. If Kosovo were a place where he could be with a Serb, then there would be no fear of beatings by the police, no threat of war and violence. Kosovo would be a place where an entire village of Albanian manhood could not be extinguished in a sudden volley of weapons fire.

In 1995, Gjorg needed a Sofia. He needed a Sofia so badly he was forced to manufacture one. I have no doubt Gjorg and Sofia met and struck up a friendship that may or may not have lasted for years. I also have no doubt that some of what Gjorg told me as fact was a myth so compelling he had come to believe it. My theory is that Sofia resided for so long in Gjorg's imagination that the real girl he met in Mitrovica blurred and became the fantasy he pined over on his farm. I don't believe Gjorg and Sofia were ever really engaged. I don't believe she really considered her blood to be mixed, nor would I think she would necessarily care if it were. I also don't think Gjorg believed he was lying to me. More precisely, I think he truly believed the lies he told me. The ruins of Yugoslavia are a place where facts are inconsequential, history is manufactured, and always for a reason. In 1995 Gjorg created this Sofia to survive. Maybe Sofia did the same. Maybe she invented the "mixed blood" story. Maybe she projected on Gjorg and used him as a haven as much as he had clung to her. I will never know Sofia's side of the story, but obviously, by 2002 Gjorg no longer needed Sofia as a person or an ideal. "I'm with Albanian people now," he had said.

I grasped Sofia's hand. I looked into those eyes that now expressed confusion and a lot of anxiety, and I said the only thing I could say. They were my last words to Gjorg. It was the only message I had any right to deliver.

"I'm sorry," I said. "I'm very sorry."

At last I understood what Gjorg was looking for when he searched for Sofia. It wasn't what the others searched for when they agreed to assist me in finding her. Sasha helped in order to understand Kosovo, a place she had never been until we went there together. Boris helped because of his desire to confront the worst the Serbs had done in Kosovo, so that the best could be appreciated. In this way Boris's motives and efforts were more sincere than mine.

This was clear on Boris's wedding day. As Boris, awkward and resplendent in his grey tuxedo, joyously danced the *kolo* and sang, I saw that he believed he had found what he was searching for—before I appeared in his complicated life, and afterwards. The wars were over, and he had survived, and most of his family was safe. Milošević was over. A Croatian friend attended his wedding. Yugoslavia was coming back together. And most of all, Boris was getting married and expecting a child.

But questions still remained unanswered that the medical student and I pondered while Boris sang. Why the wars? Why the hatred? How could it have happened—250,000 dead in Bosnia, the siege of Sarajevo, the cleansing of the Krajina, the massacres at Srebrenica, and later Rezallë?

There are clinical explanations for the Milošević phenomenon, for Tudjman and Izetbegović and Agim Çeku. But there is nothing clinical or academic about the Balkans. There are other forces at work. They are as unfathomable and potent as the *rakija* I am drinking as I watch Boris emote. The wedding was festive as soon as the music began to play, but now the party rages, it rollicks, it is feverish. Everyone is on his or her feet. Beautiful raven-haired women wave their hands in the air. Men stand on chairs. Everyone dances their own steps, but they sing an ancient mantra they have known almost from birth, and maybe they knew it before. The music, lyrics, movements, and hysteria are building towards something, but I can't imagine what.

At that moment the medical student turns to me. "You feel it?" he says. "You feel the passion. Now understand the madness."

For a moment I do. But above the marvellous din I can still hear Boris's tenor voice. It's only one voice, but it rises above the chorus and the chaos. "There was a girl from Vranje who loved me," I hear him sing.

There once was a girl from Vranje.

Death of a Prime Minister and Rebirth

After Boris's wedding I returned to Serbia one more time. After I returned home, I lost regular touch with Boris and Sasha, but, as a journalist, I kept a nervous eye on events in Serbia.

I watched as the republic failed repeatedly to elect a president to replace incumbent head of state and indicted war criminal Milan Milutinović. Surprisingly, the elections failed due to low voter turnout. But Serbia plodded on under the stewardship of Prime Minister Zoran Đinđić who had emerged as the most able politician of the post-Milošević era. Tough, progressive, and infinitely pragmatic, Đinđić eschewed nationalism, and faced one crisis after another on every imaginable front.

He launched initiatives against crime, state corruption, and sought to normalize the situation in Kosovo. He laboured to sustain a working relationship with the West, mainly through his willingness to feed the insatiable appetite of the

UN war crimes tribunal in The Hague with indicted war crim-inals. In 2003, he handed over Milutinović and the notorious radical leader Vojislav Seselj. Đinđić continued to co-operate, but his position was growing more tenuous. Extradition was becoming increasingly unpopular, and powerful men were now facing prosecution.

But Đinđić laboured on with reforms. On February 4, he presided over the dissolution of Yugoslavia in favour of a new, less centralized federation known as Serbia and Montenegro. This federation, which began with a bang as the Kingdom of Serbs, Croats and Slovenes in 1918, was renamed the Kingdom of Yugoslavia in 1929, morphed into a six-republic communist powerhouse in 1945, and then became the backdrop for unspeakable atrocities in the 1990s, went out in 2003 with the weakest of whimpers. Yugoslavia passed away so gently it was difficult to imagine that so many had died in its name.

I thought I had witnessed Serbia at its nadir, but I was wrong. On March 12, my phone rang. I answered and, although we hadn't spoken for a year, I immediately recog-nized Sasha's voice.

"They shot Đinđić," she said.

As I bolted from my chair, Sasha explained that a friend in the media had just told her the Prime Minister had been gunned down about thirty minutes before. We traded calls like siblings keeping tabs on an ailing parent. At one point in the afternoon, she confirmed what the television had already begun to report: Serbia's Prime Minister was dead.

Đinđić had been shot twice by a high-calibre rifle fired from the second-floor window of an apartment building two hundred metres away. The first bullet passed through his aorta; the second tore open his abdomen. Surgeons had refused to give up on him, but really Đinđić was dead when he arrived at hospital.

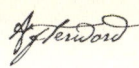

My first reaction was sadness. For the man and his family. But more so for Serbia. In a political culture still dominated by nationalist zealots and reactionaries, Đinđić was a lone voice of reason. As the sun set on March 12, he seemed irreplaceable.

His successors immediately identified the suspects: a Mafia clan headquartered in the Zemun district of Belgrade, and its maximum leader, a former-paramilitary commander known as "Legija" (or "Legionnaire"; he had served in the French Foreign Legion). Legija had succeeded Frenki Simatović as commander of the JSO or "Red Berets," the feared paramilitary *četa*/special ops unit. The strange irony of the affair became clear.

In the weeks following Milošević's ouster, I learned that the street revolt hadn't been the spontaneous implosion it had appeared. That the uprising had been bloodless was actually the result of meticulous planning. Đinđić knew he could fill the streets with protestors. But he also knew that Milošević would probably order the use of deadly force to silence them.

So Đinđić secretly met with leaders of Serbia's security apparatus and secured guarantees they would not fire on protestors. Đinđić also met with Legija, who promised the JSO would remain in its barracks on October 5, as long as protestors didn't become violent.

The JSO wasn't the only unsavoury group the opposition had conscripted, but the importance of winning their neutrality can not be emphasized enough. Đinđić admitted this himself when he said he "owed his life" to Legija. I can't imagine he liked cutting deals with the likes of the JSO, but he did it to avert a civil war that his side might have won but at a tremendous cost in lives.

Đinđić won the day on October 5, but conflict with his murderous allies was inevitable. By March 12, 2003, Legija no longer commanded the JSO. He had resigned in 2001,

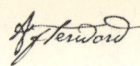

probably at Đinđić's request, and joined the board of the Zemun clan, one of the Balkans' most powerful criminal syndicates, while still calling shots with the Red Berets.

Crime was the motive, authorities said, in the hours after Đinđić's murder. Đinđić was tough on the Mafia, and the Zemun boys had decided to get rid of him. I wasn't convinced this was true. But I could only watch with amazement as the government lashed out. They declared martial law, and issued arrest warrants for Legija, who, of course, had gone underground, along with Zemun-gang cohorts Dušan Spasojević and Mile Luković. The JSO barracks were surrounded and quarantined. Within hours, dozens of crime figures were arrested and the number quickly grew. (As I write this, two thousand suspects are in Serbian lockup.) No one was immune. Arkan's pop-singing widow Ceca, the purported head of her dead husband's empire and Legija's alleged lover, was picked up. Deputy state prosecutor Milan Sarajlić confessed to being on the payroll of the Zemun boys to keep the courts off their backs. Two weeks after Đinđić's killing, the police finally caught up with Spasojević and Luković and shot them dead after the heavily armed kingpins resisted arrest.

Any doubt that Legija and the Red Berets had also orchestrated Đinđić's death was swept away when police arrested the trigger man, JSO deputy commander Zvezdan Jovanović, who told interrogators the killing was intended to spark nation-wide anarchy, a JSO-led coup, and usher in a new regime both gangsters and war criminals could trust. The conspirators had already tried to kill Đinđić four times. That winter, a hit squad had planned to use a rocket-launched grenade to blow up a car carrying Đinđić and his family on their way back from a ski holiday at Mount Kopaonik, but aborted the attack because the Đinđić car was moving too fast for the rocket to get a bead on it.

As more revelations surfaced, Legija, I soon realized, was the state security/paramilitary murderer/gangster hybrid I had always believed Momo might be when investigating his involvement in the Rezallë massacre. Three years earlier, when Zoran was acquainting me with Belgrade's "crazy bastards," I had considered Arkan's life to be the perfect archetype for Momo. But actually Legija was the better model. As a commander of the JSO, Legija was both a blood-lusting paramilitary warlord and creature of state security. His later and quite natural rise to the top echelons of the omnipotent Zemun gang completed the portrait. The real Momo had been guilty of no crimes. But Legija personified every fear I had projected onto the mythical Momo, and his fall gave me the sense that I had walked the last stretch of my search for Sofia's father.

Also as Serbian authorities dismantled the JSO and incarcerated ethnic cleansers like Frenki Simatović and Jovica Stanišić, I couldn't help but feel that Đinđić's greatest accomplishment was now being realized. Serbia was clearing away the rot that had had long stymied Đinđić's reforms. His government was fighting the civil war he had averted.

As I write this, Đinđić's forces seem to be winning. But for me personally, the most hopeful development came one afternoon when Sasha called from Belgrade to discuss some turn in the hunt for Đinđić's killers. Midpoint in our conversation I heard a howl in the background. This noise, I realized, emanated from Sasha's daughter, a youngster I had never met as she had been born since my last visit to Serbia.

Sasha paused and I could hear a quiet domestic commotion across the hundreds of kilometres of telephone line. I imagined Sasha adjusting a baby on her lap, and moving the receiver to the opposite ear. "Sorry about that," she said. "Can you hear me?"

Afterword

I told her not to worry. I didn't tell her that these gentle cries were the most persuasive argument I had heard that somehow everything was going to be all right.

NOTES

CHAPTER 2

1   Mark Schapiro, "Serbia's Lost Generation," *Mother Jones,*
    Sept./Oct. 1999.
2   The Kosovska (or Kosovo) designation distinguishes this
    Mitrovica from Sremska Mitrovica in Vojvodina.
3   *Vojska Jugoslavije* or Yugoslav Army.

CHAPTER 3

1   At the time, the soldier said the mounds contained twenty peo-
    ple. They later uncovered seven bodies.
2   The remains Habib showed me indicated that human remains
    had been burned in this hearth. But in fairness, it should be
    noted that the remains were not numerous, suggesting either
    that evidence had been carted away or that the number of bod-
    ies incinerated in this pit had been limited.
3   Later renamed Drenas, although still commonly referred to as
    Gllogovc.

CHAPTER 4

1   Initially, only weeks after the end of the war, I was told that
    eighty-four villagers had died. Later a local investigation would
    conclude that one hundred and twenty-seven had been killed in
    Gjorg's community and its immediate environs during the war,
    mainly as a result of executions.

CHAPTER 5

1   Julie A. Mertus, *Kosovo: How Myths and Truths Started a War*
    (Berkeley and London: University of California Press, 1999), p. 8.
2   Noel Malcolm, *Kosovo: A Short History* (London: Macmillan,
    1998), p. 339.

CHAPTER 6

1   Also Turiqefc on some Albanian maps.
2   November 28, 1997.
3   February 28, 1998.
4   On Jan. 22, 1998, at 5:30 p.m. Serb police reportedly went to the
    home of Adem Jashari in the village of Prekaz i Ulët (Serbian:
    Donji Prekaz) and withdrew after determining they had insuffi-
    cient firepower to fight their way into the clan's heavily armed
    compound. "According to his father Shaban, they retreated
    when Adem's 'friends from the woods' came to his aid" (Tim
    Judah, *Kosovo: War and Revenge*, p. 137). Police units returned
    in force on March 5, 1998, and opened fire with automatic
    weapons and artillery. They called on the Jashari men to sur-
    render. Several men left one of the houses in the compound,
    ostensibly to give themselves up. Police shot two of them.
    There were no more surrenders. The police—entrenched in an
    ammunition factory on a nearby hill—attacked with artillery

and heavy weapons. The Jasharis reportedly boasted an impressive arsenal of Kalashnikovs, but the police easily outgunned them. At the end of the siege the compound lay in ruins, and fifty-eight members of the Jashari family (including women, children, and elderly) lay dead.

5 Dečani in Serbian, home to the Dečani monastery.

6 Albanians call their province Kosovo. Serb residents call it Kosovo. For the sake of consistency only, it will be referred to in these pages as Kosovo.

7 Also known as the *hakmarre*.

CHAPTER 8

1 The Serbian police is widely known as the *milicija*, although it is sometimes referred to as MUP, the Serbian initials for *Ministarstvo unutrasnjih poslova,* Ministry of Interior. During fighting in Kosovo a specialized branch known as the *Posebrie Jedinice Policije* (PJP) acted as assault troops in combat situations. Although the PJP is a distinct division, for simplicity's sake I refer to police forces who fought in Kosovo as *milicija*. Note that in battle the PJP was well-armed with mortars and automatic rifles (M70, a Yugoslav version of AK47 or sometimes a Heckler & Koch MP5 submachine gun), and armoured personnel carriers (APCs). At the time of the NATO air strikes in 1999 the PJP boasted five thousand recruits, divided into six divisions in Serbia, and eight thousand reservists.

CHAPTER 9

1 Not the same cemetery where we had found the body in the open grave on the day I was reunited with Gjorg immediately after NATO's occupation of Kosovo. This cemetery was situated

closer to Gjorg's farm on the north side of the village.

2   Rukolli gave his account to a Kosovar researcher I later contracted to investigate the alleged massacre. Other witnesses I spoke to included women from Deliu's clan who were present in the village that day, and a woman who had witnessed the occupation of the northern edge of the village three days before. Only Deliu and Rukolli claim they witnessed the actual shooting.

3   Another female member of Misin Deliu's clan.

CHAPTER 11

1   A suburb of Belgrade.

2   Tim Judah, *The Serbs: History, Myth and the Destruction of Yugoslavia* (New Haven and London: Yale University Press, 1997), p. 186.

3   Ivan Čolović, "Football, Hooligans and War," *The Road to War in Serbia: Trauma and Catharsis,* ed. Nebojša Popov (Budapest: Central European University Press, 1996), p. 386. Note: many football chants were derived from WWII *Četnik* battle songs.

4   Ed Vulliamy, Stacy Sullivan, "Bloody Handiwork of Arkan," (*Observer,* Sunday, Jan. 16, 2000).

5   Federation of American Scientists.

6   Tim Judah, *The Serbs,* p. 185.

CHAPTER 12

1   Albanians were predominantly Catholic before the Turkish conquest of the Balkans beginning in the late fourteenth century brought the Islamic faith to the peninsula. Today there are still Catholic Albanians in Kosovo, but they constitute a minority.

2   *Šiptar* is derived from *Shqiptar*, the Albanian word for the Albanian people. (Albania is *Shqipëria* and the language is *shqip*.) There is little difference in the pronunciation between the two words, except for a subtle q or "ch" sound in the original. For many Albanians the Serb *Šiptar* (pronounced without the "ch" sound) is a racist pejorative, equivalent to "nigger".

CHAPTER 13

1   "The street protests were a symptom of the force of anger and resentment against the Milošević regime. . . . Under pressure, [Milošević] took refuge in a bottle of Viljamovka. 'Milošević could not handle the winter demonstrations. He was drunk a lot of the time,' said one high level source.'" Adam LeBor, *Milošević: A Biography* (London: Bloomsbury Publishing, 2002), p. 266–267.

2   Centre for Free Elections and Democracy.

3   As proof, Blagojević cited a previous vote when the state elections committee reported that a voting station in western Kosovo near the town of Junik came in nearly 90 percent for a SPS candidate. Junik was an infamous hotbed of Kosovar defiance and insurgency. In the 1998 Serbian offensive against the UÇK Junik was one of the last fortresses to fall. About to be overrun, Junik's rebel fighters and virtually its entire population crept out of the city one night and trekked over the mountains into Albania. But still the regime claimed these same Kosovars had supported the SPS at the polls.

CHAPTER 15

1   Human Rights Watch found credible accounts of ninety-six cases of sexual assault by Yugoslav soldiers, Serbian police, or

paramilitaries during the period of NATO bombing, and the actual number is probably much higher." (Human Rights Watch, *Kosovo: Rape as a Weapon of 'Ethnic Cleansing,'* 2000)

CHAPTER 17

1   *Rrahovec* in Albanian.
2   *Bjeshkët* in Albanian.

CHAPTER 18

1   UN resolution 1244, passed in June 1999, defined Kosovo as Yugoslav territory.

CHAPTER 19

1   Not Aleks who shared a room with Boris in Klina.

CHAPTER 20

1   This brief interview became the foundation for the account of his life in this book. However, we discussed these events at subsequent interviews as well. I also interviewed several members of Gjorg's family with whom he shared many of these experiences, including Ibrahim, Kadri, Shota, and Hakif. His brother Kadri drew a detailed and invaluable map of the Isufis' wanderings during the air strikes.

CHAPTER 22

1   The Serbian name for the village Albanians call Gllogovc or more recently Drenas.

CHAPTER 24

1   The artery Albanians call the Gllogovc–Skenderaj road.

CHAPTER 27

1   A civilian bus, the Niš express, was carrying seventy civilian passengers when it was struck by a missile from a NATO jet. The attack, which took place at 1 p.m. on a bridge over the Lab river near the community of Luzanë (Lluzhane in Albanian), twenty kilometres north of Priština, severed the vehicle in two. One half of the bus remained on the bridge. Another half fell into the gorge below. At the time I was inclined to believe Momčilo Neznanović died in this attack. Only later did I realize it occurred on May 1, a full month before Neznanović's death in early June as reported by Sasha's official sources.

2   I had given Boris a small camera to take with him, and he was able to use it to photograph pertinent documents relating to both Gjorg Isufi and Momir N. The photos developed clearly, and I was able to review personally the documents regarding the identity of Sofia's father.

Many thanks to

Patrick Graham, Maya Mavjee, Nicholas Massey-Garrison, Arnold Toutant, Susan Ginsburg, and Annie Leuenberger for seeing this book to publication.

The Canada Council for the Arts for its generous support; and Boris Postovnik for allowing me access to his war-time diaries, and parts of his unpublished memoirs.

Great war correspondents: Julius Strauss, Sandra Balsells, Andy Rain, Quim Roser i Puig, Plàcid Garcia-Planas, Béla Szándelsky, Mark Milstein, and Erwin Tuil.

The fine people at CanWest Newspapers: Randy Newell, Peter Robb, Aileen McCabe, Mike Blanchfield, Klaus Pohle, Norma Greenaway, Christina Spencer, and Sharon Henderson.

Family: Erika Papp, John G. Nadler III, Michael Nadler, Karen Nadler, and Karl Kulmala. And friends: Vesna Kojić, Vladimir Vlaškalić, Krisztina Kovács, Tara Toutant, Lois Toutant, Justin Hearn, Alex Todorovic, Aleksandar Brkić, Aleksandar Vašović, Saša Gleda, Ismet Shuska, Naxha Shuska, Naim Shala, and Blerim Gjoci.

The "Csanády 7" writers: Chris Condon, Adam LeBor, Olen Steinhauer, Robert Wright, Neil Barnett, and Robin Hunt.

The Ottoman Society: Randall Crow, Miles Graham, John Harrington, Dan Visoiu, Rob Scott, Christian Jacobsen, Huges Martin, Andrew Haslam-Jones, Jon Gifford, Clive Rumbold, Edit Mészaros, and Daša Andrejcova.

Gjorg, Boris, Sasha, and their families for their generosity and kindness; and the people of Rezallë and Kraljevo, two proud communities that are more alike than they'll ever know.

And a special thank you to Pam Clark and Tom Mereayi.

Author's Note

On a technical note, I've used Albanian spellings for Kosovo place names in those chapters written from the Kosovar point of view, and Serbian spellings for the Serbian chapters, with a few exceptions. Throughout the book, the Serbian "Kosovo" (in Albanian, it is "Kosova") and "Priština" (in Albanian, "Prishtinë") have been used. The English "Sasha" is used for a central character, instead of the Serbian "Saša." I've adopted these forms for the sake of simplicity so as not to confuse or distance the reader, and I join a long list of writers on the Balkans when I say that any stylistic choices I have made in no way reflect an ethnic preference or prejudice.

On a more profound note, given the sensitivity of the book's subject matter (inter-ethnic love, war crimes, and the synergy between Serbia's underworld and security apparatus), I've been forced to alter names, and make cosmetic changes to some people and places. I've done this to protect the identity of sources and subjects.

The most noteworthy example is Sofia's surname, Neznanović, which is a pseudonym. *Neznan* in Serbian means *unknown* or *anonymous*. Serb friends say that the name does not exist as an appellation. This was my intention. In masking Sofia's identity, I did not want to implicate any innocents who happened to bear an invented name.

I've also withheld some details about the search for Sofia, and the investigation into her father's alleged complicity in the executions at Rezallë, Kosovo, in April 1999. I did this partly to spare the reader some of the false leads and dead ends I encountered in my research. But, again, I've also left out facts to protect identities. Another example is Sofia's home community in northern Kosovo and her current residence in the former Yugoslavia, which I've not identified, again to preserve her anonymity.

I realize (as both Serbs and Albanians who assisted me in this project have reminded me) that Sofia and Gjorg committed no crimes and *should* have nothing to fear. At the worst, they were guilty of daring to surmount the culture of hate that surrounded them. Still, from the beginning of this project, I've obsessed over security, and decided to err on the side of safety when dealing with identities in these pages.

Subsequently, I ask readers to overlook any superficial alterations, and consider *Searching for Sofia* a personal memoir of a two-year odyssey to locate the truth about a lost woman, a terrible crime, and a great nation.

About the Author

JOHN NADLER is a correspondent for CanWest Newspapers, Canada's largest newspaper chain. He also contributes to *Variety* magazine in the US. His articles have appeared in *Maclean's* magazine, *Canadian Business*, the *Ottawa Citizen*, the *Montreal Gazette*, the *National Post*, and the *Independent* in the UK. He lives in Hungary.